G. R. Hand, G. R. Hand

The Gospel Delineator and Survey

G. R. Hand, G. R. Hand

The Gospel Delineator and Survey

ISBN/EAN: 9783743417366

Manufactured in Europe, USA, Canada, Australia, Japa

Cover: Foto ©Lupo / pixelio.de

Manufactured and distributed by brebook publishing software (www.brebook.com)

G. R. Hand, G. R. Hand

The Gospel Delineator and Survey

THE
Gospel Delineator and Survey.

A VOLUME OF

SERMONS, ADDRESSES AND ESSAYS ON
REVELATION AND SCIENCE, AND THE
SCIENCE OF CHRISTIANITY,

BY

PROF. G. R. HAND,

AUTHOR OF "TEXT BOOK EXPOSED."

SACRAMENTO, CAL.:
NEWS PUBLISHING COMPANY.
1886.

Entered according to Act of Congress, in the year 1886, by

G. R. HAND,

In the office of the Librarian of Congress, at Washington, D. C.

DEDICATION.

TO THE

YOUNG PREACHERS

NOBLY DEVOTING THEIR LIVES

TO THE MINISTRY OF

THE WORD,

IS THIS VOLUME RESPECTFULLY DEDICATED,

BY THEIR FELLOW LABORER AND

ELDER BROTHER,

G. R. HAND.

PREFACE.

ACTING upon the advice and recommendation of brethren, whose judgment I respect, I have written out a series of Sermons, Addresses, and Essays, on Scriptural and Scientific themes, and their relation to the Science of Christianity, in a volume which, with pleasure and confidence, I introduce to the reading public, under the new and significant title of THE GOSPEL DELINEATOR AND SURVEY.

A few of these, as seen by the references, appeared in my own name in *The Microcosm*, *The Christian Quarterly Review*, and in the *Text Book Exposed*, by the author.

A critical and persistent study of the Scriptures, for more than forty-five years, should, at least enable me to handle the subjects with *confidence*.

The themes have been thoroughly studied, analyzed with great care, and arranged in brief, Scriptural, Scientific, and Logical order.

While adapted to popular reading, it will furnish special aid to the Student of the Scriptures, in leading him to a clearly defined presentation of the themes discussed, to make him "*apt to teach.*"

But to the *young preacher*, it will be a valuable companion, and assistant, in the analysis, and logical arrangement of the points, in the themes and theses, and a ready reference to the *proofs*.

A prominent feature of the book, is the *Delineation* introducing the discourses, and consisting mainly of my *Blackboard Diagrams* used when discoursing on the themes they introduce, and, like the *plat of a survey*, aiding to photograph in the mind the exact features of the *Scriptural ground* to be *surveyed*.

May God's blessing accompany it, and make it an efficient auxiliary in promoting the cause of our common Christianity.

G. R. HAND.

SACRAMENTO, Cal, January, 1886.

CONTENTS.

		Page
I.	Introduction — The Divine Creed Sustained. John 20:19–31	5
II.	The Divine Message	13
III.	The Resurrection—Truths and Facts	19
IV.	The Coronation—Humiliation and Exaltation	27
V.	The Great Salvation	32
VI.	Power of the Gospel	39
VII.	Rightly Dividing The Word of Truth	49
VIII.	God Everywhere	61
IX.	The Enthronement of Mind	71
X.	Survey No. 1—Establishing the Beginning Corner	87
XI.	Survey No. II—Locating the Boundaries	92
XII.	God's Gracious Gifts	97
XIII.	The Setting Up of the Kingdom	106
XIV.	Proving the Title	115
XV.	Dominion of the Kingdom	120
XVI.	When and Why God Winked at Ignorance	125
XVII.	The Savior's Prayer for Unity	134
XVIII.	Turning to God—Conversion	145
XIX.	Ultimate Elements and Resultant Combinations — The Alphabet of the Universe	154
XX.	Equation of Life, and Keys of the Kingdom	161

CONTENTS.

XXI.	Conversion of the Gentiles	170
XXII.	A Scriptural Conversion	179
XXIII.	The Name Chistian	186
XXIV.	God's Building	195
XXV.	By Grace Ye are Saved	203
XXVI.	Substantialism	207
XXVII.	Cleansing from Sin	223
XXVIII.	The Victory—Typical and Anti-Typical	233
XXIX.	Ministry of the New Covenant	243
XXX.	Writing on the Heart	243
XXXI.	Physical and Spiritual Gymnasia	251
XXXII.	Mission of the Spirit	259
XXXIII.	The Balances of Creation	269
XXXIV.	The Tabernacle	275
XXXV.	Scriptural Forms	285
XXXVI.	True Development—Milk of the Word	291
XXXVII.	God's Drawing	302
XXXVIII.	The Great Commission	307
XXXIX.	The Three Salvations	312
XL.	Christian and Jewish Antitheses	322

INTRODUCTION.

I.

THE DIVINE CREED SUSTAINED.—John 20: 19–31.

DELINEATION:

1—Qualified Witnesses.	4—Why Written.
2—Evidence of Senses.	5—How Believe.
3—Belief on Testimony.	6—What to Believe.

THE INSPIRED CREED.

The Truths.	*What They Affirm.*
Jesus Is { 1. The Christ.	Office.
2. Son of God.	Divinity.
3. Lord.	Sovereignty

SURVEY.

AS a suitable introduction to a series of outline discourses on the gospel proclamation, and the apostles' doctrine, I introduce the reader to the Savior's interview with his apostles, on the day of his resurrection, preparatory to turning over to them the mission of salvation to a dying world, which he had inaugurated during his three and a half years of public ministry on earth. The thousands of citizens and sojourners in Jerusalem were agitated and wonderfully stirred up over the report that Jesus had risen from the dead; and society was moved to its very depths.

Fearing the vindictiveness of the Jews, the disciples were assembled in a room with closed doors. Jesus, like an apparition, appears in their midst, and speaks to them, showing them his hands and his side, convincing them of his identity, and causing great joy.

"As my Father hath sent me, even so send I you," coming from the risen Savior's lips, looks to the transfer of his earthly mission, to his disciples, who are to be apostles and witnesses.

"Whosesoever sins ye remit, they are remitted unto them, and whosesoever sins ye retain, they are retained," supplements the sending, by depositing with them the terms of remission of sins in his name, with the assurance of divine sanction. Or, as Paul expresses it: "And hath given to us the ministry of reconciliation." "And hath committed to us the word of reconciliation." (2 Cor. 5:18, 19, 20.) And, "We are ambassadors for Christ."

One vacant seat is unaccounted for, as the absence of Thomas, called Didymus, appears to be without a written excuse. Didymus means a twin, and why the twin was not there, has given rise to many conjectures. But he is reminded of the feast of rejoicing he had been deprived of, by his absence, when the other disciples therefore said to him, "We have seen the Lord." As he is one of the appointed witnesses he demands the same opportunity of assurance, which had been accorded to the others, and no more.

The religious world has done injustice to Brother Thomas. They speak of "doubting Thomas," and sing of "doubting Thomas," until "doubting Thomas" has become a synonym for incredulity. But there is no evidence that Thomas was naturally more incredulous than the others. He only asks for the necessary endowments of an original witness, which the others had received, and of which he had been deprived by his absence from that interview.

Suppose they interview Thomas on the subject. Brother Thomas, why do you hesitate to take the word of those who say they have seen the risen Lord? Because I am to be one of the chosen witnesses of his resurrection, and if I believe upon your testimony, it will not make me a witness. I must see for myself. Well, Thomas, will you be satisfied with seeing him? No. In the midst of the great excitement here, a person resembling Jesus might take advantage of the occasion, and attempt to palm himself off for the risen Savior. I saw the nails driven through his hands, and the soldier's spear pierce his side; and saw the blood and water flow; and I must see the print of those nails in his hands, and that wound in his side, that I may identify the body. But will you be satisfied with *seeing* the wounds, Thomas? No. An imposter resembling Jesus might paint the representation of wounds in the hands and the side, and attempt to palm himself off as the risen Savior, with the mutilated body. And I must avoid the deception, by being permitted to apply the sense of touch, to ascertain if they are real wounds, and not painted deceptions. The rest of the witnesses have had the same privilege.

On the next first day of the week, when the disciples are together and Thomas with them, Jesus again stands in their midst, and speaks to them. Then, addressing Thomas, he shows his wounds, and invites him to ascertain their reality by the application of his finger to the print of the nails, and his hand to the open wound in his side.

Now he has had the privilege he claimed, and which had been granted to the others a week before, and they are all qualified witnesses of the resurrection. "And Thomas answered and said unto him, My Lord and my God." He is now thoroughly convinced.

But some one may say that after all, they believed upon seeing, and did not handle him. How do you know they did not handle him? It is not said in this lesson, whether they did, or did not. So we will hear the testimony of John in another place. (1 John 1:1.) "That which was from the beginning, which we have heard, which we have seen with our eyes, which we have looked upon, and our hands have handled, of the word of life." Here, from the testimony of this same writer, it appears that they did "handle" him, and that the evidence of three out of five of their senses concurred in constituting them witnesses.

I call special attention to the reply of Jesus at this point. He says: "Thomas, because thou hast seen me, thou hast believed; blessed are they that have not seen, and yet have believed." He does not chide him for demanding the evidence of his senses. That was necessary to make him a witness. But thousands then living, and thousands yet unborn, would be called upon to believe, upon the testimony of these witnesses, without the concurrent testimony of their own physical senses. The blessings of the gospel are here promised to those who believe upon testimony, and not through their senses.

In full accord with this, the Savior had prayed for the unity of all those who believe on him through the word of his apostles. (John 17:20.)

That the testimony of these witnesses, the word of the apostles, may be forthcoming and ample, the apostle concludes our lesson thus: "But these are written, that ye might believe that Jesus is the Christ, the Son of God; and that believing ye might have life through his name."

The analysis of this sentence is outlined in the Delineation. We have seen that the *knowledge* of the witnesses was based upon the evidence of the majority of the senses, but the *faith* of the Christian, with the promised blessing, was made dependent upon the testimony.

Why is the testimony written? The apostle answers: "That ye might believe." And Paul sounds the same note in the culmination of a climax, with: "So then faith cometh by hearing." (Rom. 10:17.)

The testimony is written, and therefore in the historical form, and may be called historical testimony, the belief of which may be called historical faith. Still it is evangelical testimony or history, and therefore its belief is evangelical faith. It is also the faith by which we "might have life through his name," and is therefore saving faith.

Having taught us *how* we believe, the inspired apostle proceeds to tell us *what* we must believe in order to "have life through his name." The essential creed is brief but comprehensive. Take it *seriatim*.

JESUS is the central magnet around which the truths and facts of the gospel cluster, as steel filings cluster around a magnet. Jesus means Savior, and they were divinely instructed to "call his name JESUS; for he shall save his people from their sins." (Mat. 1:21.) Then it is important for us to learn what to believe, and what to do, to become "his people," in order to be saved from our sins.

The essential truths affirmed of Jesus, to be believed, are the following:

1. That he is *the Christ*. The word "Christ" means

anointed. God gave his ancient people prophets, and they were anointed, or christed, and each anointed prophet was a christed person, or *a* christ. Yet not one of them was *the* Christ. God also gave them priests, and they were anointed, and therefore christed persons, and called the Lord's anointed. Yet, though *a* christ, not one of them was ever *the* Christ. God also gave them kings, and these were anointed, or christed persons. Yet no one of them was ever *the* Christ.

But the prophets foretold of a coming One, who would embody in himself all these offices, and be anointed for all time, and to the exclusion of all others. This personage would be *the Christ*. And the anointing being official, our first truth: *Jesus is the Christ*, affirms *office*.

2. That he is *the Son of God*. John, here speaking in the third person, says he is the Son of God. But Peter, addressing Jesus in person, speaks in the second person: "Thou art the Son of the living God." He also uses the word "living," which John omits, but which I shall retain in the analysis.

It is not *a* son of God, in common with the children of God. Nor is it a son of *a* god, as one of the heathen gods, nor *the* son of *a* god; but "*the* Son of *the* God." The definite article is in the Greek, in our lesson, but not translated in the common version. Then, to cut off all possible reference to any of the gods of mythology, Peter says the *living* God. And our second truth, that Jesus is *the Son of God*, affirms his *divinity*.

3. That he is *Lord*. This term is not used in the sentence I am analyzing, but is implied in the phrase, the Christ, which includes the office of king, and therefore ruler, or Lord.

The news that God had made him "both Lord and Christ," was brought from heaven by the Holy Spirit on the day of Pentecost, and, by the inspired apostle, announced to the world. (Acts 2:36.)

Again, at the house of Cornelius, the same apostle says: "He is Lord of all." Thus to Jew first and then to Gentile, he is proclaimed as Lord. (See Acts 10:36.)

Paul adds his testimony thus: "For to this end Christ both died, and rose, and revived, that he might be Lord both of the dead and living." (Rom. 14:9.) Then it is clear that our third truth that Jesus is *Lord* affirms His *sovereignty*.

Practical application. As a race, we are ignorant and need a prophet to teach us. When we believe in 'our heart, and confess Jesus as *the Christ*, we accept him as our only teacher, and take his inspired word as our guide.

We are sinful beings, and need a priest to make atonement for us. When we confess Jesus as *the Christ*, we accept him as our priest, and need no other. Hence we find no official priests in his Church.

We are frail and fallible beings, and need a king whom we can trust, to rule over us and lead us on to victory. When we confess Jesus as *the Christ*, we accept him as our king, and disclaim all right to make the laws for the kingdom of heaven, of which we have acknowledged him to be the king.

When we confess Jesus as *the Son of God*, we recognize in him a divine person, and therefore infallible as a teacher, all prevailing as a priest, and all conquering as a king, and we can trust him as a safe guide, an efficient Savior, and triumphant leader.

The prophets were fallible men; our prophet is infallible. The priests were mortal and "could not continue by reason of death;" our priest is immortal, and has "an unchanging priesthood." The kings grew old and died; our king never dies, and is able to confer immortality upon his finally triumphant host. When we confess him as *Lord*, we acknowledge him as the one who was to come who had the right to rule.

Surely the platform of our Divine Creed is long enough, and broad enough, and deep enough, and high enough, and strong enough for all to stand upon, and work together. And the Divine Creed is sustained.

II.

THE DIVINE MESSAGE.—Heb. 1:1.

DELINEATION.

First Message.	*Second Message.*	*True or False.*
1—To the Fathers.	1—To Us.	1—Believer.
2—By Prophets.	2—By His Son.	2—Skeptic.
3—Divers Manners.	3—Through Apostles.	3—Infidel.
4—Sundry Times.	4—Once for All.	4—Atheist.
5—Time Past.	5—Last Days.	5—Deist.

EVIDENCES.

I. *Fulfilled Prophecy.*   II. *Miracles.*
1. On Him.   2. By Him.   3. By Apostles.
4. By other Inspired Men.

SURVEY.

"GOD, who at sundry times and in divers manners spake in time past unto the fathers by the prophets, hath in these last days spoken unto us by his Son." (Heb. 1:1.)

Messages of authority, from the king to his subjects, are usually deemed of primary importance. Here we have two messages from the Supreme Ruler of the universe. The one addressed to *the fathers*, the other to *us*. This epistle is addressed to Judaizing Christians, mainly to place in antithetical counterpoise, the two messages, showing the superiority of Christianity over Judaism; of the new covenant over the old, being based upon "better promises;" the messenger of the new, over the messengers of the old; the priesthood of the new, over that of the old; the temple, the service, the blood of the new, over those of the old; the salvation of the new, over the old; the Divine Mediator of the new, being infinitely superior to the human mediator of the old. The antithetical points in the messages, are indicated in the blackboard delineation above.

The second is *our message,* and is contained in the New Testament. Does it make any difference which message we follow? May we go indiscriminately to the old, or new, to learn what *we* must do in order to enjoy the "great salvation?" Confusion must follow every such indiscrimination.

Suppose a merchant finds upon his desk a letter ordering a bill of goods shipped to a certain point. Without noticing the *date* or *address,* he ships the goods, and draws on the ordering house for the amount. His draft is returned, not honored. They say: "We never ordered you to ship those goods." He compares the items in the letter, with the invoice, and finds that every article ordered has been shipped, and wonders why his draft was not honored. He is in trouble.

To his mortification he finds that the letter ordering the goods was of *old date,* and not addressed *to him,* but to some one else, who had filled the order long ago, and received his money. Now he has come to grief by following the wrong message, and you say he deserves it. Just so.

Now every one who goes to the old message, in the Old Testament, to find what sinners "in these last days," must do to be saved, is in company with that merchant, making a similar mistake, and with like inexcusable oversight. "Therefore we ought to give the more earnest heed to the things we have heard."

The two messages are antithetical as to recipients,

agents, mode, frequency, and period. Or, *to* whom, *by* whom, *through* whom, how *often*, and *when*.

Our proposition reads: *God hath spoken to us by his Son.* This is either true or false.

Men may be arranged into some five classes, the status of each class being measured by their relation to our proposition. These classes are, as in the delineation, believers, skeptics, infidels, atheists, deists.

1. *Believers.*—You approach a believer with our proposition, and he says: "Yes, I believe that with all my heart."

2. *Skeptics.*—The word is from *skepticos*, which means to look around. He is looking for the evidence. You ask his assent to our proposition, and he asks for the evidence. When you show him the testimany, and he accepts it, he is no longer skeptical.

3. *Infidels.*—Approach the infidel with our proposition, and he says: "I don't believe it." He does not say he *believes* it is *false*. He has no belief on the subject, usually from not having examined the testimony. It does not take *study* to make an infidel. He may be infidel from not knowing anything about it. Infidelity, from in, *not* fidelity, *faith*, or believing, means *not believing*, and is simply negative.

4. *Atheists.*—The word is from, a, *without*, theos, *God*, ist, a *person*, meaning a person without a God. Technically, the atheist is one who *affirms* that there is *no God*. He is in the affirmative, but he affirms a *negative*, not based upon *testimony*, but upon the supposed *absence* of all testimony or proof. He affirms that God has *not* spoken in the Bible, and that there is *no God*. In this he assumes the *absence* of all evidence of a designer in nature, for no man has ever yet so far

stultified himself as to undertake to prove by positive testimony that there is no God.

But in assuming that there is no evidence in the Bible that "God has spoken," he necessarily implies that he has studied every sentence in the Bible, from the first of Genesis to the last of Revelation, else the evidence might be in some verse that he had *not studied*.

In affirming no God in nature, he ignores all *teleology* in creation, and assumes that in all the sciences there is not one scrap of evidence of an intelligent designer. This of course implies that he has studied in minutia every department of every science, and every relation and potency in all nature, else the evidence might be just where he had not examined.

He must have gone through all philosophy before he can intelligently affirm the entire absence of evidence there.

He must be familiar with the analysis of every compound in mineral, vegetable, or animal chemistry, with the laws of all their potencies and activities, including those of elective affinity, before he can consistently affirm no evidence there.

Physiology must have opened her portals to him widely before he can affirm no evidence of design in the anatomy and physiology of our physical organisms, so "fearfully and wonderfully made," with the wonderful adaptation of bones, and joints, and ligaments, to their varied functions, in beautiful harmony, where blind chance might exchange the location of ball and socket, and hinge joints, respectively, and work disastrous confusion.

He must have read, and studied with close scrutiny, the story book of the geologist, and probed the igneous, and stratified, and fossiliferous rocks, the cabinet where paleontology has stored her myriads of fossil types of prehistoric life, before he is competent to affirm the universal absence of design in that book.

He must have accompanied the astronomer in his wondrous flight through flaming space, where worlds, and suns, and solar and stellar systems are but way marks in the cycles of time, as he probes the depths of the siderial heavens, and weighs planets in the balances of creation, before he can be sure that Sir Isaac Newton, the great astronomer, was mistaken when he uttered that sublime sentence of world wide fame: "The undevout astronomer is mad," or can successfully command teleology to "down at his bidding."

Assuming all this, would be virtually proclaiming himself the highest intelligence in the universe.

The insuperable difficulty in the way of the atheist may be illustrated thus: Suppose three men, representing skeptic, infidel, and atheist, are together. A stranger, who may represent the believer, tells them that a vessel containing ten thousand dollars in gold was buried, in war time, in a certain field, within three feet of the surface, and that the owners who buried it were killed in the war. He then disappears. Skeptic, looking around for the evidence, would like to know if it is true, and proposes that they all go and dig for the money and divide it among them if successful. Infidel says: I don't believe there is any money there, and do not care to spend the time and labor. Atheist says: There is no money there; that man just wanted to hoax you. Skeptic then replies: You have affirmed that it is *not* there; I challenge you to prove it. Now, to prove that the money is *not* buried there, he must dig every foot of ground within the field, to the depth of three feet. But the stranger who knew where it was, could go right to the place and find it without trouble.

5. *The Deists.*—From deus, *God,* and ist, a *person.* *Deus* is the Latin, and *Theos* the Greek for God. The deist believes in the God of *Nature,* but not in the God of the *Bible.* He does not believe that "God has spoken" in the Bible. The deist and Christian go hand in hand in nature, with the question: Is there a God? And nature answers in the affirmative, uniformly, to both. To the proposition in Heb. 11:6, "He that cometh to God must believe that he is; and that he is a rewarder of them that diligently seek him." The deist responds: I believe the first part but not the second.

As "faith comes by hearing," or *belief* is based upon *testimony,* it follows that most unbelievers are such for want of attention to the testimony. The character of the evidence may be summed up thus:

1st. *Fulfilled prophecy* concerning Christ.

2d. *Miracles,* which I would divide into the following classes:

1. Miracles terminating upon the person of the Messiah, as (*a*) his incarnation, (*b*) his inauguration at his baptism, (*c*) his transfiguration, (*d*) his crucifixion, (*e*) his resurrection, (*f*) his ascension, (*g*) his glorification.

2. Miracles performed by him in person.

3. Miracles performed by his apostles, whom he inspired, and empowered to work miracles in confirmation of their divine mission.

4. Distributed gifts among those on whom apostles had laid hands, which closes miracles for confirmation.

III.

THE RESURRECTION—TRUTHS AND FACTS.

DELINEATION.

I. SAVED BY THE GOSPEL.

II. TRUTHS—Jesus is { The Christ. The Son of God. Lord.

III. FACTS—Christ. { Died. Buried. Rose.

IV. New Facts.

V. Testimony.

VI. Witness examined.

VII. Argument.

SURVEY.

"MOREOVER, brethren, I declare unto you the gospel which I preached unto you, which also you have received, and wherein ye stand; by which also ye are saved, if ye keep in memory what I preached unto you, unless ye have believed in vain. For I delivered unto you first of all that which I also received, how that Christ died for our sins, according to the scriptures, and that he was buried, and that He rose again the third day, according to the scriptures." (1 Cor. 15:1–4; read 1–20.)

I. Here we have the gospel of *facts* as *preached* by the inspired apostle, and *received* by the Corinthian brethren, and by which they were *saved*. But we learn that in preaching this gospel of *facts* to the Corinthians, he also preached the *truths* of the gospel, for he "testified" to the great *truth* "that Jesus was the Christ," (Acts 18:5,) "and many of the Corinthians hearing believed and were baptized." (Verse 8.) By this gospel the Corinthians were saved, and by the same gospel we are saved, if saved at all, for Paul denounces a curse upon man or angel who shall preach any other gospel than that preached by the apostles, (Gal. 1:8, 9,) and says: "God shall judge the secrets of men by Jesus Christ according to my gospel." (Rom. 2:16.)

II. The leading *truths* of the gospel, as above delineated, are: 1, that Jesus is the Christ; 2, that he is the Son of the living God; 3, that he is Lord. The first of these affirms *office*. The second affirms his *divinity*. The third affirms his *sovereignty*. These *truths* were preached by the apostles, and heard, believed, and *confessed* by converts. The development of the truths must be left for another discourse.

III. The *facts* of the gospel, as in the text and delineation, are: 1, that Christ *died;* 2, that he was *buried;* 3, that he *rose* again. Some may inquire why I place *truths* and *facts* in separate classes. I answer, because of their distinctive difference, and the significant forms of acceptance and recognition. *Truths* are things that are *true*, and not necessarily expressive of action. *Facts* are actions, things done, or performed, or acted. The *truths* of the gospel were believed and *confessed* with the mouth. The *facts* were believed and *acted out*, by *dying* to sin, being *buried* in baptism, and *rising* to a new life.

IV. Gospel means *good news*, or joyful tidings. Then the gospel facts must have been *new* facts when first proclaimed, in order to be *news* at all, and fraught with *good* to man, in order to be *good* news. Besides, they were not *facts* till they transpired, and therefore this gospel could not have been truthfully proclaimed antecedent to the facts. Had any of the Old Testament prophets, or even John the Baptist, preached that Christ died, and was buried, and rose again, they would have affirmed falsely, for he had not then died.

And had the apostles, while Christ was in the tomb, gone and preached that Christ had risen from the dead, they would have proclaimed falsehood. Hence the apostolic gospel could not have been preached until after the resurrection.

But were these *new* facts? First fact.—Christ *died.* Was it a *new* fact that one should die? Men had died from the days of Adam down. So death was no new fact. We then look for the limitations in the text. Christ *died*—the fact—died *for our sins*, a limited fact. But may not some one have died for the sins of others, before this? Then we need the next limitation. Christ died for our sins, *according to the scriptures.* Here we have a limited fact, further limited, by *fulfillment of prophecy*, and beyond doubt a *new* fact.

Second fact.—Was *buried.* But dead men were buried in all ages. Then the limitation, "according to the scriptures," implied, makes this a *new* fact.

Third fact.—*Rose* again. Was this a *new* fact? Persons had risen from the dead in the days of the Savior, and in the days of Old Testament prophets. Then the limitations are needed, and are in the text. *Rose* again—the fact—rose again *the third day*, a limited fact. Is it a *new* fact, thus limited? Is it certain that none of the others rose on the third day? Here the second limitation steps in and sets it right, "according to the scriptures," or in fulfillment of prophecy. Then the limited fact, further limited, reads: "He rose again the third day, according to the Scriptures." With these limitations, it was a *new* fact, beyond all peradventure, and the *basic* fact of the gospel.

V. *Testimony* is necessary to the belief of facts, and the testimony to sustain this *basic* and fundamental fact is found in the word of God. Hence, "faith comes by hearing, and hearing by the word of God." (Rom. 10:17.)

The facts that Jesus *died* and was *buried* had no counter testimony. Those facts were patent to the multitude. But the third fact met with a determined effort at rebuttal, by the enemies, which demands attention.

VI. *Examination of Witnesses.* The body of Jesus was wrapped "in linen clothes, with spices, as the manner of the Jews is to bury." The "manner" was to take long strips of linen five or six inches wide, and wrap the limbs and body, from foot to head, and from head to foot, several thicknesses, enclosing spices and preservatives, of which, on this occasion, about a hundred pounds were used. Then a napkin, handkerchief, or towel is drawn down over the head and tied around the neck. Thus prepared, the body was placed in a new stone vault, carved out of the solid rock, and the great stone door closed.

Then the enemies of Jesus, by the authority of the governor, sealed the stone door, and placed soldiers as sentinels to guard the sepulcher till after the third day, lest the disciples come and steal him away, and report that he had risen the third day, according to his remembered promise.

Under the authority: "Make it as sure as you can," they had these elements of security: Strength of material in the solid rock, imperial authority in the seal, and representative military vigilance in the sentinels. But the authority of seal, and weight of rock, are as nothing before angels' fingers, as they open the sepulcher, for the egress of the risen Lord; and the eye of vigilance closes upon the scene, as the guards lie prostrate under the influence of divine chloroform.

Sentinels report an empty tomb, and the body gone from their custody. But they are bribed by evil counsel to report that while they slept, the disciples came and stole him away. Two conflicting reports are circulated, to account for the empty tomb. One says he was stolen away. The other affirms that he is risen.

Supposing the guard to have deposed that the disciples stole the body, I will cross examine one of the witnesses, as a specimen of all.

I say, sir, why did you not prevent them from taking away the body? We were asleep. Then why did you not pursue them, and recover the body? They were out of sight when we awoke, and we did not know which way they went. What is the penalty for going to sleep when on duty as sentinel? The penalty is death. Then you testify that you lay down and went to sleep, with death staring you in the face as the penalty? Yes, sir. How many constitute a full Roman guard? Sixty. How many of them were asleep? All of them. Then how do you know the disciples came and stole the body, if you were asleep all that time? You are not a competent witness, and such a witness would be ruled out of Court. The witness can step aside.

VII. I next present the argument on the testimony. *First*—It would be a miracle for an able bodied soldier to go to sleep under those circumstances of the death penalty. *Second*—Sixty asleep under similar circumstances would be sixty miracles, and the testimony requires to believe in sixty miracles, to avoid believing the miracle of the resurrection. *Third*—The coincidence of all going to sleep at the same time, makes it sixty miracles intensified. *Fourth*—It is further intensified by the sleep being prolonged till the disciples passed their sleeping bodies, broke the seal, rolled back the heavy stone door, entered the tomb, took off the napkin, folded it up carefully, and laid it in a place by itself, unwrapped the long bandages from limbs and body and folded them up and laid them in another place; then took up the body and carried it away, passing between the sleeping bodies of the sentinels, as they lay on the ground in the moonlight, without awakening one of them, and arriving at some place of safety, out of sight and hearing, before the sleeping guards waked up. *Fifth*—The witnesses admit they were asleep all the time the facts to which they testify are said to have been transpiring, and it is sleepy testimony. So we are asked to believe all these miraculous inconsistencies, rather than believe the miracle of the resurrection! *Sixth*. The probabilities are all at fault. Suppose the disciples had undertaken to steal away the body; several difficulties would stare them in the face. 1. What time in the night shall we go? The nearer midnight the lighter, for it is always full moon the time of the passover. 2. How shall we elude the guards in bright moonlight? Coming in sight, they see the guards all lying on the ground with their faces upturned to the light of the moon. How fortunate! They glide between the sleeping bodies like ghosts by moonlight. 3. Who will have the courage to break the seal, and thus defy the authority of the Roman empire? But they conclude to share that responsibility. 4. How can we remove the great stone without waking the sleepers? With their combined strength they roll it away, and not one sleeper stirs. 5. They enter and commence unwrapping, as above described. Stop! Right there the story breaks down and falls to pieces. Had they succeeded in gaining access to the body, the first impulse would be to seize the body, wrapped as it was, and convey it away without stopping to unwrap it there. But this is the best they have on that side of the question.

We now turn to the testimony on the other side. Brother Paul, summon your witnesses—you are the affirmant. You say he arose from the dead. Who saw him? Peter saw him. Who else? The twelve saw him. Well, twelve living witnesses should be good testimony. Call another witness. James saw him. Any others? Yes; above five hundred brethren saw him at one time. Are they still living? Yes, most of them are alive, and could be summoned to testify. Any other interviews? Yes, again he was seen by all the apostles. Paul, did you see him yourself? Yes, I saw him. Here we have a galaxy of living witnesses who saw him after his resurrection. Many of them laid down their lives in attestation of the truth, sealing their testimony with their blood. Follow Paul in his preaching tours. A mob sets upon him, and he persistently affirms: "I saw Jesus." They stone him and leave him for dead. The like is oft repeated, till he can say "in deaths oft." Again and again he is imprisoned for preaching a risen Savior, till he can say: "In prisons more frequent." Chastisement with rods, administered so freely that in his inventory of his effects he writes down: "Thrice was I beaten with rods." And still he persists in sayin, "I saw Jesus." See him as they deliberately tie him to the whipping-post and upon his bare back administer thirty-nine lashes, each followed by a flow of blood, while at each successive stripe he reaffirms: "I saw

Jesus." Again and again is he treated to a like indignity, till he deliberately records: "Of the Jews five times received I forty stripes, save one." Follow him to Rome, and see him incarcerated in prison, where he writes: "For I am now ready to be offered, and the time of my departure is at hand. I have fought a good fight; I have finished my course; I have kept the faith. Henceforth there is laid up for me a crown of righteousness, which the Lord, the righteous judge shall give me in that day." Then follow him to the execution—his head placed on the block. As the executioner's axe that is to sever his head from his body begins to descend, he reiterates for the last time: "*I saw Jesus!*" And his head rolls from his body, crimsoned with the spouting gore.

Such is the character of the testimony and witnesses for "Jesus and the resurrection."

IV.
THE CORONATION—HUMILIATION AND EXALTATION.

DELINEATION.

Phil. 2:5–11;	CORONATION	Eph. 1:19–23.
1 Equal with God.		Head. 8
2 Form of God.	*Humiliation.* *Exaltation.*	Body. 7
3 Disrobed.		Name. 6
4 Form of Servant.		Dominion. 5
5 Likeness of Men.		Might. 4
6 Humbled.		Power. 3
7 Obedient.		Principality. 2
8 Death.		Dead. 1

SURVEY.

"CROWNED with glory and honor," is predicated of "Jesus, who was made a little lower than the angels for the suffering of death." (Heb. 2: 9.) And, as He stooped to conquer, or, "was made lower," *antecedent* to being "crowned," I will glance briefly at the *humiliation* before the ascent, or *exaltation* to the throne.

Equality with God, from being in the divine form, might be predicated without usurpation. But through unexampled philanthrophy, he *disrobes* himself of His garments of royalty in the palace royal of the universe, descends to earth, in *human* form, to *serve* the race, and *humbly* renders *obedience* to the law, until the *death* of the cross proclaims of His voluntary servitude: "It is finished." Having conquered death, He is entitled to *our obedience.* "Wherefore God hath highly exalted Him, and given Him a name which is above every name," and ordained that, "every tongue should confess that Jesus Christ is Lord, to the glory of God the Father." (Phil. 2: 5–11.)

We are now prepared to witness the *Coronation* so sublimely portrayed by the inspired apostle: "According to the working of his mighty power, which he wrought in Christ, when he raised him from the dead and set him at his own right hand in the heavenly places, far above all principality, and power, and might, and dominion, and every name that is named, not only in this world [age] but also in that which is to come; and hath put all things under his feet, and gave him to be the head over all things to the church, which is his body, the fullness of him that filleth all in all." Eph., 1: 19—23.

Enraptured inspiration seems to have illuminated the apostle's pen, as in one grand sweep he carries us from the grave to the throne of the universe, in a single sentence. He seems to have placed the foot of the ladder in the tomb and leaned the top against the throne of God, while a halo of sublimity encircling the top flashes its radiance over the intervening steps into the dark charnel house of the race, to reveal the basic stratum of all-conquering power, and pioneer the pathway of the conqueror from the grave to the throne of universal sovereignty. As the eagle, soaring "far above," may contemplate the mountain peaks below, so the apostle contemplates Christ as "far above" all these intermediate steps as outlined in the delineation.

1. *Dead.* In the cold embrace of death he meets the grim monster—the king of terror, and terror of kings—in his own dominions and conquers him, carrying away the keys of death and hades. Then, after

the figure of Oriental conquering kings, drags him, as a trophy, chained to his chariot wheels. Escorted by a convoy of agels to his heavenly home—from which he had been absent some thirty-three years, on his mission of the world's redemption—approaching the battlements of heaven, the heralds proclaim: "Lift up your heads, O ye gates, and be lifted up ye everlasting doors; and the King of Glory shall come in." The response from the sentinels on the watch towers is returned: "Who is this King of Glory?" The heralds send back the triumphant answer: "The Lord strong and mighty—the Lord mighty in battle. Lift up your heads, O ye gates; even lift them up ye everlasting doors; and the King of Glory shall come in." Psalm 24:7—9. Such was the vision of the approaching coronation scene, as painted by the psalmist more than a thousand years antecedent to its consummation.

2. *Principality.* Unquestioned superiorty is expressed by the term "far above." It is not expressive of a bare majority, but an overwhelmning majority that overrules every doubt. Principality is government. When he was on earth the Jewish government assumed jurisdiction over him, and the Roman government still higher sovereignty. But now the tables are turned, and he is above, and *far* above, Jewish and Roman government, and all government. Shall we acknowledge his sovereignty?

3. *Power.* The original is *authority.* They claimed authority over him once, but now he is above *all* authority. Bring on the authority of magistrates, and governors, and kings, and emperors the world over, and our leader is "far above" them all. Can we trust him?

4. *Might.* This is the word for ability, or power, and may represent the military power of the governments. But the available power of the captain of our salvation is "far above all;" for, even when on earth, he claimed his Father would honor his draft for more than twelve legions of angels." Mat., 26:53.

5. *Dominion.* Etymologically, this means lordship. Now, bring all the lords and lordships in the world, and our Lord outranks them all.

6. *Name.* Here name means *authority*, as agents act in the name of those they represent. Rulers transact their legal business in the name—that is, by the authority of the government they represent. To illustrate: A mob had collected in a great city to do violence to a certain house, and thousands passing by had stopped in the crowd to see what was going on. The leaders were about to smash doors and windows, when the voice of the Mayor of the city was heard above the hum of the crowd, and the multitude listened to a short speech, delivered in a clear, strong, and forcible style, in these words: "In the name of the State of Ohio, I command you to disperse." And that crowd did disperse. It was a short speech, but it had power in it. And the power was in the *name*. They knew that the *name* was backed by the military power of the State. And acting in the *name* was taking refuge in that power. Do you say there is nothing in a name? The *name* of Jesus Christ is high authority. To act in his *name* is to recognize his authority and take refuge in his authority. The first time his authority was ever made known on earth those who were baptized in his name took refuge in his authority. Acts, 2:36, 38. And his name, or authority, is supreme.

7. *Body.* The Church of Christ is his *body*, and is subject to the head, *in heaven.* A church with a head on earth must be something else than the Church of Christ.

8. *Head.* Crowned heads of the Old World claim great authority over nations and kingdoms and empires. But Christ has been crowned head over all things to the Church, and made "both Lord and Christ." Acts, 2: 36. And this exaltation, glorification, and coronation—in a series of events—culminating in putting the reins of government and universal sovereignty into the hands of the Christ, as prophet, priest, and king, took place after his ascension, and constituted the chief burden of the message of the Holy Spirit, born from heaven, and first made known to men on the day of Pentecost.

The prophets speak of a time coming when the kingdoms of this world shall become the kingdoms of the Lord Jesus Christ, and when all dominions shall serve him. Will we acknowledge his headship, recognize his authority, and obey his commands? Let us not be like those who said, "We will not have this man to reign over us." May suffering and dying love draw us to willing obedience.

V.
THE GREAT SALVATION.—Heb. 2:1-4.
Corollary to Proposition in Heb. I:2.

DELINEATION.

Terms.—or *Ages*.	Illustrations.
1—Adamic.—Gen. 2:17.	1—Noah—Gen. 6:1-4.
2—Patriarchal—Gen. 4:7.	2—Lot—Gen. 19:12-16
3—Jewish.—Lev. 4:27-31.	3—Egypt—Ex. 12:7.
4—Christian { Alien—Acts 2:36-38 / Citizen—Acts 8:22.	4—Naaman, 2 Ki. 5:10

SURVEY.

"THEREFORE we ought to give the more earnest heed to the things which we have heard, lest at any time we should let them slip. For if the word spoken by angels was steadfast, and every transgression and disobedience received a just recompense of reward; how shall we escape if we neglect so great salvation; which at the first began to be spoken by the Lord, and was confirmed unto us by them that heard him." (Heb, 2.1-4.)

Here the apostle introduces, with "therefore," a corollary to his proposition in first sentence of previous chapter: "God hath spoken to us by his son." This "great salvation" is salvation from *sin*, or remission of sins *in the name of Jesus*, which "*began* to be spoken by the Lord" to the apostles (see Mk., 16:15, 16, and Lk., 24:46-49), and *by them* confirmed miraculously and authoritatively to us and to the world. See Acts, 2; 36-42. An induction of these passages and others will show positively that this "great salvation" was never offered to the world till the day of Pentecost.

And the terms of that salvation were made known by the Holy Spirit that day, fresh from the courts of heaven. That no *non-essentials* are in these requirements, is assured by the apostle in the significant question: "How shall we escape if we neglect so great salvation?" enforced by the fact that in the former dispensations "every transgression and disobedience received a just recompense of reward." Not a *non-essential* there.

A few of these terms may be enforced by analysis: 1. *Disobedience.* The base of the word is *obey*, which, as every child knows, means to *do* what is required. The prefix, *dis* (not), makes *disobey*, meaning *not to do* the requirements. The suffix, *ence* (the act), makes obedience mean the act of obeying. Then *disobedience* means the neglect, or *not doing*. For these *neglects* they were held responsible. 2. *Transgression. Trans* (over or beyond), *gress* (to go or step), *ion* (the act). Combine these and we have *transgression*, the act of stepping over, or going beyond, and doing what is forbidden. These are sometimes distinguished as sins of *omission* and sins of *commission*, both of which were *responsible* sins. 3. *Neglect.* From *neg* (not), and *lect* (to choose). Hence, to neglect is to *not choose*. This shows conclusively that the "great salvation" is offered upon terms that may be *accepted* or *neglected.* We may *choose* or *not choose*, and be held responsible for our choice. I knew a man once who, speaking of the *obedience* of the gospel, said he did not *choose* to go to heaven by water. It is possible that others do not choose that way. It is also barely possible that some of the Israelites, on the hither side of the Red Sea, did not *choose* the *water route*, in which case it may be questionable whether they joined in the song of rejoicing on the other side.

Salvation implies suffering, or danger, from which to be saved. We may then raise a few questions, to each of which there can be but one of two answers. 1. Does man need salvation? 2. Has God offered him salvation? 3. If so, has he offered the salvation conditionally or unconditionally? 4. If conditionally, has he revealed the terms, or conditions? 5. If the terms are revealed to us in the word "spoken to us by his son," may we reasonably expect to enjoy that salvation without complying with the terms? Or, as Paul expresses it in the text, "How shall we escape if we neglect so great salvation?"

This last question will now be our theme, assuming it as admitted that the four antecedent questions have been correctly answered, and that God has revealed the terms upon which he has offered conditional salvation to man who was in need of salvation. *What* the terms are we do not discuss in this discourse, but refer you to the citations in the *delineation* above, where you will find the terms given in each dispensation thus: *Adamic*—Prohibition of the fruit of one tree. *Patriarchal*—Animal sacrifice offered by the person, or head of the family. *Jewish*—Sacrifice offered through the priest. *Christian*—Dispensation for the *alien*, faith in Christ, repentance toward Christ, and baptism into Christ. For the *citizen*, repentance and prayer. The terms are not under discussion in this discourse; you can turn and read them for yourselves. Our question is, are they *essential* or *non-essential*, or may they be *neglected* with impunity?

1. Was it essential in the *Adamic* age to refrain from eating the forbidden fruit, in order to continue in God's favor? They transgressed and suffered the penalty. Then "how shall we escape?"

2. In the first example under the *Patriarchal* was it *essential* for Cain and Abel to offer the bleeding victim? By *faith* Abel offered an acceptable offering, which shows that he knew the requirement, and that "without the shedding of blood there is no remission." Cain came with a *substitute*, in which he *sinned* and was rejected, and "sin is the transgression of the law." Cain's "*neglect*" then was *transgression*, and he suffered the penalty. Then, "how shall we escape?"

3. Under the *law*, the Jew who complied with the terms of forgiveness and brought his lamb to the priest, had the word of God for it that when the priest had made the atonement for him he was forgiven, and rejoiced in the remission of sins understandingly. But, if he failed to comply with the terms, he despised Moses' law. And Paul says: "He that despised Moses' law died without mercy." Then, "how shall we escape, if we neglect?"

1. Dark clouds of vengeance brooded over the earth, threatening destruction to the race, when God gave Noah specific instructions for the building of an ark. And Noah never inquired whether that was *essential*, or whether a canoe or a steamship would do as well, but "prepared an ark to the saving of his house," in the *neglect* of which he could not have hoped to *escape*. Then, "how shall we escape, if we neglect?"

2. Terrible was the cloud of sin that enveloped Sodom and called for divine retribution, when not ten righteous persons could be found in all her borders. Fiery billows will soon roll over the devoted city. God sends a warning messenger to Lot and family, with terms of escape from the impending ruin. They are explicit: Arise, and flee from the city! Lot

and his wife and two single daughters accept the terms and escape, while sons-in-law and married daughters who neglected, or did not choose, were left behind and involved in the great conflagration.

This salvation of Lot and family was clearly conditional, and terms made known that could be neglected or complied with. And in view of the facts, it is needless to inquire for the *non-essential*. But "how shall we escape?" Apropos, at this point, is the following graphic poetical description, which I stored away, years ago, in my boyhood's memory:

> A sound of mirth was heard by night,
>   Its merry peals rang high;
> And song, and dance, and sinful rite,
>   Bade the wingéd moments fly.
>
> Glad Sodom, in her pomp and pride,
>   Gave up her soul to glee;
> And proud Gomorrah, by her side,
>   Rang with the revelry.
>
> Thy streets, Zeboim, too, were glad—
>   Glad with unholy mirth;
> And Admah's drunken sons were mad,
>   And ruled upon the earth.
>
> The night passed on; the torches' light
>   Flashed far from tower to wall;
> And gay forms, gliding to the sight,
>   Glanced bright from bower to hall.
>
> The morning came, and all was still,
>   Save those warned from on high,
> Who, fast toward the distant hill,
>   With hurried steps, flew by.
>
> The sun arose, and fiercely swept
>   Along his red'ning path,
> While riot's drunken sons still slept,
>   Nor dreamed of coming wrath.

There is a dark cloud rolling on,
  Swift as a rushing flood;
Its heaving bosom, dim and dun,
  Seems filled with flame and blood.

It closes o'er them, fierce and fast,
  Red streams of sulphur pour;
Lightning, and smoke, and fiery blast
  Mix with the thunder's roar.

But hark! a deep yell rends the sky—
  Ten thousands shriek aloud!
The cry of mortal agony—
  Man struggling with his God!

'Tis done. That cloud has rolled away;
  But where, Oh where are ye?
Yon dark, black lake alone can say,
  Ye cities of the sea.

3. When the dark-winged angel of death was commissioned to enter the houses of Egypt, at dead of night, and slay the first-born of every family, exemption from this death was offered to the families of Israelites, upon terms announced. The terms were to place blood upon the two side-posts and the lintel of each door, and the destroyer would pass over every door thus protected and not enter. Did anyone hint *non-essential*, or *neglect* either door, or side-post, or lintel. Compliance with the terms secured safety.

4. Naaman, captain of the Assyrian host, makes a raid into the land of Israel, and among the captives carries home a Jewish girl, who becomes a waiting maid in his family. Naaman is a leper, and learning, through the little Jewess, that the prophet in Israel could cure him, marches to the residence of Elisha, and in due form announces his arrival. The prophet sends by the servant the terms—"Go wash seven times

in the Jordan, and be cured." Naaman at first declares it a *non-essential*, and then asks if something else will not do as well. He proposes to go home and wash in Abana and Pharpar, instead of the Jordan. Finally the sober second thought prevails, and he complies with the prescribed terms. "Then went he down and dipped himself seven times in Jordan, according to the saying of the man of God." As soon as he had complied with the terms strictly, and not before, he was cured.

With such examples as these recorded for our admonition, how can we reasonably expect to enjoy the "great salvation," the remission of sins, without complying with the terms? Or, in the language of the text: "How shall we escape if we neglect?" Then, let us "give the more earnest heed to the things which we have heard."

VI.
POWER OF THE GOSPEL.—Rom. 1:16.

DELINEATION.

I. Power Moves { 1. Matter. 2. Spirit. }

II. Spirit { 1. Divine. 2. Human. 3. Satanic. }

III. { 1. Divine 2. Human 3. Satanic } Physical Power.

IV. { 1. Divine 2. Human 3. Satanic } Spiritual Power.

SURVEY.

"FOR I am not ashamed of the gospel of Christ; for it is the power of God unto salvation to every one that believes." (Rom. 1:16.)

What does the apostle mean by "the gospel?" In the preceding verse, he says: "I am ready to preach the gospel to you that are at Rome also." In the following verse, he says: "For therein is the righteousness of God revealed." Then the gospel reveals God's righteousness, and when preached, becomes his power for salvation. In full accord, the same apostle says: "In whom ye also trusted, after that ye heard the word of truth, the gospel of your salvation." Eph. 1:13. Then by "the gospel," Paul means, "the word of truth."

What is "power?" Here I send you to philosophy, where you learn that power is that which *moves*, or sets in motion. Then without power there is no motion. The power and the object moved must have a mutual adaptation. No man thinks of applying steam power to propel machinery adapted to water power, without change in adaptation. The overshot wheel, undershot wheel, and breast wheel, have each a different adaptation to water power. The spring of the watch, and weight of the clock, are differently adapted to the application of power.

Antithesis in the analysis of the text may assist us just here. (*a.*) The gospel is *God's power*, not *man's* power. (*b.*) It is *the* power, not *a* power, or one of the powers, as though God had put forth some other power for the same purpose. Logically, then, we are not at liberty to look for some other power for that purpose, unless God has, somewhere in his word, told us that he has put forth such power.

But you ask: Are you not limiting God's power? I answer: It is not my limitation, but that of the inspired apostle. You ask again: "Has not God, at some time, put forth some other power?" I cheerfully concede that he has. In the morning of creation, when the heaven and the earth stood forth at his bidding, he put forth creative power. Then, on the first day of cosmic formation, he said: "Let light be, and light was." On the second day he caused the firmament, or atmosphere, to encompass the earth, and on the third day created vegetation without the seed. In each of these, he put forth absolute power, and not the "power of the gospel."

But at this point he limited his own power by a law of reproduction, ordaining that created vegetation should thenceforth bring forth seed after its kind. And man, to this day, respects that law, and sows his wheat, and plants his corn, never dreaming that grains of corn will produce wheat, or oats, or acorns produce apple trees.

A farmer is sowing wheat, if you please, and a neighbor comes along and inquires why you are sowing wheat. You say you sow it to procure a harvest of wheat. He says he thinks the grain is not necessary to secure a crop. You say the germ contained in the seed is God's power for vegetable life. He replies that you are limiting God's power. Did not God create vegetation at first without the seed? Yes. Has he not as much power now as he had then? Yes. Then can he not give me a crop of wheat without the seed? Yes, he *could*, but *will* he, since he has given you the power in the germ, the law of reproduction? It is not a question of *can*, but of *will*.

He says he has more faith than you, and intends to pray God to give him a crop without the seed. He wants it by *faith alone*. We leave him in the field to pray daily for a crop, and to report when he gets it without the seed.

Christ, while here, claimed and exercised power on earth to forgive sins, but not in his own name. Before his ascension, he merged his power to forgive sins into a law of "forgiveness of sins in his name," and left it in the hands of his apostles to be promulgated after his glorification, which they did on the day of Pentecost, and it is now a part of "the word of truth, the gospel of our salvation," the power of which for salvation, Paul says he is not ashamed. Now, suppose some one, "ashamed of the gospel," persists in praying to God for remission of sins without complying with the terms. Will he not be like the man we left in the field? We will leave them out there together, both equally inconsistent, and possibly they will report together.

Next: Suppose a man, determined to be independent of God's power, taxes his skill and makes a grain of corn, just like a natural grain in size, shape, color, hardness, and weight, and plants it and fails. What is the trouble? It did not contain the *germ*, which is God's power. Man may make a grain, but cannot place the *germ* in it, and it will be not God's power, but man's power, and inoperative. So man may make a system of religion resembling the gospel in some respects, but it will only be *man's* power, for the gospel is God's power.

Our friend, if you please, next experiments on the natural grain. He plants it in dry sand, and makes a failure. Why? He ignored one of the conditions of vegetation. Moisture is necessary to the development of the germ. Grains of wheat have been found among the mummies in the catacombs of Egypt, where they had lain in the dry, for thousands of years, without growing, and containing the germ all that time, for when brought out and planted, under right conditions, they grew, and produced the kind of wheat they raised in Egypt four thousand years ago.

He next plants in soil in a box, and waters it well, but lets it freeze, and fails again. Now what is the trouble? Another condition is ignored. Warmth is required for vegetation.

Again, he plants in a box of well watered soil, down in a deep, dark cellar, free from Jack frost, and makes another failure. This time light was the desideratum ignored. Light is necessary to healthy vegetation.

Lastly, he plants his grain out in the open air, in soil watered by the rains of heaven, and warmed and lighted by the genial influences of the sun, and a healthy growth rewards his labor.

So the word of God, the "seed of the kingdom," though eighteen hundred years old, is still "living and powerful," yet requiring the right conditions in order to become "the power of God unto salvation."

But this is God's power for *vegetable* life we have been considering, which is not the power of the gospel. We then return to the text, and look for another limitation.

(c.) It is the power of God for *salvation*. But here again you ask, has not God put forth power for salvation other than the gospel? I answer yes. He put forth power for the salvation of Noah, and Daniel, and the three Hebrew children, which was not the power of the gospel, even though it checked the seven-fold heat of the fiery furnace, tamed the ferocity of lions in their den, and swept from the earth a sin cursed race.

(d.) To whom, then, is it power for salvation? "To every one that *believes*." Here, then, we have the final limitation. To the *believer* it is the power for salvation, for it tells him what to do to be saved. To the unbeliever it is the power unto believing, as John says: "Written that you might believe that Jesus is the Christ." Jno. 20: 31.

I might take a short route here, by showing that it tells men what to do to be saved; but I wish to trace the power home. To this end I call attention to the Delineation.

I. Power is that which moves something, for some purpose, and may act upon or move either matter or spirit. All objects liable to be moved by power may be classified into two classes, known as *matter* and *spirit*. Power acting upon matter is called *physical* power, but acting on spirit, it is *spiritual* power. This gives us two classes of power as to the objects upon which it terminates.

How are these classes distinguished? What are their differentia? I again send you to philosophy. Ask the school children who are studying philosophy to give you the essential qualities of matter, and among them they will name *inertia*. Ask them what they mean by *essential*, and they will tell you it means that which belongs to all matter, and without which matter does not exist. Then ask them to define *inertia*, and they will tell you it means the want of power—the absence of power—and that no particle of matter, small or great, can move itself.

From this we see that power cannot originate in the material world, and we must therefore trace power to the spirit world. We understand spirit to be essentially active, and capable of moving itself, and acting upon either matter or spirit.

II. All the spirit powers may be arranged in three classes. 1. God, the Holy Spirit, and all the holy angels, may constitute the first class, which we will call *Divine* spirit power. 2. Man has a spirit within him, and the whole human race may compose the second class, which we will call *Human* spirit power. 3. Satan is regarded as a spirit, and having angels or messengers subject to him, and these may be grouped into a third class, and called *Satanic* spirit power. This gives us *Divine* spirit power, *Human* spirit power, and *Satanic* spirit power, making three classes of power as to the source.

Then as each of these classes of power may act upon either of the two classes of objects, making three classes of physical power and three classes of spiritual power, we have six classes of power all told. And this is an exhaustive classification.

III. If divine, human, or satanic power acts upon matter, it gives us these classes, as in the Delineation: 1. Divine physical power. 2. Human physical power. 3. Satanic physical power.

IV. Divine, human, or satanic power, acting upon spirit, gives us: 1. Divine spiritual power. 2. Human spiritual power. 3. Satanic spiritual power.

In one of these classes, then, we must look for the power of the gospel. As the gospel is not addressed to inanimate objects, but to intelligences, we may dismiss the three classes of *Physical* power, and search in the three classes of *Spiritual* power.

The power of the gospel, then, is either Divine, Human, or Satanic spiritual power. If I begin at the lowest, and assume that it is Satanic, you will all say no. Then we have but two left. If I next assume it to be Human, you all say no. Or if any one assumes it, for the sake of argument, the text denies it, for it says it is God's power. Then we have traced it home. And beyond all peradventure, the Divine spiritual power is put forth in the gospel.

Power requires a medium of communication. Physical power requires a physical medium. But as the gospel does not propose to move inanimate objects, we do not look for a physical medium.

The normal medium of spiritual communication is *language.* Jesus recognized this distinction when, at Capernaum, he healed such multitudes of all kinds of diseases. The physical maladies he cured with a touch—a physical medium. But when he came to those possessed of evil spirits, he *spoke* to the spirits, and commanded them to come out, and the record says, "they obeyed him."

Suppose you see a friend passing your store, hastening to the depot, and you say, please step in and we will arrange that little business. He says, I have not time now. I have barely time to make the train, and it will be at least five dollars out of pocket if I miss this train. You pull out a twenty dollar gold piece and give him, saying take that; it will be worth more than that to me to have the business attended to now. He then cheerfully goes in and attends to your business, and waits for the next train. Now you have worked in him both to will and to do your pleasure. And the medium through which you communicated that power that turned him was language.

Suppose I convince the hearers in a large audience that I am authorized to bestow upon them as a Christmas gift, ten thousand gold dollars, and that I will throw them broadcast in the aisles, and they are at liberty to leave their seats and pick up the dollars, and get all they can, and keep all they get. Then, suiting the action to the word, I scatter the dollars on the floor, and watch the results. Would anybody be moved? Do you say everybody would be moved. Perhaps not. Who would not be moved with such a dollar argument as that?

Three classes might not be moved. First, a man might be asleep, and not hear the argument and proposition. Second, a deaf mute might be present and not hear. Third, a foreigner, or Indian, who did not understand a word of the English language, might be present, and not be moved by the proposition.

In these supposed cases the power was a *motive* put forth in language that moved them to action. A *motive* means something that *can move*, and these were pecuniary motives.

Now the gospel contains *motives*, high as heaven, deep as the grave, vast as the universe, and weighty as a world of gold, and are put forth in language which must be heard, understood, and acted upon, in order to be the power of God unto salvation.

Paul says, when the spiritual gifts have passed away, Faith, Hope, and Love remain. Then the gospel, to be the power of God, must contain the faith producing power, the hope producing power, and the love producing power. And it does.

The faith producing power is presented in the miracles wrought in attestation of the divine mission and the fulfillment of prophecy.

The hope producing power beams forth in the evidences of the resurrection.

The love producing power hangs like a convoy of beckoning angels around the story of the cross. Love is the strongest power in man, and in suffering and dying love, that power is intensified. Christ said: "I, if I be lifted up, will draw all men to me." Here the lifting up on the cross is a *drawing* power.

We sometimes sing, "I yield, I yield, I can hold out no more; I sink by dying love compelled, and own thee conqueror." Conquered by love, the true and efficient "power of the gospel."

We have now reached the penetralia, the inner temple of gospel power, and deem the sentiments of the following hymn an appropriate ending:

> Plunged in a gulf of dark despair,
> We wretched sinners lay,
> Without one cheering beam of hope,
> Or spark of glimmering day.

With pitying eyes, the prince of peace,
Beheld our helpless grief.
He saw, and oh! amazing love,
He ran to our relief.

Down from the shining seats above,
With joyful haste he fled,
Entered the grave in mortal flesh,
And dwelt among the dead.

O, for this love, let rocks and hills,
Their lasting silence break,
And all harmonious human tongues
Their Savior's praises speak.

Angels, assist our mighty joys,
Strike all your harps of gold,
But when you raise your highest notes,
His love can ne'er be told.

VII.
RIGHTLY DIVIDING THE WORD OF TRUTH.

DELINEATION.

I. *Paths Illuminated.*	II. *Lamp Adjustments.*
1—Faith in God.	1—Old Testament.
2—Faith in Jesus Christ.	2—The Four Testimonies.
3—Terms of Remission.	3—Apostolic Practice.
4—Christian Duty.	4.—The Epistles.
5—Our Heavenly Home.	5—Revelation.

SURVEY.

"STUDY to show thyself approved unto God, a workman that needeth not to be ashamed, rightly dividing the word of truth." (2 Tim. 2:15.)

"Thy word is a lamp to my feet, and a light to my path." (Psalm 119:105.)

While the apostles of Christ could speak infallibly by direct inspiration, all other preachers must *study* the apostles' teaching, in order to be master workmen approved of God. And the secret of success in becoming an "approved workman, that need not be ashamed," lies in "rightly dividing the word of truth," which requires "study."

The Bible, the word of truth, is a large book, containing sixty-six different books in one volume, thirty-nine of them in the Old Testament, and twenty-seven of them in the New Testament. These books were written by many different men, in different periods of time, and running through many centuries. These books, though inspired of God, were written for different purposes; and to simply direct the inquirer to the

Bible for information would be very indefinite instruction. The Christian teacher must be able to direct the inquirer to the particular part or division of the word of truth, in which the desired information may be found. Then he "need not be ashamed." In default of this preparation he ought to "be ashamed" and go and "study" his lesson better before attempting its public rehearsal.

The psalmist says the word of God is both a *lamp* to the *feet* and a *light* to the *path*. These two expressions are not identical, and are wisely put in. The psalmist refers to the oriental custom of horsemen riding at night with lamps attached to the stirrups of the saddle. In the saddle, and feet in the stirrups, he has a *lamp* to the *feet;* but the lamp must be lighted and properly adjusted before it can be *also*, or "and" a *light* to the *path*.

So God's lamp, the "word of truth," must be "studied" in its adjustments by "rightly dividing" in order to make it "a light to the path."

Some of us can remember when lanterns were made of tin, with holes punched through to let the faintly glimmering light shine out. Then came the glass lantern; then a reflector was added. Now the headlight of the locomotive, with its great concave reflector, gathers the radiant rays and throws them all forward in one concentrated "light to the path" of the fleet iron horse.

As oil without lamp, and lamp without oil, gives no light, but oil must be in the lamp to give light, so the Spirit of God, the oil, to illuminate, must be in the *word*, the lamp, in order, through the word, to be a *light* to the path. Word alone, or Spirit alone, illuminates not. Divorce the Spirit from the word, and call it the *mere word*, and we will find ourselves, like the foolish virgins, in the dark.

The anointing with oil, or the Spirit, for official sanctification, is a different thing, and does not represent its *illuminating* prerogative.

The Christian teacher is liable to be called upon to throw the light of the divine lamp on the various paths in which the inquirer needs to travel, for which emergency he must prepare himself by studying the lamp adjustments, and "rightly dividing the word of life."

To facilitate this preparation, I call attention to the delineation, and inaugurate a series of illustrations for practical application.

First—I will suppose an honest, intelligent, and highly educated inquirer after the truth calls upon you for instruction. He is familiar with the sciences, and with Grecian mythology, but knows nothing of the Bible. He says: Sir, I understand that you claim to worship a God that created all things, and rules in heaven above and on the earth. Now if there be such a God, it is worth all else beside to know and serve him. And if you believe in him you must have some evidence upon which you believe, for men cannot believe without evidence or testimony. Will you do me the favor to refer me to the book containing the evidence.

Now you are called upon to adjust your lamp to shine upon path number one, that leads to *faith in God*. Having "studied" the right divisions, you give him a copy of the Old Testament, and tell him to read first the historical and prophetic portions, beginning with the first chapter of Genesis.

Our friend takes the book and retires to his studio in the midst of his library, and commences the study in good earnest. He reads the first sentence. "In the beginning God created the heaven and the earth." He is struck with the majesty of the proposition, and begins to contrast it with mythology. It never has been predicated of Jupiter on Mount Olympus, that he even made the *mountain* on which he is said to be enthroned, much less that he created the *heaven* and the *earth*. If this be true of him, it places him so far above Jupiter, and all the thirty thousand gods of Grecian mythology, that his pre-eminence will wipe out all other gods, and monotheism stand unrivaled.

He then remembers that some skeptical geologists say that the Bible account of creation, is contradicted by geology, in that the former makes the earth only about six thousand years old, while the latter, in the strata of rocks, carries its antiquity back through many cycles into the middle of a past eternity. He reads the proposition again, and begins to question the votary of the stony book. You admit, according to the nebular theory, that the earth had a beginning, beyond which period, matter spread far and wide in the form of incandescent vapor. How far back do you place that beginning? If you say ten thousand millions of years, drive down your stake and stand by it. If that is the beginning, then that is where the Bible says God created it, for it says he created it "in the beginning," but does not say *when* that beginning was. It affirms the *fact* of the creation, but does not locate the *antiquity* of that inaugurating fact. There can therefore be no contradiction.

He next compares the six days of cosmic formation, with the pages of the stony book, and finds no contradiction there, but God's creative and organic power manifest throughout.

First day—While darkness was upon the face of the deep that surrounded the earth, God said: "Let light be, and light was," of course *where* the darkness was before. Light exists now, and the stony book testifies not on the subject of its introduction, and therefore cannot contradict the Bible account.

Second day—God said: "Let there be a firmament, and it was so." The firmament, or atmosphere exists now, and the pages of the stony book, bear no testimony concerning the time of its beginning, and cuts off contradiction.

Third day—Land emerges from the deep, and vegetation covers the dry land at the command of God. The leaves of the stony book, in fossil remains, bear testimony to the pre-adamic existence of vegetation, without giving its *date* or disputing the *fact* of its Divine creation.

Fourth day—God said: "Let there be lights in the firmament, and it was so." The mists that rolled in splendor during the *translucent* period, had rolled away, or were precipitated, till the sun, moon and stars, now visible through a *transparent* atmosphere, become lights in the firmament. Those twinkling lights have not yet winked out, and the leaves of the stony book are as silent as the grave, on the subject of their first appearance as lights in our firmament, and no contradiction.

Fifth day—God commanded the waters to bring forth fish to swim in the great deep, and fowl to fly in the upper deep, and they are here yet. The leaves of the stony book in fossiliferous rocks, accord to fish and fowl, an antiquity anterior to man upon the earth, as the Bible does, but contradicts not either the *fact* or *period* of creation.

Sixth day—Creation of land animals affirmed. The fossiliferous leaves of the stony book show land animals as pre-existent to man, but locates not the *period*, and contradicts not the *fact* of their creation. So the charge that geology contradicts the Bible account of creation is without foundation.

Our friend goes to the prophecies and reads predictions concerning men, and cities, and countries, and nations, which, in course of time, are fulfilled with wonderful minutia, each receiving the judgment pronounced against *it*, and not what was spoken of *another*.

As an example, he reads Isaiah's description of the fall of Babylon, uttered about a hundred and seventy-four years before its fulfillment, in which the prophet speaks of drying up its rivers, loosing the loins of kings, opening the two leaved gates, breaking in pieces the brazen gates, bringing to light the hidden treasures, and making Babylon a desolation for coming ages, even giving the name of the besieging general, Cyrus, more than a hundred years before he was born. Isa. 44: 24, 28, and 45: 1, 4, and 13: 1–22.

He finds the fulfillment of this in the fifth chapter of Daniel, when, on the night of Belshazzar's feast, Cyrus dried up the waters of the Euphrates and marched his army into the city through its channel, and performed all and singular the predictions, all of which are further corroborated, both in sacred and profane history.

Second—Our friend comes to you again and says: O sir, you gave me the right book. I now believe that God, who created the heaven and the earth, rules in heaven above, and on the earth beneath, and even brings a wicked nation to chastize another wicked nation. But I come to you for further information. In the book you gave me, the prophets foretold a coming Messiah, a Redeemer and Savior, but they all close without announcing his arrival. I understand that you believe he has come. If so, you must believe on testimony. Have you the book containing the evidence? Please refer me to the testimony.

Now you are called upon to adjust your lamp to shine upon the path that leads to *faith in Jesus the Christ*, and you give him a copy of the four testimonies known as Matthew, Mark, Luke, and John, the last of which says: "These are written that you might believe that Jesus is the Christ, the son of God, and that believing you might have life through his name." Jno. 20: 31.

He reads of his prophetic and miraculous birth and childhood, his public divine recognition at his baptism, by an audible voice from heaven. He then follows him through the many recorded miracles, most of which he wrought in the presence of the multitudes, each one of which is another link rivited in that golden everlasting chain that binds the faith of man to the throne of the universe. He sees him stand on the deck of a little vessel in a storm, as one born to rule the elements, while winds and waves yield swift obedience to his command. He sees him curing all kinds of diseases, expelling demons, raising the dead, and finally entering the grave himself and conquering death, returns to heaven.

Third—Our friend comes to you again and says: You have given me the right book again. Now I believe upon the testimony, that Jesus is the Christ the son of the living God. But I come to you for further information. In the book you gave me, I learn that Jesus gave his apostles a commisssion to offer remission of sins in his name, but required them to wait and remain at Jerusalem until endued with power from on high, and then ascended to heaven out of sight, and left them waiting for the celestial telegram. I do not learn from Matthew, Mark, Luke, or John, that the apostles have yet commenced preaching remission in the name of Jesus, and no one can learn from the book you gave me what a man must do for remission of sins in the name of Jesus. If you have learned it, you must have been taught it through some other book than what you have thus far given me. I desire to know *what to do to be saved*. I do not ask for your opinion, or what Brother A or B may think, but if you have another book from the pen of inspiration that gives that information, I desire to have access to it and read it for myself.

Now you are called upon to adjust your lamp to shine upon the path that leads the believer *into the remission of sins*, and you correctly give him a copy of *apostolic practice*, known as "Acts of Apostles." He reads, and at the end of the first chapter finds the apostles still waiting.

The second chapter brings the holy spirit, and they commence preaching. With intense interest our friend watches every step, as the Holy Spirit, by Peter, makes known, for the first time on earth, the terms of remission of sins in the name of Jesus, as that day brought down from heaven. The oracle says: *Hear* these words, and proceeds with the testimony. Our friend *hears*. The oracle says: *Believe*, or be assured that Jesus has been made both Lord and Christ. Our friend *believes*. The oracle says: *Repent*. Our friend resolves to *repent* or change his mind, and follow the Lord. The oracle says: *Be baptized* in the name of Jesus Christ for the remission of sins. Our friend gladly *obeys*, as three thousand did who gladly received his word and were baptized. He now *rejoices* in citizenship in which is remission of sins, just as all may *rejoice*, who have been "instructed into the kingdom."

Fourth—Our friend comes to you again saying: You have given me the right book again. Now I have learned the way into the kingdom by the teaching of the Holy Spirit, and have obeyed, and by *faith* in God's word am enjoying the remission of past sins in the kingdom. But I come to you for further instruction. In the book you gave me I learn that those who had complied with the *terms* of remission or citizenship, "continued steadfastly in the apostles doctrine," which will be the *service* of citizenship. If you have a book on that subject, written by inspired apostles, I desire the benefit of its instruction.

Now you are called upon to adjust your lamp to shine upon the path of *Christian duties*, which are constantly *recurring* duties, requiring *steadfast* service; and you give him a copy of the *Epistles*, which are all addressed to christians or churches, to teach them how to *live* Christainly.

He reads and practices day by day, and year by year, and finally comes to you for the last time, and says: O, sir, you have given me the right book every time. This last book you gave me says; "Add to your faith virtue; and to virtue, knowledge; and to knowledge, temperance; and to temperance, patience; and to patience, godliness: and to godliness, brotherly kindness; and to brotherly kindness, charity." All these I endeavor "steadfastly" to practice, that I may attain to that abundant "entrance into the everlasting kingdom." 2 Pet. 1:5–11.

It also instructs Christians to "run with patience the

race that is set before us." Heb. 12:1. I am practricing on that race, with the crown in view.

Fifth—In this fifth and last visit of inquiry, he adds: I read in the last book you gave me, 2 Pet. 3:1-14, that the heavens shall pass away, and the earth be burned up, and that we look for new heavens and a new earth. Now if you have a book of apostolic writing that sheds light on that subject, and opens the vision of the "everlasting kingdom," I am anxious to have a glance at it before I go hence.

Now you are called upon for the last adjustment of your lamp to shine upon the path that leads into *our heavenly home*, a path starting in this life but disappearing amid the fogs of the valley of the Jordan of death. Lift the lamp higher and throw its flashes nigher to the other shore. You now give him a copy of the book of *Revelation*, the *ne plus ultra*, of the revealed will of God to man, the last division of *"the word of truth."*

With ecstatic delight our friend revels in the delineations and panoramic views, that spring to life before him, as the old apostle turns the divine telescope to the prophetic heavens, draws rays of light from the far distant Hebrew prophets, and with the spectroscope of testimony weaves them into the web of time, on which, with chromatic tints drawn from the millennial and everlasting ages, he paints a panoramic view of the world's history and the conflicts and triumphs of the Church.

In telescopic photograph, the new heaven and new earth stand forth in life like proportions, and graphic rainbow sheen. And there is no more sea. The great commercial highway of nations will not be needed there. No more curse, no more death, no more sorrow, no more crying, no more pain, are seen or known.

The New Jerusalem, the capital of the new earth, fifteen hundred miles square, and same in elevation, with gold paved streets, and open pearly gates inviting happy entrance, and lighted by the glory of God and the lamb, shines from its lofty summit, like a city set on a hill, and cannot be hid. Another glance through the telescope presents an interior photograph, in which the throne of God, once more among men, looms up as the great commanding central figure, honored with the presence of God and the Lamb. The good and the holy of all ages are there; our loved ones gone before are there, and Jesus our best friend is there, in "the realms of the blest," of which we sing, with responsive echo: "But what must it be to be there?"

Then the *bill of fare* presents rich viands and sparkling nectar, delicious enough to tempt the delectation of an epicure. The ambrosial fruit of the tree of life, of perennial verdure, yields monthly supplies. And the "sweet and sparkling water" of the river of life, clear as crystal, supplies tempting nectar fit for gods.

Separation from the tree of life in the first Paradise caused man to be *mortal*. "Dying thou shalt die." The flaming sword still keeps the way of the tree of life, and man is still mortal. Admitted to the tree of life again he becomes *immortal*. But the tree of life is still within the Paradise of God, and man, to have access must be permitted to enter through the gates into the city. Is there a passport provided? Yes. "The word of truth" extends from the first of Genesis to the last of Revelations, and carries man *from* the tree of life *to* the tree of life, giving the terms of *separation* (Gen. 2:17), and the terms of re-admittance (Rev. 22:14), which admitting passport reads: "Blessed are they that do his commandments, that they may have a right to the tree of life, and may enter in through the gates into the city."

Fellow mortal have you secured your passport? If not, it will stare you in the face from the "great white throne," which is not a "throne of *grace*," but a throne of *justice*, from which earth and heaven shall flee away. Then secure your passport, and

> "When wrapt in flames, the realms of ether glow,
> And heaven's last thunder shakes the earth below,
> You, undismayed, shall, o'er the ruins smile,
> And light your torch at nature's funeral pile."

VIII.
GOD EVERYWHERE.—Jno. 4:24; Ps. 139:1-12.

DELINEATION.

Illustrations.	*Illustrations.*
1. Entomology.	7. Attenuation of Matter.
2. Microscopic Animalcula.	8. Electrical Experiments.
3. Solars System.	9. Electric Telegraph.
4. Telescopic Sidereal Heavens.	10. The Train Dispatcher.
5. Hydrostatics.	11. Electro-Psychology.
6. Pneumatics.	12. Teleology.

SURVEY.

MATERIALISTIC skepticism, shrinking from an effort to comprehend the idea of an omnipresent God, asks the question: How can God be everywhere at the same time?

The question is significant, but has its birth in materialism. As we cannot conceive of a man, or any material object, being in different localities at the same time, so it is difficult to think of God as in all places at the same time. But the difficulty lies in the conception of God as a material being, like a man. I purpose, therefore, in this paper, to examine the subject from a scientific standpoint, and from the material, progress up to the immaterial substances.

The inspired Psalmist grasps the idea when he says: "Whither shall I go from thy spirit? or whither shall I flee from thy presence? If I ascend up into heaven, thou art there. If I make my bed in hell, behold thou art there. If I take the wings of the morning and dwell in the uttermost parts of the sea, even there shall thy hand lead me, and thy right hand shall hold me. If I say: Surely the darkness shall cover me; even the night shall be light around me. Yea, the darkness hideth not from thee, but the night shineth as the day; the darkness and the light are both alike to thee." (Ps. 139: 7-12.)

This is sufficient to show that the thought, if not the phrase, "God Everywhere," is in the Bible, whether it is to us a thinkable entity or not. But Jesus says: "God is a spirit," (Jno. 4: 24), literally rendered, *God is spirit*. This lifts us out of the material or physical, and carries us into the realms of the spiritual, or immaterial substances. I now proceed to draw some illustrations from several of the sciences, to aid us in grasping the thought, or, if you please, enable us to apprehend the incomprehensible.

1. ENTOMOLOGY.—Go with me, if you please, and stand beside a city of millions of diminutive inhabitants, the home of a colony of *ants*. As you stand by this ant hill, and watch the movements of these little architects engaged in building and repairing their city, and storing up food, you see myriads of them, in regular order, marching to and fro around their city, as busy as ants, and all apparently unconscious of your presence. Now imagine yourself listening to the conversation of a little group of ants on the opposite side of their city, as they receive, with amazement and incredulity, the report of one of their number, that there was a living being standing near their city and watching them, who was capable of seeing them all at once, and noticing all the movements of the whole colony at one glance. Just then a spruce little ant steps to the front and says: You can't stuff me with that. We can

see only a small distance, and I can't think of a being so large and far-seeing as to take in our whole colony at one view! Perhaps you pity his incredulity. But then remember, he is only a skeptical ant, and perhaps he may be as excusable as skeptics who have had better opportunities.

2. MICROSCOPIC ANIMALCULA.—We next visit a colony of animalcula in a glass of clear water. Here, possibly, we may find some human beings skeptical in regard to the very existence of these animalcules in the water. But the oxy-hydrogen microscope reveals them. I have seen the image of a single drop of water, magnified to about twenty feet in diameter, cast upon a screen, and the shadows of the invisible inhabitants, of various sizes and shapes, living and moving, and chasing each other, and fighting, like uncaged animals in a menagerie. And all these in one drop of water. We now return to our glass of water. And here comes our little ant for a drink, and falling in, struggles hard on the surface of the water to get out of the tumbler. Now we ensmall ourselves, and get down into the water among the invisible denizens, and hear their surmises, and theories, and doubts. As they look up and see that great monster, the ant, struggling on the surface like a great black cloud in agony, one expresses the opinion that it must be a thunder cloud stranded. One ventures to suggest that it is a living being, as its actions resemble those of live animals. Another says: You can't convince me of the existence of a living being as large as that, and so many thousand times larger than we are! This is a skeptic of diminutive size, it is true, and the magnitude of our former skeptical ant is the subject upon which he is skeptical. Possibly he is a confirmed skeptic.

From this lesson we learn that organic life exists far removed into the realms of invisibility, and in organisms so infinitessimally small as to require magnifying some hundreds of times, to bring them within the scope of human vision. Then, why should a man doubt the existence of organic beings in the spirit world, though, as yet invisible to fleshly eyes?

3. THE SOLAR SYSTEM.—Now, go with the astronomer into the solar system. He measures the distances of the planets from the sun, computes their periods of revolution, weighs them in the balances of creation, and admits that the sun, the great central orb, exerts a power over them all that holds them in their orbits, regulates their speed, and maintains the harmony of the system with the accuracy of a perfect chronometer; and that even Neptune, running on the outside track, twenty-eight hundred and fifty millions of miles away, yields to the potency of this solar influence, and is conducted safely along its remote and solitary way on a journey of one hundred and sixty-five years in a single revolution.

Admitting this wonderfully accurate and all-pervading influence of the sun, an inanimate object, is it not almost self-stultification to deny the existence of an overruling intelligence?

4. TELESCOPIC SIDEREAL HEAVENS.—We accompany the astronomer into the sidereal heavens. After persistent efforts for years, he conquers a parallax, and measures the distance of a few of the fixed stars lying on the hither verge of the illimitable. He then turns his telescope to take in the stellar inhabitants of the realms beyond. As, with increased magnifying power, he probes the depths of the heavens, star after star comes into view, lying far off upon the frontier of

hitherto unexplored invisibility, until he seems to have almost reached the bounds of flaming space and gauged the contents of the immeasurable sphere of the sidereal heavens. Then, admitting that each fixed star is a central sun to some stellar system, as our sun is to the solar system, he sees those stars clearing the way before us, and closing in behind us, as our sun, like a great locomotive, with its train of planetary and cometary cars, rushes along its track in a great orbit that spans eternity, around some other great center, which may possibly be the throne of the God of the universe. With such a field before him, the great astronomer, Isaac Newton, unbosomed the sublimity of his impressions in the significant expression, "The undevout astronomer is mad." But grosser minds than his may gaze, perhaps, unmoved, and cling to the sensuous and material.

5. HYDROSTATICS.—Returning from our sidereal excursion, we draw a lesson from Hydrostatics. I construct a box one foot square inside, and a thousand feet long. I place this in a horizontal position, with the lid screwed down tight, and fill it with water, leaving a small aperture through the lid at each end. I stand at one end and you at the other. I press the water in the aperture with a force of, say ten pounds to the square inch; and you perceive the water forced up through the aperture at your end of the box with the same force, though a thousand feet away. You apply your hand to the orifice to hold the water down, and every impulse I give the water here, you feel with equal force against your hand. I insert a tube in each orifice, and as I fill my tube with water yours fills at the same time to the same level. If I force water down my tube with any given force, I, at the same instant,

force it up yours with like power; and yet I am a thousand feet away.

6 PNEUMATICS.—We go to the air pump for a lesson. Suppose the receiver of the air pump has a capacity of one cubic foot, and the exhausting cylinder a capacity of one-tenth of a cubic foot. Then, at the first stroke of the piston, one tenth of the air would be withdrawn from the receiver, but the remaining nine-tenths would, by its elasticity, occupy the entire space in the receiver. And the next stroke of the piston would take out one-tenth of the remainder, and so on till you can exhaust no more. And still a small fraction of the air remains, and occupies the entire space of the receiver. If, then, a portion of the atmosphere can adjust itself to fill the entire space, whether large or small, and we call it a material substance, can we not conceive of an immaterial substance, as spirit, occupying the entire space of a human body, whether large or small, in infancy or manhood, as taught in the *Problem of Human Life*, or of the Divine Spirit, God himself, pervading all space.

7. ATTENUATION OF MATTER.—I now return to our hydrostatic box, one foot square in the clear, and one thousand feet long; take off the lid and empty out the water. I will now fill the box five times without emptying it, and then send another substance through from end to end without the least interference from the presence of those five substances. I commence with the grossest material. I have here a mountain or pyramid of cannon balls, four inches in diameter. Three of these will just reach across the box, and twenty-seven will just fill a cubic foot. And, as the box is one thousand feet long, twenty-seven thousand cannon balls will just fill it full, with room for not one

more. I next fill it with bullets, which will roll down and fill the interstices amongst the cannon balls. I then fill it with small shot, which will permeate the spaces amongst the bullets. I now pour in sand to fill up the spaces amongst the shot. I finally fill it with water, even full, and screw down the lid, and then perform all the experiments suggested in the lesson on hydrostatics. I now insert a wire in each end of the box, reaching into the central cannon ball, and connect the other ends of the wires with the positive and negative poles of a galvanic battery, or heavily charged Leyden jar, and send a current, or a charge, of electricity through the box from end to end. Thus from the grosser material we have introduced those more and still more refined, until electricity, more refined or sublimated than either, walks through the midst of them unmolested, and with a power that bids defiance to either and all of them.

Then can we not conceive of spirit as still more sublimated than electricity, and a more permeating, all-pervading, and enduring substance, with a power more persistent, self-asserting, and vitalizing?

8. ELECTRICAL EXPERIMENTS.—The lecturer, with his electrical machine and Leyden jar, will send a charge of electricity through the muscles and nerves of a row of ladies and gentlemen extending around a large hall, clasping each other's hands, and connected with the opposite poles of the battery. And each will have a feeling sense of the presence of electricity, while the last one in the circuit and the first, precisely at the the same instant, would act out the involuntary promptings of electro-muscular dynamics. He will exhibit the electrical kiss, the magic dance, the insulated human electrical reservoir, the magazine explosion,

and numerousother fantastic feats of that highly attenuated substance called electricity.

9. ELECTRIC TELEGRAPH.—From the time Franklin lassoed the lightning steed with his kite string, it had scarcely risen above the dignity of a scientific plaything, till Morse harnessed it to his telegraph, and bid it bear the messages of "thoughts that breathe in words that burn" along the trembling wire. Now, this highly attenuated substance, pervading the whole atmosphere, though not supposed to think for itself, has become the custodian of human thoughts in their transit from point to point, over mountains, and rivers, and valleys, and plains, and under ocean's depths, till the ubiquity of man is almost practically established.

10. THE TRAIN DISPATCHER.—In no position in life, perhaps, does man approach nearer to omnipresence than in that of the train dispatcher. He holds in his hands the lives of thousands of human beings. He knows in his office, at every hour of the day and night, just where every train on his road is moving or standing. The conductor of a train, though hundreds of miles away, is warned of a broken bridge, a washout, a wrecked train, or other obstructions, and he avoids the danger and saves the lives of his passengers.

But the train dispatcher can will the destruction as well as the safety of his passengers. He can order a train to a certain point in a given time, knowing that the result will be the collision of two trains in rounding a point over a mountain precipice, where both would be precipitated into certain destruction. The conductor who would disregard the warning of the train dispatcher, and stubbornly run his train into danger and imperil the lives of his passengers, would be held culpable. God, the great train dispatcher of the universe, has warned men of the danger of continuing in a certain course. If they will not heed it, will they not be as culpable as the conductor who disregarded the warning?

The train dispatcher is only a human being, and if a man can thus know the whereabouts and control the destinies of thousands of his fellow beings, though hundreds of miles away, can we not conceive of a being superior to man, who knows and controls our destinies? And is it not more reasonable to believe in such a being than to suppose that we are the highest intelligences in the universe?

11. ELECTRO-PSYCHOLOGY.—A book was published some years ago on electro-psychology, taking the position that God is a spirit, and that electricity is his body. As electricity pervades the whole atmosphere, so the Divine Spirit, more sublimated, is more omnipresent and powerful, and being an intelligent entity, rules and controls all else. I merely refer to this as a kind of stepping stone in the transition from material substances to immaterial substances and intelligent entities, and the final great intelligent first cause, the controller of all, the being we call God.

12. TELEOLOGY.—A thousand years before the star of Bethlehem led the Magi of the East to inaugurate that thousand mile journey to see the Babe of Bethlehem, the poet laureate of Israel wrote: "The heavens declare the glory of God and the firmament showeth his handywork." (Ps. 19:1-6.) David saw teleology, or evidence of design, in the works of creation. The *works* of God and the *word* of God shed mutual light upon each other. And the intelligent student of the Bible sees evidence of design in all departments of nature. Confiding in the divinely confirmed proposition, that

"God hath spoken to us by his Son," he walks abroad under the starry dome of the temple of God's creation, amid countless manifestations of creative power, and draws inspiration from both volumes, whose pages are radiant with the light of eternity, proclaiming the majesty and goodness of a *God everywhere.—Published in Christian Quarterly Review, January,* 1883.

IX.
THE ENTHRONEMENT OF MIND.

Baccalaureate Address delivered before the Graduating Class of Daughters' College, Platte City, Mo., June 15th, 1882,

BY G. R. HAND.

Young Ladies and Gentlemen of the Graduating Class: Cycles of days, and weeks, and months, and even years have rolled into eternity, burdened with the memory of your earnest struggles, and heartaches, and headaches, and triumphant masteries you have achieved in overcoming the obstacles that obtruded themselves defiantly in your pathway, since you entered upon the curriculum of your college course. And now the time has arrived, when your successful triumph, attested by your diplomas, shall introduce you to society and to the world, and invite you to step forth into the arena of active life, and *commence* the varied and arduous duties of real and earnest life, and the labors of love in the respective fields for which your past achievements have qualified you.

Young ladies and gentlemen, as a theme appropriate to the occasion, I have selected "The Enthronement of Mind," to the consideration of which I now invite your earnest attention.

In "The Empire of Mind" we might, perhaps, find a wider field. But in "The Enthronement of Mind" we shall find more active and earnest work.

ANALYSIS OF THE THEME.

Those familiar with mental and moral philosophy,

require at my hands no definition of mind in its antithetical relation to matter. We will let it stand forth as the regnant entity in the dominion of thought. Throne implies eminence, elevation, control, authority, power, dominion. Enthronement means on the throne, and may imply the act of placing upon the throne, or the state of occupying that eminence.

And now, young ladies and gentlemen, in all these years of your literary calisthenic exercises, and scientific gymnasia, the cynosure, beaming from the Hill of Science, and upon which your eyes have been steadily fixed, has been the enthronement of your minds.

You this day pause upon the eminence you have attained, and retrospect the path that lead you up, and the activities that enabled you to reach, and stand upon the first summit in your upward course, which is but the commencement of the main struggles of life, in scaling those loftier heights which your present elevation brings within the scope of your vision. Hence, this day, though closing your college course, has been very appropriately called "Commencement Day."

In the order of creation we find first the mineral kingdom. But, from the forms of inorganic matter, igneous] or stratified rock, aquatic, or aerial oceans, with the potencies that upheave, depress or agitate them, there comes no evidence to us that they exercise the prerogative of mind, which we call thought. And we conclude that in this vestibule of creation, we have not yet penetrated the dominion of mind.

Next in order comes the vegetable kingdom. Here, organic forms of vegetable life, numerous, various, multiform, look down upon us from their mountain homes, peep up at us from the valley beneath, or smile in our faces along our pathway, as if they would speak to us; while the atmosphere, redolent with the rich fragrance of blooming flowers, bears to our nasal organs a voluptuous cargo of exhalations, like the odors wafted from the garden of the Hesperides. But, from all the forms and potencies of the vegetable kingdom, there comes no evidence of the exercise of thought on the part of vegetable life. We conclude then, that in God's arbor, we have not yet entered the domain of mind.

Next comes the animal kingdom, and earth, sea, and air, are all vocal with the evidences of animal life. But, from zoology, ichthyology, or ornithology, from the roaring of the lion in the forest, the barking of the sea lion in his aquatic home, or the carol of the timid warbler upon his aerial perch, man has hitherto failed to draw from these animals, through any interpretation of their language, the first evidence of the exercise, on their part, of those thinking and reasoning faculties which we attribute to that spiritual entity in man, denominated mind. We realize then, that even in this third vestibule of creation, we have not yet penetrated the domain of mind.

Last comes man. And now we begin to feel that after passing through devious windings, portals, labyrinths, and vestibules, the pentralia of the inner temple begins to unfold and reveal to us the light of the presence chamber, the citadel of the empire of mind, and we begin to look around for the evidences of the Enthronement of Mind.

As man is the first being we have found in our upward progress through the halls of creation, in which reason, or mind, is the distinguishing characteristic, it will be in order, at this point, to consider the question:

WHAT IS MAN?

More than a thousand years before the introduction of the Christian Era, the poet laureate of Israel, the prophet and king, asked the question in this style: "When I consider thy heavens, the work of thy fingers, the moon and the stars which thou hast ordained; what is man that thou art mindful of him? and the son of man that thou visitest him? For thou hast made him a little lower than the angels, and hast crowned him with glory and honor. Thou madest him to have dominion over the works of thy hands." (Ps. 8: 3–5.)

Here is the authorized enthronement of mind, by the mandate issued at the beginning of creation. And man is crowned and given dominion over the works of creation, including by special mention, in the context, the whole animal creation, terrestial, marine, and aerial. It should be noticed that while this recognizes mind in nothing below man, it does recognize mind above man, the Creator.

With the question, What is Man? I invite you, young ladies and gentlemen, to accompany me on an excursion of inquiry. God has furnished us with two volumes from which material may be drawn to replenish the great storehouse of knowledge. These are the volumes of nature and of revelation. They will throw light upon each other. Into this field, then, I invite you to enter, with the injunction that in all your excursions, explorations and examinations in the great laboratory of nature, the machine shop of the universe, you avail yourselves of the advantage of the rays of light from the volume of inspiration, by which new lustre and radiant beauty will be added to the works of grandeur and magnificence.

In the passage quoted, the status of man is given as between angels and the animal creation; a little lower than the former, and regnant over the latter. The term *man* is used in its generic sense, including the race. In the realm of mind, women may honorably compete with men for the literary crown, and I have seen young ladies excel young gentlemen in the same class in geometry.

What is man?

1. From the standpoint of the chemist in the laboratory of nature, the answer, as extorted by retort and crucible, gives the analysis of a few elementary solids and fluids, and their combinations.

2. The physiologist subjects him to the lancet, the knife and scalpel, and evolves an answer freighted with flesh and blood, bones and sinews, muscles and tendons, veins and arteries, joints and ligaments, nerves and brain, tissues and membranes, cellular and fibrous, vital organs and organs of locomotion; all wrapped in an envelope of epidermis and cuticle, with an ornamental label of nails and hair.

3. You ask the naturalist for a definition of man, and he tells you that man is an animal. But that definition will not distinguish a man from a horse. It is sufficiently *inclusive* but not *exclusive* enough. Then we will select some variation, and eliminate from a group, including man, all that vary in that particular. And from the group forthwith are eliminated all the quadrupeds, decapods, centipedes, millepeds, and multipeds in general, and man is left with the bipeds. But bipeds will include the fowls; so we select another variation, and eliminate the feathers, and man stands before you with the invisible garb, and euphonious ap-

pellation of Plato's man: "A two-legged animal without feathers."

4. The scientist, thrusting aside the recognition of the superior mind of a creator, attempts to bring man through by some sort of overland route; and protoplasm, primordial germs, monerons, mollusks, monkeys and men, with innumerable multitudes of intermediate and *invisible* flag stations all along the interminable route, flit by like stations on a railroad, till, at the terminus, your imagination is invited to accept as man, the spectre of evolution that stands before you, a veritable tramp, without so much as a check for his trunk, to show that he came by that road.

5. Now let the light from the other volume be turned on, and see how beautifully it illuminates the dark picture, and dispels the mists and fogs that overhung that obscure and semi-invisible road we were trying to explore. Accompany me, if you please, to the world's great zoological garden at the original homestead of father Adam, the representative man, and see him reviewing his stock as the animals pass before him in pairs, each with its companion. As the last pair disappears, the organic truth is impressed upon his mind, that it was not good that man should be alone, while companionship blessed all the lower orders of creation, supplemented by the further fact that, among all the happy group there was not found a companion suitable for man. Already God had given man dominion over all the animal creation, and "put all under his feet." A companion suitable for man can hardly be expected from a class of animals divinely placed "under his feet."

Now just at this place the development theory might crop out. There seems to be a dilemma, or trilemma.

Either the potencies of development had forgotten to develop a companion for man, or one must now be developed, or else a creator must step in and provide one for the occasion. But our young man Adam would have a lonesome time in spending the years of his adolescence, waiting through a few millions of cycles, for the development of a companion. In mercy God cuts short the period of bachelorship, by placing Adam under the influence of divine chloroform, and performing the first surgical operation known to our race. And from the rib taken from his side near his heart, is formed a companion suitable for the man, to greet his waking with her smiles. Thus, not from "under his feet," but from his side, under his arm, and near his heart, is taken the one who is entitled to walk by his side, under the protection of his arm, and in the enjoyment of mutual affection.

6. We now transfer our investigation to another field, and endeavor to learn what man is, by what he is capable of doing, and what he has done. In former days might be seen the slow team wending its way *over* the *hills* and *through* the *valleys*. Now, at the bidding of man, the ubiquitous iron horse comes bounding along on his iron track and, reversing the former practice, plunges *through* the *hills* and *over* the *valleys*, and bounds away over the plains with a speed that almost laughs at the wind.

Not satisfied with the speed already attained, which outstripped all other locomotion, the ambition of man begins to look around for something to head off the iron horse; and not long is he compelled to wait. For our American philosopher, Franklin, had lassoed the lightning steed with his kite string, and brought it to the earth, where it stood champing and prancing, and ready for service, till Morse comes along with his wires and batteries, and harnesses it to his telegraph, and bids it dash along its course upon the trembling wire with lightning speed, bearing its burden of "thoughts that breathe in words that burn," to be distributed along the way, or duly deposited at the far away terminus.

At this juncture, the iron horse discovers in the lightning steed a companion to accompany him in his rapid perigrinations. He wooes and weds her, and a new era in railroading celebrates the nuptials.

To some things there is a limit; but it would seem that the rapid excursions of the lightning steed are destined to be limited only by the circumference of this great round globe on which we live.

A Cyrus Field conceives the idea of extending the telegraph across the ocean, to bring "good news across the deep blue sea" from our cousins on the other shore. But the rolling billows of the ocean furnish rather precarious footing for telegraph poles. Yet mind is bound to triumph over matter, and from the depths of the ocean is revealed a secret which had lain hidden for ages.

The thermal waters of the Gulf stream meet the Arctic current at Newfoundland, compelling the icebergs to dissolve, and discharge their cargoes of gravel, sand and soil, thus forming and extending the Grand Bank of Newfoundland. The sediment carried by the combined current had been deposited in the depths of the ocean and formed a plateau, extending from the American shore to the coast of Ireland. This plateau is just in the place it is needed, and discovered by the deep sea soundings of Lieut. Maury of the U. S. Navy, furnishes the bed upon which the trans-Atlantic cable is laid, through which submarine telegrams leap with lightning speed, to bring young America face to face with the potentates of the old world.

In this grand triumph of mind over all obstacles on earth, in air, or in ocean's depths, the first telegram that "passed through the sea," and, like Moses and the Israelites, sung the song of rejoicing on the other side, recognized the superior mind of him who "plants his footsteps in the sea and rides upon the storm." That queenly telegram, brief, pointed and suggestive, that pioneered the pathway of thought through the labyrinths of ocean's dark abysmal depths, was couched in the memorial and ever cherished language: "What hath God wrought?"

The highly cultivated and finely polished minds of Grecian mythology, recognized superhuman mind in their deities, notwithstanding "the world by wisdom knew not God," and they offered sacrifice to an "unknown God." They represented their Jupiter, with his throne on Mount Olympus, panoplied with the scathing lightning and awe-inspiring thunderbolt. The aspiring poet mounted his Pegasus and scaled the lofty heights of Mount Parnassus, the home of the Muses, to inhale more lofty draughts of poetic inspiration.

But mind, as represented by young America, outstrips Pegasus, challenges the lightning, scales the lofty summit, besieges Jupiter on his mountain throne, spikes his thunder cannon, and wrests from his hands his death-dealing thunderbolt, bearing away his trophy as a present to science and the world, henceforth to do service in the capacity of a scientific international football.

Perhaps it is in astronomy that the mind approaches

nearer the mind of God than anywhere else in the wide range of science. Into those realms where Newton learned and expressed that sublime sentiment of world-wide fame. "The undevout astronomer is mad," let us now enter with modest reverence, as in the presence chamber of the regnant mind of the universe.

With pedestal firmly based on the earth, and surmounted by the far-reaching telescope, man turns the great glassy eye to any designated point of right ascension and declination, and at his call the inhabitants of the stellar regions come floating into the field of vision. With carefully measured base line on the earth, and telescope at each extremity, he constructs a triangle with the apex at the moon, and now with two angles and included side measured, he is master of the whole triangle, and the 240,000 miles to the moon becomes an assured element.

With this as a base, and the moon in its quadrature, he constructs another triangle, with the apex at the sun, and the hypothenuse measuring its distance from us. Finally, with the diameter of the earth's orbit as his yard-stick, he enters the sidereal heavens, and, by dint of perseverance, succeeds in conquering the parallax of a few of the fixed stars. As, with increased magnifying power, the great glassy eye of the telescope is turned to the sidereal heavens, and new stars, worlds, and stellar systems rise to view, until the immensity of space merges into the illimitable, and the illimitable becomes an unthinkable entity.

A decade of centuries before the "star of the east" inaugurated that thousand-mile journey of the Magi to the land of Judea, to see the infant Savior, the youthful shepherd poet had looked into the heavens, from the fields of Bethlehem's flocks, until his soul had become suffused with that deep inspiration that, in his riper years, enabled him to give birth to the sublime language of the 19th Psalm: "The heavens declare the glory of God," etc. When he says: "There is no speech nor language, their voice is not heard," [correctly rendered] he seems to be laboring to express the majesty of silence. Though they talk about the great mind that regulates them, yet, "their voice is not heard." No vocal sound from the revolving spheres of our solar system reaches our ears, though we might, on some clear night, listen to catch some floating sounds from the "music of the spheres." Then we may conclude that the "harmony of the spheres" may be found in the movements of the planets and stellar spheres, in loyal harmony with the law of their existence, which is the true "poetry of motion." Recognizing this, the Psalmist, as a connecting link between the reference to the *works* of God and the *word* of God, says: "The law of the Lord is perfect," and we recognize this as true in the kingdom of nature, as well as in the kingdom of grace.

The astronomer announces that at a given hour, on a certain night, in the coming year, there will be a total eclipse of the moon, visible on certain portions of the earth's surface, and the inhabitants of the designated localities, will rise from their slumbers, in the dead of night, to see the queen of the heavens veiled in the shadow of our earth. He foretells a total, annular, dark, or partial eclipse of the sun, visible along a designated line on the earth's surface, and at the given time, the inhabitants of the favored regions, armed with improvised telescopes of smoked glass, will be on hand to witness the moon, in contravention of royal etiquette, pass between the audience and the face of his majesty, the sun.

A transit of Venus over the sun's disk, is predicted, and the enthroned mind of the scientific world, steps forth, at the call of the nations, to furnish representative men to make the required observations. The enthronement of mind assumes new radiance as we enter the Holy of Holies, or the presence chambers of the universe, and converse with the regnant mind of creation.

We recognize enthroned mind, as a "power behind the throne," presiding over, pushing forward, and directing all the potencies and activities of man.

Mind speaks, and the hidden power of steam bursts forth, and the steamer, the locomotive, the mill, the factory, yield to its impulse, until the earth almost trembles beneath the rolling wheels of agriculture, manufacture, and commerce, under the steady control of the enthroned mind.

The lightning steed played wildly in the atmosphere, till the enthroned mind of a Franklin curbed its wild career, a Morse harnessed it, and a Cyrus Field sent it on its submarine mission, and to this day, it conveys its messages at the mandate of enthroned mind, at every depot or station the world over.

The printing press that daily, weekly, monthly, and yearly rolls out streams of instruction for the eager minds of teeming millions, is but the instrument through which enthroned mind proclaims its sovereignty, asserts its potency, and sends forth its power to move the world.

Since we are compelled to recognize the controlling power of mind, in the adaptation of all the machinery, potencies and industries of man, how is it possible for us to regard the more perfect adaptation of the powers, and accurate movements of the planetary system, as the result of chance?

We are constrained to look once more into the solar system. While Uranus was regarded as the exterior planet in our system, some unaccoutable perturbations were discovered in its movements. Leverrier set out to discover the cause, in full confidence that "the law of the Lord is perfect" in this field. The solar system, as then known, was weighed in the balances of creation, and found wanting. To complete the harmony of the system, a planet of a certain size, revolving in an orbit of over twenty-eight hundred and fifty millions of miles from the sun, performing a revolution in one hundred and sixty-five years, and now in a certain part of its orbit, must be discovered. "The law of the Lord is perfect." Mathematical science demonstrates it, and it must be there. He writes to an astronomer in charge of an observatory, directing him to turn his telescope to a certain point in the heavens, giving right ascension and declination, and discover a new planet as above described. Soon the penetrating eye of the telescope rests upon the unknown wanderer of the skies, within on degree of the designated place, fully answering the description, and accurately running on schedule time. And now, while the planet Neptune continues to roll its ample rounds on the outside track of creation, and "hum the wild eternal bass in nature's anthem," does not teleology in the machinery of the universe compel us to recognize the controlling influence of enthroned mind at the helm to guide it all.

But God has "visited" man in the person of Jesus the Christ, through whom the regnant mind of the universe, has come into communication with the enthroned mind of man. "God hath spoken to us by his Son," and the words of the message were providentially crystalized in the Greek language, which afterwards ceased to be a living and changing language. And now the unchanged thoughts of God, are brought to light through the analysis of those crystals, and, though the current of modern theology may become turbid, we can go to the fountain head.

Those of you who have earned the Baccalaureate degree, have enthroned your minds on this vantage ground, and secured the key that unlocks this storehouse of knowledge, and confers a power and influence that almost enables you to move the world.

Rising above the smoke of Babylon, and the fogs of the valley below, you can quaff, fresh at the fountain head, the streams of inspiration as they leap, sparkling and bright, from the crystal fount. You can leave behind you many of the vexed questions of modern theology. They sprang up amid the dark mists of the valley below, and, at the fountain head, will not appear as disturbing elements, or as factors in the great problem of Christianity, as you imbibe the health inspiring streams of salvation, just as they flowed from the lips and pens of Jesus and the apostles. In this, as a mirror, you behold the glory of the Lord. Here you learn what God has done for the salvation of men, in sending his son; what Christ has done for us in his life, sufferings, death, burial and resurrection and glorious triumph over death; and what man must do to enjoy that salvation. The question: "Will not something else do?" or, "Can't I be saved without obedience?" will not meet you there, as it is the offspring of a semi-disloyal spirit of a post-apostolic period.

And now, young ladies and gentlemen, our pleasant excursion must soon terminate, and you will be introduced to the world to go forth and fill your places in the busy walks of life, to act your parts in the moving scenes of the world's great history. Let me impress upon you this parting injunction: Determine to *be* something and *do* something in the world. Be living, active factors in the great problem of life. Resolve to make your mark in the world, and set that mark high, and show what man, or woman, is capable of doing, by acting it out in the living present, and illustrating it in the usefulness of a well spent life. So live that when you depart, the world will be better for your having lived in it. In all your doings, keep before you, as an ever present reality, the example of the Great Teacher who "went about doing good." Combine in your lives, the Philosopher and the Christian. To the bold and aggressive spirit of philosophic inquiry, add the soul-subduing and soul-renewing spirit of the meek and lowly Jesus. Let your lives be so inwrought with the pure, and the good, and the holy in society, as to impress upon the great heart of the Christian community, a realization of the necessity of your living and active presence as constituent elements.

Let your lives be so blended with the lives and sympathies of mankind, and the living issues of the day, as to embalm your memories in the affections of the great brotherhood of man, that, when you shall be called upon to pass over the river and gather fresh laurels on the other shore, you will need no monument of cold marble, to point future generations to the particular spot where repose the mortal remains of your once active body. But better, far better than marble monument or brazen pedestal, you will have erected a living monument, in the living and glowing hearts of an appreciative community. Your labors of love will have so enthroned you in the hearts of the living, that your fond memory will float upon the breezes as they sing your requiem, and deeply enthroned in the affections of succeeding generations, as the years roll along, you will be "Ever remembered by what you have done."

X.
SURVEY NO. 1, ESTABLISHING THE BEGINNING CORNER.

DELINEATION.

$S.\ 9,\ T.\ 3\ N.,\ R.\ 4\ W.$

SURVEY.

"THUS saith the Lord: Stand ye in the ways, and see and ask for the old paths, where is the good way, and walk therein, and ye shall find rest for your souls. But they said: We will not walk therein." (Jer. 6:16.)

Here is the divine authority for the survey. There were too many ways then, as now. We are instructed to inquire for the *old* paths. Some of them are *too new;* but they are still in the *plural* number. We are next to ask for *the good way*, and walk in it, and find rest. This shows that amidst the plurality of human ways, God has *one way*, in which we may find rest, and that is the *Scriptural* way, which it is my purpose now to survey, notwithstanding many say, "We will not walk therein." They love their own ways better.

I now call your attention to the *Delineation* or plat of the survey, using the plan of the United States survey of public lands for illustration.

A public survey consists of a whole State or part of a State. The first thing done is to run a true meridian line near the center of the survey, known as the *prime meridian*, indicated in the delineation by the heavy north and south line, marked N. and S. All ranges of townships count east and west from this line throughout that whole survey.

They next run a line east and west, called the *base line*, indicated by the heavy line, marked E. and W., intersecting the *prime meridian* at *a*. All townships count north and south from this line, as indicated by the figures.

Now, suppose a man applies to a surveyor to locate and survey for him a piece of land, designated by the initials and figures at the head of the delineation. They are the abbreviations of section nine, township three north, range four west.

The surveyor finds the right *number* of section, township, and range, and surveys the land. After a time the man comes to the surveyor and says: "Sir, you have surveyed the wrong land for me; another man has come with a patent for that section." The surveyor examines and finds his survey is all right in course and distance, and will close and prove, according to deed or patent. He then examines the *abbreviations*, for there are many sections, townships, and ranges of the *same number*—many "ways," and he must inquire for the *right one*. Section 9, all right; township 3, all right; north, all right; range 4, all right.

"I have given you the right number of section, township, and range: then where is the trouble?" "But what about that W. at the end?" "Ah, there is the mistake, sure. I did not notice that; having never surveyed west of the prime meridian, it never occurred to me that it might be west instead of east. From overlooking a single letter, W., as though it were a non-essential, he has located the land just *forty-two miles* out of place. The townships are six miles square, each divided into sections of one mile square, making thirty-six sections, and numbered as indicated by the figures in "township sectionized," above.

Now, for the *infallible* reading and following: Stand at the intersection of the prime meridian and base line at a, and read the abbreviations reversed. W. says go west, and R. 4 tells you how far to continue west, and brings you to range 4 west. Now you know the land sought is somewhere in that range. You are now at the point b, and N. turns you north, and T. 3 continues you on that line to township three, at the point c. We now enlarge that township and sectionize it, as seen on the right. You now run west from c, which is the southeast corner of the township already found, to the point d, due south of section nine. Then run north to e, which is the southeast corner of the section sought. Now you *know* you are at the right corner to begin.

With like certainty I now proceed with the scriptural survey to establish the "*place of beginning.*"

At the intersection of prime meridian and base line I read: "I will raise them up a prophet from among their brethren, like unto thee, and I will put my words in his mouth; and he shall speak unto them all that I shall command him. And it shall come to pass that whosoever will not hearken unto my words which he shall speak in my name, I will require it of him." (Deut. 18:18-19.)

As all are required to hear that prophet, we go in search of him, and survey the way to find him, that we may walk in his way. As all the stakes at corners of townships and sections in timber countries have *witness trees*, so we will examine the scriptural witness trees at each point.

First stake to establish—*Who* is that prophet, and has he come? Witness trees *a* (Acts, 3:22), Peter quotes this language and applies it to *Jesus;* *b* (Acts, 7:37), Stephen quotes it and applies it to *Jesus.* Drive down your stake there.

Second.—Has he received the words? Witness trees *a* (John, 6:68), Peter said: "Thou hast the words of eternal life." *b* (John, 12:49), Jesus says: "The Father who sent me gave me a commandment, what I should say and what I should speak." *c* (John, 17:8): "For I have given to them the words which thou gavest me." Drive down a stake there.

Third.—Did Moses, the former law-giver, ever acknowledge the *transfer* of the authority to *Jesus?* Witness tree, Mat. 17:1-9. On the mount, with Peter, and James, and John, Moses and Elijah present and concurring, God made the transfer to Jesus, in a voice from heaven, in the authoritative language, "Hear ye him." Drive down your stake.

Fourth.—Where has he deposited the words? Witness trees: *a* (John, 17:8): "I have given to them [the apostles] the words." *b* (John, 17:14): "I have given to them thy word." *c:* "As thou hast sent me into the world, even so also have I sent them into the world." (John, 17:18.) *d* (2 Cor. 5:19): "And hath committed unto us [the apostles] the word of reconciliation." So he gave the words over to the apostles. with like authority, so all are required to hear them. Drive down your stake.

Fifth.—Has he formulated these words of authority in the apostles' hands? Witness trees: *a* (Mat. 28:18-19): The commission is that summary. *b* (Mk. 16:15-16): Terms of salvation in the commission. *c* (Lk. 24:46-47): Remission in his name, in commission. *d* (John, 20:21-23): Authority to announce terms of remission, given to the apostles, in the commission. So the commission conveys the terms, or words of authority. Drive a stake there.

Sixth.—Were they required to begin at any certain *place?* Witness trees: *a* (Lk. 24:47-49): "And that repentance and remission of sins should be preached in his name among all nations, beginning at Jerusalem." *b* (Acts, 1:4), Jesus "commanded them that they should not depart from Jerusalem, but wait for the promise of the Father." *c* (Acts, 2:1): Then Jerusalem was to be the *place* of beginning. So you may drive down another stake.

Seventh.—Was the *time* to begin enjoined? Witness trees: *a* (Lk. 24:49): "But tarry ye in the city of Jerusalem until endued with power from on high." *b* (Acts, 1:4–5): "But wait for the promise of the Father; * * * but ye shall be baptized with the Holy Spirit not many days hence." *c* (Acts, 2:1-4): "When the day of Pentecost was fully come, * * * and they were all filled with the Holy Spirit, and began to speak with other tongues as the Spirit gave them utterance." Then, beyond all peradventure, the day of Pentecost was the *time* when "remission of sins in his name" should first be preached, and it did there begin. So you may drive down your final stake. The beginning corner is established by *Scriptural Survey.*

XI.
SURVEY NO. II. LOCATING THE BOUNDARIES.

DELINEATION.

1. ☞ Acts 2:14; 22.
2. ☞ Acts 2:36.
3. ☞ Acts 2:38.
4. ☞ Acts 2:38.

```
          3. ☞
        ┌─────────────┐
     ☞  │    For      │  4.
    2.  │  Remission  │
        │  of Sins.   │
        └─────────────┘
               ☞ 1.
```

SURVEY.

HAVING, by divine authority, located the beginning corner, proved by the Scriptural witnesses, we are now prepared to see the surveyor general, Peter, locate the boundary line with like authority and certainty. In the Delineation, the beginning corner, already established, is at the southeast corner of the plat, and numbered 1, in the diagram.

Suppose a colony, located and working, on this tract of land before the boundary lines are definitely staked out. The Government surveyor comes to run out the lines. The settlers all gather around him and follow him, and watch with intense interest to see how the locations of the lines shall effect their homes. The surveyor sets his transit instrument at the corner, No. 1, and runs the boundaries in the direction of the ☞ and order of the figures, the rule in surveying being to keep the land on the right. At each corner, some who are located along the next line, ask permission to look through the telescope of the transit. One says: Mr. Surveyor, if you run the line where the instrument points you will cut me off; that leaves my house on the wrong side of the line. Can't you bend the line a little to take me in? The surveyor replies: I am not authorized to bend a line for the accommodation of any one. I must run straight lines from corner to corner.

When he comes round to the place of beginning, the settlers all gather round the surveyor and intercede in behalf of neighbor Smith, whose house proves to be on the wrong side of the last line. They say he is a hard working man, with a large family, and all he is worth is in that residence, and he honestly thought he was in the right place. Are you going to cut off an honest man in that way? What are you going to do with him?

The surveyor says: I am not going to do anything with him; he don't belong to me, and I am not responsible for him being on the wrong side of the line. I have no discretion in the matter. I am only authorized to survey these lands and show where the boundary lines are, but not to put settlers on or off. They say: Have you no advice to give? Oh yes, he replies, I can give advice; and my advice is, if not too late, for him to transfer his residence across the line as soon as possible, for the title does not secure to him the land he is now occupying.

Now Peter, as Surveyor-General, will proceed to locate the boundaries of the christian inheritance; and all who feel an interest in the subject can follow and know certainly whether they are in the right place. The inheritance sought is that in which we enjoy remission of sins in the name of Jesus, and on which there is no mortgage to annoy us with doubts and fears.

Peter stands at the established corner, and runs as per field notes indicated in numerical order in the delineation. *First line* (Acts 2: 14, 22), "Harken to my words," and "Hear these words." These words are the words of Peter, and of the Holy Spirit, and therefore the words of God, and are the words Jesus received from the Father and gave to these Apostles, all of whom were now present, and are the words that God requires all to hear. Possibly some one on the wrong side of this line may be ready to say: I do not like to follow the word; it is the "mere word," and will "lead men to hell."

Seeond line (Acts 2: 36), "Therefore let all the house of Israel know assuredly, that God hath made that same Jesus, whom ye have crucified, both Lord and Christ." This believe, or know *assuredly*, is a very strong belief, amounting to the faith of *assurance* of the *divinity* of Christ, based upon *divine* testimony. Are there any on the wrong side of that line repudiating the testimony of the Holy Spirit, and of the apostles, and requiring the bending of that line to take in some other *assurance* before they act?

Third line (Acts 2: 38). Pierced to the heart through the truth they have now believed, they inquire: "What shall we do?" And the response promptly comes: "Repent." Does any one charge Peter with locating this third line in the wrong place?

Fourth line (Acts. 2: 38). Now we are on ticklish ground or disputed territory. Will Peter answer right? He speaks as the Holy Spirit gives him utterance. Will the Holy Spirit answer right? "Then Peter said unto them, repent and be baptized every one of you in the name of Jesus Christ for the remission of sins." Is there any one on the wrong side of this line, sitting in judgment on the decision of the Holy Spirit, and pronouncing it a nonessential, and thus resisting the Holy Spirit?

Should some of my religious friends and neighbors ask me what I am going to do with the many good, pious lovers of Christ, who are honestly on the wrong side of this line, and have never been baptized, I reply as the surveyor did, or as Peter would do under the circumstances: I am not responsible for their mistakes? I must leave them in the hands of God. But I would advise them to put themselves on the right side of that line as soon as possible, and not run the fearful risk of being found on the wrong side in the day of judgment, for we shall then be judged by the gospel as preached by the apostles.

The divine *order* established is, as in the order and direction of the numerals and ☞ in the delineation: 1. *Hear;* 2. *Believe;* 3. *Repent;* 4. *Be baptized.* This order completed, closes the survey, and encloses the inheritance, in which is *assured* the remission of sins.

Do you ask: Is the *order* of these lines essential? May we not run them the other way, so we get round the land and enclose it? I reply: 1. This is the scriptural order and has the divine sanction. 2. Look at the diagram, and from the beginning corner run in the reverse order and note what will be the practice. It will be: *First*—Baptize in infancy or unbelief. *Second*—When old enough they should repent. *Third*—Pray the Lord to give them faith. *Fourth*—Preach the gospel to them and teach them the Christian duties.

Such a perversion of apostolic teaching can scarcely claim the sanction of honest inquirers after truth.

Let us then look well to our teaching and practice, lest haply we might be found fighting against God.

XII.
GOD'S GRACIOUS GIFTS.

DELINEATION.

I. *The Giver.*	II. *Good Gifts.*	III. *Perfect Gifts.*
1. Father.	1. Light.	1. Word of Truth.
2. No Parallax.	2. Atmosphere.	2. Able to Save.
3. No Tropics.	3. Vegetation.	3. Gospel Mirror.
4. No Solstice.	4. Astronomy.	4. Perfect Law.
5. No Eclipse.	5. Fish and Fowl.	5. Blessed in doing.
	6. Beasts, Man, Society.	

SURVEY.

"Do not err, my beloved brethren. Every good gift and every perfect gift is from above, and cometh down from the Father of lights, with whom is no variableness, neither shadow of turning." (Jas. 1:16-17.)

The apostle enjoins upon the brethren the precaution not to *err*, using the word πλανετη [planetee] which means to *wander*. The ancient astronomers mapped out the starry heavens, and finding that some of the stars would not stay in their places among the *fixed* stars, but would *wander*, they called them *planets*, that is, wandering stars. James uses this astronomical term in his *precaution*. He then introduces two classes of gifts, and the character of the giver, to which I call attention in the order presented in the Dilineation:

I. *The Giver*—Some of the oriental nations, observing the influence of the *lights of heaven*, sun, moon and stars, upon vegetation, climate, &c., became sun-worshippers. From this *error*, or wandering, the apostle now desires to call away the minds of the Christians. He tells them it is true these gifts come 'from above," though not from these "lights" which, they worship, but from the "Father of the lights." This carries their minds far above "the lights," or "the host of heaven," to the great giver or maker of the lights. In presenting the attributes of the giver, he draws some contrasts between him and the lights.

1. *Parallax.* "With whom is no variableness." Here, "variableness," is a very tame rendering of the original *parallax*, which is another astronomical term, and may be fairly represented by the word parallax, in English. It means the difference between the apparent position of one of the heavenly bodies when viewed from different standpoints, by which the astronomer can construct a triangle, and measure its distance. While the lights of heaven have their parallax, God their author has none.

2. *Tropic.* Here is another astronomical term used: "Neither shadow of *turning*." The word τροπη [tropee] means to *turn*, and is the word from which come our word trope, a figure of speech in which one word is used for another, or *turned* from its meaning, also our word tropic, a turning. Even the sun, the greatest of "the lights," has its tropics, or "turnings." It crosses the meridian, a little farther north every day, till midsummer, when it *turns back*, and crosses a little farther south, each day till it reaches its extreme southern point, and again *turns back*. These turning points are called tropics, and because the former occurs when the sun is in the sign of Cancer, and the latter in Capricorn, they

are called the Tropic of Cancer and the Tropic of Capricorn, and the lines vertically under these points, on the earth and parallel to the equator, are called by the same names.

3. *Solstice.* At each tropic, or turning point, the sun crosses so nearly at the same point for three days in succession, that it seems to *stand still* and then turn back, hence the time of turning back is called *solstice*, from *sol*, the sun, and *stice*, a standing, sun standing still. As one of these occurs in midsummer, and the other at midwinter, they are called summer solstice, and winter solstice.

4. *Eclipse.* "Neither *shadow* of turning." In the "turning," or changing position of some of these lights or heavenly bodies, *shadows* are cast upon others, and we have eclipses, transits, occultations, resulting. The Father of the lights, having neither parallax, tropic, solstice, eclipse, transit or occultation, may always be relied upon implicitly.

II. *Good Gifts.*—Temporal blessings received in conformity to the laws of nature, constitute good gifts. Turn to the first chapter of Genesis and find them so classified. At the close of each day God pronounced it *good*, and we accept the decision.

1. *Light.* The work of the first day was *light*. Then all the blessings pertaining to light, may be classed under the good gifts of the first day. To obtain a measuring unit in making an inventory, let each one answer the question: How much would you take in United States gold coin, to permit your eyes to be put out? Then think of all the blessings of sight, the beautiful landscape, the starry heavens, the variegated flowers, the radiant rainbow, the panoramic views, the lifelike pictures in the arts gallery, and the

"human face divine." These with others in endless variety, may be set down, under the head of good gifts of the first day.

2. *Atmosphere.* The work of the second day was the firmament or atmosphere. Without the atmosphere to breathe, we would die, lamps would go out, fire would not burn, vegetation would expire, and sounds of sweet music would fail to reach our ears, as it is the medium of sound transmission. But the principal use of the atmosphere, as given in Genesis, is to separate the waters above, from the waters below. The water exhaled from ocean and sea, in the form of invisible vapor, is borne up by the atmosphere, and carried over the land where it is condensed and let fall in fertilizing showers. To approximate an estimate, suppose the ground is becoming very dry. Farmers say: "If it does not rain in a week or two, the corn crop is gone up." In a few days there comes a fine rain, and the corn is revived. Now the farmers say: "That shower of rain made the corn crop." Now ask each farmer how much corn that shower made for him. Multiply the amount on one farm by the average number of farms in the township, and that by the number of townships in the county, and set down the result under the good gifts of the second day.

3. *Vegetation.* The third day brought vegetation. Now approximate an inventory, by ascertaining the value of the vegetables of every kind, on one farm, and multiply by the number of farms in the township, and again, by the number of townships in the county, and place to the account of the good gifts of the third day.

4. *Astronomy.* Translucency yields to transparency on the fourth day, and the lights of heaven appear in

our firmament. Of what use is their appearance to us? The record says: "For signs, and for seasons, and for days, and for years." This expresses their relation to the earth, and to us, and from our standpoint. (a.) The sun passes through the twelve signs of the zodiac, annually, and the moon monthly, thus marking *signs* to us. (b.) The obliquity of the axis of the earth to the plane of its orbit, causes the changes of the *seasons*. (c.) The revolution of the earth on its axis, measures out the *days*. (d.) The revolution of the earth in its orbit around the sun, rolls out to us the *years*.

Had man been on the earth before the fourth day, and present when the curtains of the translucent period, in rolling mists, were folded up to let the lights of heaven appear, he might have gazed upon the canopy of night's star gemmed diadem, and fancied it but the ornamentation or finishing touch, as the Almighty had dipped his hand in the golden reservoir of ethereal light of eternity, and sprinkled it broadcast over the heavens, and set the twinkling stars in nature's diadem. But the marshalled hosts of stellar sentinels, in stately steps of measured march through the corridors of creation, proclaim the accuracy with which the diamond set jewelry of God's chronometer, registers time, as *signs*, and *seasons*, and *days*, and *years* are steadily rolled out upon the terrestial dial plate, while Bethlehem's astronomer, and Israel's king, breaks forth in admiration: "The law of the Lord is perfect."

The astronomer announces an eclipse of the moon at a given hour, some night during the coming year, and people will rise at the dead of night to see the moon wade through the *shadow* of our earth.

The astronomer describes an eclipse of the sun at a

given hour and minute on a certain day in the year, and visible along a certain line on the earth's surface, and the inhabitants of the favored district, armed with improvised telescopes of smoked glass, will be promptly at their posts to witness the queen of the heavens, in contravention of royal etiquette, pass between us and the face of his majesty the sun. And the *change* occurs on time, even in the face of the wind and weather, for, "The law of the Lord is perfect" in the kingdom of nature as well as in the kingdom of grace. And good gifts of the fourth day are assured.

5. *Fish and Fowl.* The fifth day witnesses the divine fiat calling fish and fowl "like spirits from the vasty deep." Now make an approximate estimate of the value, to man, of the inhabitants of aqueous and aerial oceans, and place to the account of good gifts of of fifth day.

6. *Beasts, Man and Society.* On the sixth day the domain prepared for man, is stocked with land animals. All being in readiness, God makes man, and constitutes him the lord of creation, or landlord of the furnished domain, with ownership in fee simple. Now before us stands the world's first millionaire, the world's proprietor, who can say:

"I am monarch of all I survey;
My right there is none to dispute."

No fear of litigation, or questioning of title. Is he happy? If wealth could make a man happy, surely he has the elements of happiness. But wealth *alone* will not bring happiness. The land lies before him, the animals in pairs pass before him, all happy in society. While each has a companion, he looks in vain for a companion suitable for the man, and now realizes "that it is not good for the man to be alone," while all the animals enjoy companionship. A rib from near the heart, forms the basis from which is built, a companion suitable for the man, to greet him with her smiles on his awaking; and society is inaugurated, the blessings of which may now be added to all the previous gifts. Now it is pronounced "very good."

III. *Perfect Gifts.*—These are spiritual blessings enjoyed in obedience to "the word of truth;" and the points referred to in the Delineation, are in verses 18–25, immediately following our text.

1. *Word of Truth.* "Of his own will begat he us with the word of truth." For the perfect gifts then James at once refers us to the word of truth, and says we are begotten by it. Peter says we are begotten "by the word of God." Paul says: "I have begotten you through the gospel." To be "begotten," means to "believe that Jesus is the Christ." (1 Jno. 5: 1), and the same writer tells us that this being born or begotten of God, gives us "the privilege of becoming children of God," (Jno. 1: 12–13), a privilege they could not have, if this believing had already made them children.

2. *Able to save.* The apostle says: "Be swift to hear, slow to speak." An old proverb says, we should hear twice to where we speak once. This is also indicated by our having two ears and but one tongue. Again, God has placed one ear on each side of the head, showing that we should hear both sides of a question. A man who is afraid to hear any but his own side, is somewhat lop-sided, and hardly a full man. The apostle further says: "Receive with meekness the engrafted word, which is able to save your souls." Well, says one: "If the word of God is able to save my soul, I will just wait and let it save me." Then you

spoke too soon, and was about to deceive yourself in supposing you could be saved without doing anything, for the apostle immediately adds: "But be ye doers of the word, and not hearers only, deceiving your own selves."

3. *Gospel Mirror.* He next carries us to the gospel mirror, illustrating by a common mirror. The man consults his mirror to see that the toilet is properly arranged, before starting to his place of business, but in the busy counting-room or office, he forgets all about that fine face he saw in the mirror. So the one who hears without doing. The impressions are made, but unless he obeys the gospel, the impressions soon vanish away. The common mirror reveals *one* image, and that is your own image. But the gospel mirror presents *two* images. One is the image of a full grown Christian, in all of its perfections. The other is the image of our own defective selves in contrast, that we may see the defects and improve according to the model before us. Or, as Paul expresses it: "Beholding as in a glass the glory of the Lord, are changed into the same image." (2 Cor. 3: 18.)

4. *Perfect Law.* This gospel mirror is more perfect than a common mirror, in that it presents a perfect character. Hence the apostle calls it "the perfect law of Liberty." We have clearly arrived at the "perfect gifts," and find them portrayed in the "perfect law." When God makes a law, he makes it perfect for the purpose for which it is appointed. But this is also called "the law of liberty," inasmuch as under the gospel, we are liberated from the burden of the Mosaic law, of which Peter says: "Which neither our fathers nor we were able to bear." (Acts 15: 10.)

5. *Doer Blessed.* James clinches the do-nothing nail, he had just driven, and closes our lesson thus: "But whoso looketh into the perfect law of liberty, and continueth therein, he being not a forgetful hearer, but a doer of the work, this man shall be blessed in his deed," or in the doing, not *for* the doing. The blessings of the gospel, or the "perfect gifts" are promised in the doing. Let us then be up and doing while it is called to-day, for the night is coming on, in which none can work. And may the Lord preserve us from wandering into the shadowy path of do-nothingism.

XIII.
THE SETTING UP OF THE KINGDOM.

DELINEATION.

*The King's Guide Board to the setting up of the Kingdom.**

B. C.	A. D.												
1451	725	603	519	32	32	33	33	33	33	60	64	64	64	64	96
Duet	Isa.	Dan.	Zech.	Mat.	Jno.	Mat.	Lk.	Acts	Acts	Rom.	Eph.	Ph	Col.	Heb.	Rv
18:18.	28:16.	2:44.	6:13.	16:18.	7:39.	28:18.	24:47.	1:8.	2:36.	14:9.	1:20	3 2:8.	1:13.	4:14-16.	1:9

SURVEY.

IN the delineation, we have a diagram of the way marks, or finger boards along the "King's Highway," pointing the traveler to "The Good Way," that he may "walk therein and find rest for his soul." (Jer. 6:16.)

Gold, silver, brass and iron are the component parts of the great image in Nebuchadnezzar's dream, which Daniel interpreted to represent four universal monarchies that should rule in succession upon the earth. The Assyrian, Medo-Persian, Grecian and Roman Empires, in like chronological order, filled this programme in the world's history, and passed away. A stone, from God's mountain, impinging upon the feet of this image, with crushing and destructive results, is interpreted to mean the fifth universal empire, the kingdom which the God of heaven shall set up.

---
*Diagram in "Text Book Exposed," by the author.

The time of the setting up of this universal empire in the world's history is the theme of this investigation. The four kingdoms have gone, and as the blow upon the feet occurred while the image was standing, the stone kingdom must have been set up while life remained in the empire.

"And in the days of these kings shall the God of heaven set up a kingdom which shall never be destroyed; and the kingdom shall not be left to other people, but it shall break in pieces and consume all these kingdoms, and it shall stand forever." (Dan. 2: 44.)

This is the initial point of divergence of some of the modern human ways. But we will examine the guide boards to find the right way. Adventists switch off the track here, strangely enough assuming that "these kings" refer to the *toe* kingdoms, and that these are yet future, making the setting up of the kingdom yet future, thus dethroning Christ. But the toes are not called kingdoms, nor is it intimated that they represent kings or kingdoms. Only four kings or kingdoms had been mentioned, the four empires, and must therefore be the antecedent to "these kings." Some even reverse the wheels of time and take the back track, and imagine the kingdom set up in the days of Abraham, and thereby get infant membership in the kingdom. Others locate the setting up, in the ministry of John the Baptist; and still others place it in the personal ministry of the Savior, and before his crucifiction, thus avoiding Pentecostian responsibilities.

The spirit of universal empire, the divine right of kings, human government based upon the principle that "might gives right," is embodied in chronological order in the image, beginning at the head and terminating at the feet. Then clearly the kingdom must be set up during the existence of universal empire, and before the smiting took place. The blow struck upon the *feet*, which locates it in the latter part of the Roman Empire, and before the division into the kingdoms of Europe. The empire suffered this terrible blow, when the Emperor Constantine dethroned Paganism and made Christianity the religion of the empire.

Now refer to the Delineation and read the guide boards and notice that all antecedent to the setting up of the kingdom look forward, and all subsequent to that event look back, with indices suggestively pointing in the right direction.

1. "I will raise them up a prophet from among their brethren, like unto thee, and I will put my words in his mouth; and he shall speak unto them all that I shall command him. And it shall come to pass that whosoever will not harken to my words, which he shall speak in my name, I will require it of him." (Deut. 18: 18–19.)

That this refers to Jesus, the king of the stone kingdom, is evident from the fact that Peter and Stephen both quote it and apply it to him. (Acts 3: 22–23 and 7: 37.) It was clearly future when this prediction was uttered, B. C. 1451.

2. "Therefore thus saith the Lord God, behold I lay in Zion for a foundation a stone, a tried stone, a precious corner stone, a sure foundation; he that believeth shall not make haste." (Isa. 28: 16.)

This prophetic laying of the foundation was then most undoubtedly future.

3. "In the days of these kings shall the God of heaven set up a kingdom, etc." (Dan. 2: 44.)

If the *shall set up* of this text does not locate it in the then future, no language can.

4. "Then take silver and gold and make crowns, and set them upon the head of Joshua, the son of Josedech, the high priest, and speak unto him, saying thus speaketh the Lord of hosts, saying: Behold the man whose name is the Branch; and he shall grow up out of his place, and he shall build the temple of the Lord; even he shall build the temple of the Lord; and he shall bear the glory, and shall sit and rule upon his throne; and he shall be a priest upon his throne." (Zech. 6: 11–13.)

This is given to show that he was to be a priest and a king at the same time.

5. "Upon this rock [the rock] I will build my Church, and the gates of hell [hades] shall not prevail against it [it the rock]. And I will give unto thee the keys of the kingdom of heaven; and whatsoever thou shalt bind on earth shall be bound in heaven; and whatsoever thou shalt loose on earth shall be loosed in heaven." (Mat. 16: 18–19.)

Here kingdom and Church are used interchangeably, and the building of the Church future, and the laying of the foundation still restrained, for the next verse says: "Then charged he his disciples that they should tell no man that he was Jesus the Christ."

6. "But this he spake of the Spirit, which they that believe on him should receive; for the Holy Spirit was not yet given, because that Jesus was not yet glorified." (John 7: 39.)

Then the kingdom was not yet set up, for the king was *not yet glorified*, though, a few days after the Spirit was given on the day of Pentecost, Peter says: "The God of our fathers hath glorified his Son Jesus." (Acts. 3: 13.)

7. "And Jesus came and spake unto them, saying: All power [authority] is given unto me in heaven and in earth. Go ye, therefore, and teach all nations, baptizing them in the name of the Father and of the Son, and of the Holy Spirit." (Mat. 28: 18-19.)

This was subsequent to the resursection, but only preparatory; they had to wait.

8. "Then opened he their understanding, that they might understand the scriptures, and said unto them: Thus it is written, and thus it behooved Christ to suffer, and to rise from the dead the third day; and that repentance and remission of sins should be preached in his name, among all nations, beginning at Jerusalem. And ye are witnesses of these things. And behold I send the promise of my Father upon you; but tarry ye in the city of Jerusalem until ye be endued with power from on high." (Luke 24: 45-49.)

So the kingdom is still future, as remission of sins is an act of executive clemency of the ruling monarch, in his own name, and that is still withheld, waiting for the power from on high. And that power cannot come till after the ascension. (John 16: 7, and Acts I: 8.)

9. "When they therefore were come together, they asked him, saying: Lord wilt thou at this time restore again the kingdom to Israel? And he said unto them: It is not for you to know the times or the seasons which the father hath put in his own power [authority]. But ye shall receive power after that the Holy Spirit is come upon you; and ye shall be witnesses unto me, both in Jerusalem, and in all Judea, and in Samaria

and unto the uttermost parts of the earth." (Acts 1: 6–8.)

This still points forward, for the apostles are restrained and waiting for the Holy Spirit and the power, and innocently inquiring of the Savior if he *will restore* the kingdom to Israel.

10. "Therefore let all the house of Israel know assuredly that God hath made that same Jesus, whom ye have crucified, both Lord and Christ." (Acts 2: 36.)

Having waited for the power from on high as directed, the apostles are now filled with the Holy Spirit, which now infallibly directs their speech. Among the utterances of the Holy Spirit on that memorable occasion, was the world startling fact, fresh borne from heaven, that Jesus, the crucified and risen one, had been divinely constituted both Lord and Christ. "The Christ," means the annointed one, the one annointed to all the offices of *prophet, priest* and *king.* To these offices Jesus had been annointed in heaven since his ascension, the official report of which the Holy Spirit brought from heaven to earth that day, as had been promised. Now all restraint is removed, every "until" taken out of the way, the high priest is on the throne, "both Lord and Christ." Terms of citizenship, and remission of sins *in his name* can now be offered for the first time on the face of the earth. Now the kingdom has been set up and become a present reality. From this on the ☞ will point back.

11. "For to this end Christ both died and rose, and revived, that he might be Lord both of the dead and living." (Rom. 14: 9.)

Here are three facts referred to as now in the past and antecedent to his being Lord of the dead and living, and consequently antecedent to the setting up of the kingdom, which at this time had become an established fact.

12. "According to the working of his mighty power, which he wrought in Christ, when he raised him from the dead and set him at his own right hand in the heavenly places, far above all principality, and power, and might, and dominion, and every name that is named, not only in this world, but also in that which is to come; and hath put all things under his feet, and gave him to be the head over all things to the Church, which is his body, the fullness of him that fills all in all." (Eph. 1: 19-23.)

No longer as a future contingency, but as a past event is this grand coronation scene, here referred to as the culmination of a series of grand displays of the mighty energy of God, reaching from the grave to the throne of the universe. The crucified one, the ascending one, the conquering one, the glorified one, head over all—dynasties and governments—all subordinated to him, and his name transcendantly above every name in the present or allcoming ages; and all this majesty conferred upon him since his ascension.

13. "And being found in fashion as a man, he humbled himself, and became obedient unto death [until death], even the death of the cross. Wherefore God also hath highly exalted him, and given him a name which is above every name; that at the name of Jesus every knee should bow, of things in heaven, and things in earth, and things under the earth; and that every tongue should confess that Jesus Christ is Lord to the glory of God the Father." (Phil. 2: 8-11.)

While in mortal flesh he was *obedient until death*, and therefore could not have been king till after his death. Conquering death for us he acquires the right to rule, and now in his glorification demands the obedience of others to his authority.

14. "Who hath delivered us from the power [authority] of darkness, and hath translated us into the kingdom of his dear Son; in whom we have redemption through his blood, even the forgiveness of sins." (Col. 1: 13–14.)

It is here referred to as a past event, for the Colossians were in the kingdom when Paul wrote, and enjoying "forgiveness of sins" *in* and not *out of him*, "through his blood," which could not avail for that purpose before it was shed, for "without shedding of blood is no remission." (Heb. 9: 22.)

15. "Seeing then we have a great High Priest, that is passed into the heavens, Jesus the Son of God, let us all hold fast our profession [confession]. For we have not a High Priest who cannot be touched with the feelings of our infirmities; but was in all points tempted like as we are, yet without sin. Let us therefore come boldly unto the throne of grace, that we may obtain mercy and find grace to help in time of need." (Heb. 4: 14–16.)

I give this to show that Christ is King and Priest at the same time, according to the prophecy and illustration (Zech. 6: 11–13), presented as No. 4 in this series of proofs. Since Jesus has passed into the heavens, a great High Priest, we have a *priest* on the throne, and therefore a *throne of grace* or favor, otherwise it would be only a throne of *justice*.

16. "I, John, who also am your brother and companion in tribulation, and in the kingdom and patience of Jesus Christ." (Rev. 1: 9.)

Our last finger board points back some sixty-three years, to one that perhaps you overlooked, and to which point, if you are seeking the beginning, you must return. John was in the kingdom at the time of this writing, about the year ninety-six, and had grown old in the enjoyment of citizenship.

With these guide boards the King's highway is so plain that the way-faring man shall not *err therein*, or *in it*. But should he despise the guide boards, and trust to men, he may miss the way, and not being *therein*, but *out there*, his error may prove disastrous.

XIV.
PROVING THE TITLE.—Gal. 4: 24–29.

DELINEATION.

Steps to the Heirship.

1—By Faith.	5—Are Christ's.
2—Baptized Into.	6—Abraham's Seed.
3—Put On.	7—Heirs.
4—In Christ.	8—The Seal.

SURVEY.

INHERITANCE to a landed estate is held in such high estimation that a man will pay a lawyer five or ten dollars to examine the record, that he may be sure that his title is legally made out and recorded. More important is it to us that we examine the record and be sure that we can read our title clear to a greater inheritance.

"For if the inheritance be of the law, it is no more of promise; but God gave it to Abraham by promise." (Ver. 18.) That promise reads: "And in thy seed shall all the nations of the earth be blessed; because thou hast obeyed my voice," (Gen. 22: 18.) Then our inheritance is through this promise, and not through the law. And of this promise and seed, Paul says, verse sixteen: "He saith not, and to seeds, as of many; but as of one, and to thy seed, which is Christ." That locates the inheritance in Christ, and not through the law.

But some one is ready to say: "Wherefore then serveth the law, if we seek not our inheritance there?"

Paul answers; "It was added because of trangressions till the seed should come." (Verse 19.)

Then the law was an addition to the promise, made four hundred and thirty years after, added because of transgressions, with the limitation, "until the seed should come." And when Christ the seed shall come, the law expires by limitation, and men look for the promised inheritance through Christ.

Utilizing this thought, the apostle proceeds: "Wherefore the law was our schoolmaster [pedagogue] to bring us to Christ, that we might be justified by faith." The pedagogue was not the educator, but a servant employed to lead the children to school, to be educated by the Philosopher, and his services as child leader continued "till" the children were led to the academy to be educated by the teacher. So the law was added to lead these wayward children of Israel "till" the seed, Christ, should come, that we might be educated by the great teacher, and justified by faith in him.

The apostle adds: "But after that the faith is come, we are no longer under a schoolmaster" [pedagogue]. The law that *was*, not *is*, our pedagogue, having expired by limitation, we are no longer under it. "For ye are all the children of God by the faith [through the faith] in Christ Jesus."

But how had they become the children of God through the faith? Through what steps had they come? The apostle answers: "For as many of you as have been baptized into Christ have put on Christ," and that, too, without regard to sex, race or previous condition.

What is now the condition of those who have put on Christ? They are joint heirs: "For ye are all one in Christ Jesus. And if ye be Christ's, then are you

Abraham's seed, and heirs according to the promise."

Here then are heirs of the promised inheritance through Christ, made of God to Abraham two thousand years before the Christian era. Starting by faith they did not jump at conclusions, but came through the steps that mark the way from the faith to the inheritance. Baptized into Christ, they put on Christ; are clothed in his righteousness. They are then in Christ, and belong to Christ. And as Christ is the promised seed, they become Abraham's seed by being in Christ's family, which constitutes them heirs.

Now retrospect the steps. Who are heirs? They that are "Abraham's seed." Who are Abraham's seed? Those who "are Christ's." Who are Christ's? Those that are "in Christ." Who are in Christ? Those that have "put on Christ." Who have put on Christ? "As many as have been baptized into Christ." Who have been baptized into Christ? All who are the "children of God by faith in Christ Jesus."

Can you prove your inheritance? Does your experience run through these steps? Are you an heir? Are you Abraham's seed? Are you Christ's? Are you in Christ? Have you put on Christ? Have you been baptized into Christ? Was it by faith you came through these steps? No guess work along here. Are you on sure ground at every step? Do you say there is doubt about your baptism? Then you should examine the record and have the doubt removed. Do you say you think you was baptized in infancy? You don't know that; you only have the word of others for it. And if you was, it was no act of yours, and not by faith, and therefore you cannot prove your heirship. Do you say you had water sprinkled on you for baptism? then doubt will hang over that step till you die, and you will go to the judgment without a record. For the same apostle that, in our lesson, said: "As many of you as have been baptized into Christ have put on Christ," has also written: "So many of us as were baptized into Jesus Christ were baptized into his death, therefore we are buried with him by baptism into death." (Rom. 6: 3-4.) You know whether you was buried when you was baptized.

Take an illustration. A gentleman dies, leaving a will bequeathing a vast estate, to his legal heirs, children and grandchildren, great-grandchildren, etc., either by consanguinity or marriage. The executor of the will, makes the usual announcement for the benefit of heirs and claimants. A young man from a foreign country comes to the executor, claiming to be one of the heirs. The executor says, you are a stranger, I do not know who you are. The young man says, my father was a grandson of the testator, and went to a foreign country, lived and died there, and I am his heir and legal representative, and have lived in expectation of being put in possession of my share of that estate. The executor says, that may be all right, but before you can be recognized as an heir, you must produce living witnesses, or documentary evidence from that country, that you are there known as the son of this grandson, who went to that country. When that is done, your name will be placed on the list of heirs.

Now to prove that you are an heir to the Abrahamic promise, you must prove that you are Abraham's seed, by proving that you are Christ's through the above steps of faith. Can you do it? Before the great white throne, you will be "judged out of the things which were written in the books." (Rev. 20: 12.) And your book will be the gospel as preached by the apostles:

"In the day when God shall judge the secrets of men by Jesus Christ according to my gospel." (Rom. 2: 16.) Then it will be safe to follow the apostolic practice.

Take another illustration. Three men are passing a splendid palatial residence, and one says: I am an heir to that property. My father has always told me I was an heir, and I rejoice in the anticipation. The second man pulls out a deed, saying here is my title to that property, and claiming that a written title is better than hearsay and impressions. The third man produces a deed for the same property, and shows by the endorsement on the back, of date, book, and page, that it has been placed on record by the Recorder of Deeds. Now which has the safest title, the one who has certain verbal assurances and impressions, the one with a pocket title unendorsed, or the one who can read his title clear on the official records of the county? Most assuredly the latter.

Then we want to be able to read our title clear, and to read it in God's book. Then we can sing:—

> "Since I can read my title clear,
> To mansions in the skies,
> I'll bid farewell to every fear,
> And wipe my weeping eyes."

THE SEAL.—The title made out, the seal is forthcoming. Having taught these Gentile Christians clearly the steps by which they became children, and heirs, he further says: "And because ye are sons, God hath sent forth the Spirit of his son into your hearts." (Gal. 4: 6.) Here then is the seal applied after the terms of the title are complied with. See also Eph. 1:13, where the same apostle says: "In whom also after that ye believed, ye were sealed with the Holy Spirit of promise." Let us be careful to have a Scriptural title to our inheritance.

XV.
DOMINION OF THE KINGDOM.

DELINEATION.

1—Four Beasts — Dan. 7: 1-18.	6—The Armies—19: 14.
2—Dominion—Dan. 7; 27.	7—Opposing Powers — 19: 19.
3—Unclean Spirits—Rev. 16: 13.	8—Beast Captured—19: 20.
4—White Horse—19: 11.	9—Dragon Chained—20: 1-3.
5—Rider—19: 11-13.	10—Millennium — 20: 4-10.

SURVEY.

1. "Daniel spake and said: I saw in my vision by night, and, behold, the four winds of the heaven strove upon the great sea. And four great beasts came up from the sea, diverse one from another." (Dan. 7: 2-3.) Beasts represent kingdoms, or governments, and these represent the four universal empires, the Assyrian, Medo-Persian, Grecian and Roman; being the same represented by the Gold, Silver, Brass, and Iron, in the image as seen in Nebuchadnezzar's dream, and explained by Daniel.

These beasts "came up *from the sea;*" did not "rise up *out of the sea,*" like the Papal beast of Rev. 13: 1. So we regard them as *politcial* governments, rising out of *the earth.* They are explained thus: "These great beasts, which are four, are four kings, which shall arise out of the earth." (Verse 17.)

2. "And the kingdom and dominion, and the greatness of the kingdom under the whole heaven, shall be

given to the people of the saints of the most High, whose kingdom is an everlasting kingdom, and all dominions shall serve and obey him." (Dan. 7: 27.) Here the final triumph and dominion of the kingdom is confidently and unequivocally foretold.

3. We next go to Revelation to see the exciting and acting agencies, and opposing forces in the struggle that triumphantly inaugurates the universal reign of Christ on earth. "And I saw three unclean spirits like frogs come out of the mouth of the dragon, and out of the mouth of the beast, and out of the mouth of the false prophet. For they are the spirits of devils, [demons] working miracles, which go forth unto the kings of the earth, and of the whole world, to gather them to the battle of that great day of God Almighty." (Rev. 16: 13–14.)

Here are the exciting agencies, inaugurating a simultaneous opposition of the whole anti-Christian world, that shall result in their disastrous defeat. These agitating spirits may be recognized by the source whence they emanate, and whose spirit they disseminate. The dragon represents open *infidelity*, its embodiment being Pagan Rome. The Beast I understand to be Papal Rome in its ruling power. The false prophet, *pseudo propheta*—would be teacher—I regard as the assumed authority to teach and formulate doctrines and dogmas authoritatively, whether papal or protestant. These three spirits are now abroad in the world, urging on, the war of Armageddon, which is a war of doctrine, and to that extent a bloodless war. But with *triple* leaders we naturally look for a *triparty* division as the result. So we read: "And the great city was divided into three parts, and the cities of the nations fell." (16: 19.) "The great city," is defined to be the apostate church, the woman in "the wilderness," on the "scarlet colored beast." "And the woman which thou sawest, is that great city, which reigneth over the kings of the earth." (17: 18.) Then if the Roman Catholic Church is "the great city," clearly "the cities of the nations," that fell, are the national denominational churches, and when mother church goes down, her daughters fall with her.

4. "And I saw heaven opened and behold a white horse." (19: 11). The white horse comes out again, representing the spirit of truth and purity, upon which the word of God will be carried to final triumph.

5. "And he that sat upon him was called Faithful and True, and in righteousness he doth judge and make war." (19: 11.) He has "many crowns" on his head—his name, "The Word of God"—his title, "King of Kings and Lord of Lords." (19: 12-16.) This well describes the incarnate Word, that was with God.

6. "And the armies which were in heaven followed him upon white horses." (19: 14.) Here the followers of Christ, have taken the field and are following their leader to the conflict and to final victory. The word of God in the hands of the white horse army of Christians, is to triumph over all the heirarchies of men, human creeds, and open infidelity, and every opposing power.

7. "And I saw the beast and the kings of the earth, and their armies, gathered together to make war against him that sat on the horse, and against his army." (19: 19.) Here the opposing powers include the Papal power, which will fight against the pure word of God in the hands of the people, to the bitter end, and the kings of the earth, who, jealous of their

own authority, will not yield to the sovereignty of Christ through his word, without a desperate struggle.

8. "And the beast was taken, and with him the false prophet that wrought miracles before him, with which he deceived them that had received the mark of the beast, and them that worshiped his image." (19: 20.) The capture of the beast will make the *crisis* in the war for the dominion of the word, for with his fall, sounds the surrender of the "false prophet," and "the image of the beast," or "cities of the nations."

It is a significant fact that the false prophet wrought his false or deceptive signs, before, or in the presence of the beast and image, and deceived both beast and image worshipers. The false prophet is clearly the ally of the beast and image, works with them and for them, and shares their fate. In face of this, I fail to see how men can make Mahomet the false prophet, who is neither the ally, nor in the presence of the Papal power.

9. The capture of the beast and the false prophet, has paved the way for an easy conquest over the dragon. An angel with a chain and key in his hand, apparently without resistance, leads the powerful dragon to his millennial term of imprisonment. (20: 1–3.) As the dragon personates open infidelity, it is easy to see that a chain of testimony and fulfilled prophecy, is the only chain with which he can be bound and receive his quietus; and that the capture of the beast and false prophet removed the last obstacle in the way of his capture.

Ask a non-professor, perhaps a moral skeptic, why he is not a Christian, and perhaps, nine times out of ten, the answer will be, that there are so many different churches, different creeds, and different ways, that he don't know which is the right one. But these many creeds and ways owe their existence to the beast and false prophet of human authority, and they being now out of the way, he cannot fall back upon the many human creeds for an excuse. It is now the word of God or nothing religiously, it is either true or false. Upon examination of its claims, he surrenders, and is led by the chain of testimony into quiet acquiescence. And infidelity is out of sight.

10. "And I saw thrones, and they sat upon them, and judgment was given unto them; and I saw the souls of them that were beheaded for the witness of Jesus, and for the word of God, and who had not worshiped the beast, neither his image, neither had received his mark upon their foreheads, or in their hands; and they lived and reigned with Christ a thousand years. But the rest of the dead lived not again until the thousand years were finished. This is the first resurrection." (20: 4–5.)

Now the dominion of the kingdom has come, and the Millennium has been inaugurated, with no opposition in all God's holy mountain.

XVI.
WHEN AND WHY GOD WINKED AT IGNORANCE.

"THE times of this ignorance God winked at; but now commands all men everywhere to repent." (Acts 17: 30.)

Unquestionably there have been times of ignorance at various periods of the world's history, and men have arisen to teach the ignorant; but whether they have been able to see their error and "repent," may perhaps be a mooted question, as applicable to the present or any past age.

Historically and scripturally, I shall limit the investigation to the particular period covered by the phrase: "The times of this ignorance," which spans over seven hundred years.

But why should God "wink at," or overlook this particular period of ignorance any more than ignorance in general? Clearly because God had given the world a problem to solve, more than seven hundred years before, and allowed them all that time to prove that men cannot find out God by their own wisdom. God had said: "For the wisdom of their wise men shall perish, and the understanding of their prudent men shall be hid." (Isa. 29: 14.) This was uttered seven hundred and twelve years before the Christian era, and in view of the fact that their fear toward God, was "taught by the precept of men."

This problem looks to the development of two kinds of religion. The one, a religion based upon the discoveries, reasoning, and experience of men, in their vain attempt to find out God by wisdom. The other, a religion based upon the revelation of God to man, in his word. These may be placed in antithesis by the phrase: "Experimental religion," versus "Revealed religion."

Pending the solution of this problem of the race, God throws around the people of the Ionian Isles the most favorable facilities for learning, until under the fostering influences of freedom and science, the Greeks become the most learned people the world ever saw.

If the idea that man can find out God, had been a plant of human cultivation, most assuredly it would have been developed in that soil. After a century of preparation, in clearing, and grubbing, and planting, the era of Grecian Philosophy is inaugurated six hundred years before Christ, with Thales at the head of a long list of about thirty Philosophers, including such men as Pythagoras, Socrates, Plato, and Aristotle. It is a little remarkable that ancient Philosophy is exhausted in Grecian Philosophy, and that Grecian Philosophy exhausted itself inside the period covered by our phrase: "The times of this ignorance," or, within the six hundred years, from Thales to Christ.

That God should select this period, the most brilliant in philosophic discoveries, and sparkling with the diamond-like splendor of polished intellect, as the period in which to allow the representative intellect of the world to demonstrate the utter inability of man to find out God by his own wisdom, is wonderful indeed, from any other than a providential standpoint.

With all these Philosophers, the great leading object of investigation, was to try to find out God, or, as frequently expressed by themselves, "the source of all things."

Elevated upon the highest pedestal of science, this Greek nation was finally and within this period, elevated to the throne of the world's great empire, having conquered the Medo-Persian Empire; and all the appliances of wealth, and power, and grandeur, and imperial influence, were laid under contribution at the feet of Science and Philosophic discovery. What success they made in finding out God, may be gathered from Grecian Mythology.

Theistic investigation, evolved polytheism, pantheism, deism, and atheism. But in the shafts and drifts of their mines in delving after Theism, they had succeeded in stumbling upon some thirty thousand gods, until it was once said by a facetious writer, that it was easier to find a god in Athens than to find a man—the greater gods being represented by temples, and the lesser ones by altars.

Pestilence rages in that city, and the smoke from thousands of altars may be seen daily mingling and ascending as a grand holocaust to heaven, to propitiate the favor, and deprecate the wrath of their gods, but all to no purpose. The pestilence continues. There the melancholly fact is realized and admitted, that the representative wisdom of the world had failed to find out God. And in the pale grief of despair, they erect an altar "To THE UNKNOWN GOD," the inscription on which is the culmination of their ignorance, and their own acknowledgment of their failure to find out God.

Pending this brilliant period of man's efforts to find out God, and its splendid failure which remanded the experimental religion of the Philosophers, to the shades, God was training another people on the problem of revealed religion. These, the Jews, were separated hundreds of miles from the Greeks, and without their philosophy. But, while God gave the Greeks some thirty learned Philosophers inside the six hundred years of their probation and splendid labors on the problem, he gave nine Prophets to the Jews in the same period, but under very different auspices. At the introduction of the brightest period of Grecian Philosophy, with Thales in the lead, God removes the Jews a thousand miles farther away, into Babylonish captivity, for seventy years. But they are cured of idolatry, and trained in Monotheism through the revealed word of God.

Simultaneously their lines thus begin to trend in courses strangely divergent. The Greeks, nestled in freedom in the bosom of the Ionian Isles, commence scaling the grandest heights, of cultivated intellect and philosophic investigation the world had ever seen; while the lights of Jewish supremacy and regal splendor at Jerusalem are extinguished; and as a conquered people, divested of privilege, and wealth and splendor, they commence a downward career trending in the direction of a long, dreary, and gloomy bondage among the heathen.

But antithetical as these two races may appear from a human standpoint, they both had a mission from God, in working out the answer to his great problem.

Yet the strangely divergent lines of these two races are destined, after six hundred years, to converge and blend together. When in the fullness of time, the Greeks had failed with all their wisdom to find out God, and plead guilty to their failure, by publicly recording upon an altar "TO THE UNKNOWN GOD," (the sublime culmination of Philosophic ignorance;) the

Messiah comes, who had. through all the dark days of captivity, been promised by the Hebrew prophets. He comes to solve the long pending problem of Deity and Humanity.

Comes he to the learned Greeks, and in the wisdom of Philosophy? No; Philosophy had exhausted her resources and failed. And God had promised to disparage the wisdom of men, because they had relied on "the precepts of men." Gathering around a company of illiterate fishermen, and unlearned Galileans, to be witnesses, of his life and teaching and miracles, he finally qualifies them miraculously to preach him to the world. Not one Philosopher, not one wise man, not one learned man among those called to the apostleship.

For some seven years these illiterate but inspired apostles preached Christ to the Jews only. He had promised to settle this question without the wisdom of men, which was done during the first seven years of apostolic preaching. To this the Apostle Paul refers when writing to the Corinthians, a Church among the Greeks. He says: "For it is written, I will destroy the wisdom of the wise and bring to nothing the understanding of the prudent." (1 Cor. 1 : 19.) Upon this he comments thus: "Where is the wise? where is the scribe? where is the disputer of this world? hath not God made foolish the wisdom of this world? For after that in the wisdom of God, the world by wisdom knew not God, it pleased God by the foolishness of preaching to save them that believe."

Here the apostle says that God had done what he had promised more than seven hundred years before, and that he had done it without the Philosophers, or the learned men of this world, but through inspired illiterate Galileans. For "not many wise men after the flesh, not many mighty, not many noble are called. But God hath chosen the foolish things of the world to confound the wise." (1 Cor. 1: 26–27.)

Thus Paul reminds this Grecian church that God had fulfilled his promise, that in his wisdom he had permitted the word, for six hundred years, and in the most learned nation the world ever saw, to try its hand at finding out God, and fail, and forever demonstrate the impossibility of finding out God except through his word. After that problem was settled, it pleased God by the foolishness of preaching the gospel, to save them that believe; and Greek Philosophy waned, and Grecian Philosophers, having fulfilled their mission, disappeared from the earth.

Apostolic preaching of the gospel, "in demonstration of the Spirit and of power," for some seven years, had laid the foundation of their faith in God, not in the wisdom of men, but in the power of God; and the time had come for the divergent lines of the Jews and Greeks, to converge in Christ. Illiterate Jews, inspired of God, had laid the foundation among Jews who "require signs," but now the Lord wants a man to go to the Greeks, who "seek after wisdom," and preach "Christ the power of God and the wisdom of God." Looking to this service, Jesus laid his hand upon Saul of Tarsus as his man. Learned in the Jewish literature, and familiar with the Greek Philosophy and Mythology, Saul can step into the college of Philosophers, and discuss with them, their abstruse questions; and from human or divine standpoint, clearly we have the right man in the right place, when Saul is divinely installed into the office of Apostle to the Gentiles.

Now follow Paul to Athens, the literary metropolis of the world. (See Acts 17: 15-31.) Here Christianity is brought face to face with Grecian Philosophy, in the hands of one who is familiar with both. Distributed over the great city are monumental evidences of the progress these Philosophers had made in their six hundred years labor on the problem of finding out God. Gloriously had they labored, made a splendid failure, and lapsed into idolatry. His eyes take in evidences of idolatrous worship on every street. He is antagonized by epicureanism and stoicism; two of the leading schools of Grecian Philosophy of the above period, which, though antagonistic to each other, could unite in opposing the gospel. The preaching of Jesus and the resurrection, was construed into "setting forth of strange gods," and curiosity is excited.

The learning of the world is represented at Athens, and Philosophers come there to report their discoveries, and to hear the report of discoveries made by others. In this spirit of inquiry they are anxious to hear Paul, and invite him to deliver an oration in the public forum before the Court of the Areopagus.

These learned Philosophers are informed that they are too devotional; too much devoted to demon-worship; worship too many gods; that after a search of six hundred years, and the discovery of some thirty thousand gods, they had failed to find out God, and had gone to worshiping "an unknown god." Him, Paul had come to declare to them, a God that can be revealed and declared, but not found out by experimental philosophy; a "God that made the world and all things therein;" the very thing that Grecian Philosophers for six hundred years had been trying to discover, but which the Jews had by revelation in the first chapter of Genesis. The proprietor of heaven and earth does not need anything at our hands, but "gives to all life, and breath and all things," and has distributed the nations over the earth to seek the Lord, and even permitted them, if possible, to "feel after him and find him." In this distribution, he had taught the Jews how to seek the Lord through his revealed word, but had permitted the Greeks to feel after him and reason after him in nature, and fail.

Some of these Philosophers had come to the conclusion that there must be an intelligent first cause of all things, and that "we are also his offspring." Paul quotes this on them, from their own accepted poet, and then shows the absurdity of admitting that we are the offspring of God, and yet supposing that the Deity can be represented by such images as they worshiped.

Having reached the culmination of their ignorance, and reduced their mythology and idol-worship, to absuruity, he coolly lays them in the shade, in utter amazement, with the grand climax: "And the times of this ignorance God winked at; but now commands all men everywhere to repent; because he has appointed a day in the which he will judge the world in righteousness by that man whom he hath ordained, whereof he hath given assurance unto all men, in that he hath raised him from the dead."

Having laid out the Greeks to cool amid the departed shades of giant intellects, our great apostle and Christian Philosopher turns and wraps the winding sheet around the retiring cotemporary, Judaism, and thus chants its requiem: "God who at sundry times and in divers manners in time past spoke to the fathers by the prophets, hath in these last days spoken to us by his Son." (Heb. 1: 1.)

Now all ye Philosophers, who cut loose from the word of God, and seek to find God some other way, can ye not see that "the times of this ignorance," covers the brightest period of the world's history, during which God permitted the giant intellect of the world to try its hand and fail, but does not wink at your ignorance? for he now commands all men everywhere to repent and follow the Christ, a greater leader than all the Philosophers combined.

Thus God winked at the splendid period of Philosophical ignorance while, by divine permission, the representatives of science without revelation, wrought his problem to its disastrous solution. But that period closed when the divergent lines of Jew and Greek, under the leadership of Christ, "the light of the world," had formed a permanent convergence in a common path illuminated by the light of revelation which renders ingnorance culpable and inexcusable.

The votary of Materialistic Philosophy, who has been delving in the dark and dreary depths of spontaneous generation and evolution, vainly searching for the potencies of life, and creative possibilities, among the impotencies and impossibilities of blind unconscious matter, may here take up the cue and follow it through the labyrinths of beauty and grandeur and sublimity, in the great machine shop of creation, and with the aid of the light from both volumes, science and revelation, see constantly rising before him, in ever varying forms, corroborative evidences, and innumerable manifestations of creative power and providential wisdom, until THE PROBLEM OF HUMAN LIFE HERE AND HEREAFTER, shall no longer sojourn in the nebulous realms of hypothetical postulata, but, like a demonstrated proposition in Euclid, may be rounded up with a triumphant Q. E. D.—*Published in the "Microcosm," May*, 1883.

XVII.
THE SAVIOR'S PRAYER FOR UNITY.
John 17: 1-21.

The night in which he was betrayed, and at the close of his valedictory address, the Savior uttered that remarkable prayer contained in the seventeenth chapter of John, a brief analysis of which, will now claim our attention.

DELINEATION.

1—The Glorification.	5—Exclusive Prayer.
2—The Name.	6—Sanctification.
3—The Men.	7—The Apostolic Mission.
4—The Words.	8—Inclusive Prayer.

SURVEY.

1. We love to dwell on the last words, and latest advice of dear departed ones. Here we have the valedictory prayer of our Savior. In the first five verses he prays for his own glorification with his Father, in the glory that antedates his incarnation, and which he enjoyed before the birth of cosmos, and predicates his petition upon the completion of the work of his divinely appointed earthly mission. "I have finished the work which thou gavest me to do. And now, O, Father, glorify thou me with thine own self with the glory which I had with thee before the world was."

2. The Name. "I have manifested thy name unto the men whom thou gavest me out of the world." (Verse 6.)

What name had he manifested to these men, that they were not already familiar with? Not the name

God, for Moses had manifested that in the first chapter of Genesis, and they were already familiar with that. In like manner the name of Lord God had been manifested by Moses in the second chapter of Genesis, after God as creator, had become Lord or owner and ruler of the works of his creation, and they were already familiar with that name. So the name Jehovah, and the name of God Almighty, had been manifested by Moses. Then what new name, and what new relationship is here implied? Clearly the name Father by which Jesus addresses him in this prayer. In the beginning it was God, and the Word, and the Holy Spirit. But the incarnation of the Word, introduced a new relationship, of Son of God with its correlative Father, which name in its new relationship, Jesus had manifested to these men. And under the new family relation, we read of Father, Son, and Holy Spirit.

3. The Men. Jesus says he had manifested the name to the men his Father had given him out of the world. These men were the apostles who were present with him, and whom the Father had given to his Son, "out of the world," and out of the Jewish world at that, for they were Jews, and never were in the Gentile world, and at that time, "Jew and Gentile" was an exhaustive classification of the human race, though after the introduction of the new family, the exhaustive classification reads: "Jew and Gentile, and the Church of God." Now we have the nucleus of the new family. The Father in heaven, the Son on earth, surrounded by his apostles, into whose hands he is about to commit his mission for the salvation of the world.

4. The Words. "For I have given unto them the words which thou gavest me." God had said to Mo-

ses: "I will raise them up from amongst their brethren, a prophet like unto thee, and I will put my words in his mouth and he shall declare all the words that I cammand him, and it shall come to pass that whosoever will not hearken to my words which he shall speak in my name, I will require it of him." (Deut. 18: 18.)

Peter and Stephen both quote this as applying to Jesus, in the third and seventh chapters of Acts respectively. And now in this prayer, Jesus acknowledges the receipt of these words, which all are required to hear, and their transfer to his apostles.

5. The Exclusive Prayer. "I pray for them; I pray not for the world, but for them whom thou hast given me." Here is an exclusive prayer, for the apostles alone, having reference to their apostolic mission.

6. The Sanctification. "Sanctify them through thy truth; thy word is truth." He had given them the words received from his Father, which he declared to be *the truth*, and through which he desires their sanctification for their mission. So every one who undertakes to preach the gospel should endeavor to be sanctified through the word of truth, for their responsible ministry.

7. The Apostolic Mission. "As thou hast sent me into the world, even so have I also sent them into the world." Here he turns his mission over into the hands of his apostles, as his ambassadors, or ministers plenipotentiary, with like power to declare the words of authority.

8. The inclusive Prayer. Having prayed exclusively for the panoply and sanctified efficiency of the apostles, he now extends the prayer to include one

more element of addition in contemplation through their agency to be made to the new family, and only one. "Neither pray I for these alone, but for them also who shall believe on me through their word; that they all may be one; as thou Father art in me and I in thee, that they also may be one in us; that the world may believe that thou hast sent me." (Verses 20-21.)

Here the Savior predicates the salvation of the world upon the unity of his people, thus placing Christian unity upon a platform of first importance, and making it virtually responsible for the success or failure of the gospel mission.

But who are included in this prayer for unity? The great heart of the Christian world is beating in the direction of unity. And in union meetings, men of different denominations, pray for unity, and for the time to come when the Savior's prayer for union shall be realized in the union of "all believers," and then go home and work for their respective divisions, and sects, and parties, and human creeds.

But did the Savior pray for the unity of all believers? No. Nor for all his followers, nor for all denominations, nor for all professed Christians. But you say: Did he not pray for "those who shall believe on me?" No, he did not pray that either. He only prayed for those who believe "Through Their Word." That is, through the word of the apostles. And beyond that class he prayed not. Then it is as clear as sunlight that a faith that is obtained in some other way than through the word of the apostles, does not bring its possessor into the unity of the Savior's prayer, while those who believe through their word, are included, and from the nature of the case will be one.

Looking to this end, John wrote: "These are written that you might believe that Jesus is the Christ, the Son of God, and that believing ye might have life through his name." (Jno. 20: 31.) Here the faith by which we may have life through his name, is received "through their word," and therefore brings us into the unity for which the Savior prayed. In full accord with this, Paul wrote: "So then faith cometh by hearing, and hearing by the word of God." (Rom. 10: 17.)

To test the absolute and reliable truth of the position here affirmed, call a meeting of representative men of all denominations, and ply them with questions such as the following:

a. Brother A. do you believe on Jesus Christ? Yes. Bro. B. do you? Yes. Bros. C., D., E., and each brother from every denomination, do you? Yes, every last one responds. But, do you believe through the word of the apostles? Yes, is the unanimous re-reply, we believe upon their testimony. So you are one.

b. But *what* do you believe about him? Do you believe that "Jesus is the Christ, the Son of God?" Yes, I believe that, responds Bros. A., B., C., and all of them. Do you believe that, upon their word? Yes, they all reply again. Then you are one in that, as the Savior said all would be, who believe through their word.

c. Now that you are a unit on the basic *truths*, what *facts* do you believe concerning him? Do you believe that "Christ died for our sins according to the Scriptures, and that he was buried, and that he rose again, according to the Scriptures?" Every one responds in the affirmative again. But do you believe that upon their word? All respond yes, we believe that upon the testimony of the apostles.

Now you are all together on *the truths*, and on *the facts*. And John says by the faith in these truths, you may have life through his name. And Paul calls these facts, the gospel "by which you are saved." Then surely here is a platform broad enough for all to come together and stand upon. And being inspired and authoritative, it can receive no element of strength by the addition of human opinions.

d. But some one suggests that we are not all one in *name.* We represent many different denominations, each honestly believing that it is right for him to work for the Lord, under the respective denominational name of the church of his choice, and not right for him to assume the name of any other denomination. It is therefore impossible to be one under so many different names, and impossible to unite under any one denominational name.

Now apply the Savior's test. You honestly believe that you are doing right in wearing your different names, but do you believe it "through their word?" You say you never thought of that? Then read "their word" carefully from the time they commenced preaching the gospel of Christ, and teaching the churches whose members "continued steadfastly in the apostles' doctrine," and see if your name is anywhere taught by them. Do you say your name is not found in "their word?" Then it does not bring you into the unity for which the Savior prayed, and it might be safe to abandon that name before it is too late.

But if we abandon these divisive names, can we find a unifying name, under which we can all unite? Now read "their word" again, and if there is such a name you will find it there. If it is not there the Savior's unity is a failure, and the conversion of the world hopeless. But your search is successful, the name is there, the name *Christian*, upon which the desired unity is possible. "The disciples were called Christians first at Antioch," and that, too, under the eye and sanction of Paul, an apostle of Christ, and Barnabas, an apostle of the Church. So the bride and the bridegroom were both represented at the naming of the united family. (Acts 11: 26.) Then some twenty years later the Court at Cesarea knew by what name the disciples of Christ were known, when Agrippa said to Paul: Almost thou persuadest me to be a *Christian*. (Acts 26: 28.) And still later by about two years, Peter encourages the brethren to glorify God in that name, the name *Christian*. (1 Pet. 4: 16.)

Now brethren, one and all, what are you going to do about it? Can you consent to be Christians? As with one voice they all respond: Yes, we all want to be Christians. Then why not unite under that name, and be Christians, nothing more and nothing less, and march forth shoulder to shoulder to convert the world?

We find then, as a rule, that what we receive "through their word," unites us, and human opinions introduced into our creeds, divide us. Is it not safe then, to abandon the human creeds, and accept the inspired word of the apostles as our guide, and "continue steadfastly in the apostles' doctrine?" Thus did the early Christians.

Take an illustration. You place upon the surface of a vase of water, a pair of toy ducks, at the rim, on opposite sides of the vase, and facing from each other. As you stand off and look at them, they both deliberately turn round and swim towards each other, come together and kiss each other. Now what caused this action? It was produced by the attraction of magnet and steel, deposited in their heads. You now place a number of these toy ducks around the rim of the vase, all facing outward, and plant a fixed magnet in the centre. They now all turn round and swim towards the centre. And the nearer they come to this central magnet, the nearer they come to each other.

Now this central magnet may represent Christ, and his name, and all that centres around the name of Jesus, and the ducks with the magnetic steel in their heads drawn to the magnet, may represent Christians, in whose heads and hearts, the love of Christ, as the motive power is drawing them towards him, as the steel turns to the magnet. And the nearer we draw to him, the nearer we are to each other.

Now instead of the central magnet, plant four fixed magnets, at different points in the vase. Instead of all coming together around the centre, they now separate, and form four separate groups around as many different magnets, and the work of division is accomplished. These separate magnetic centres may represent that number of different denominational names, around which, sects are formed. And the greater the number of sects into which the body of Christ, the church, is divided, the more the body is weakened.

As an example, suppose in a city of two thousand inhabitants, there are four churches of different denominations, having four houses, and employing four preachers, when for the number of inhabitants, one church, and one preacher would be amply sufficient. This division saddles upon the people four times the burden of expense necessary for the home work. And by uniting in one church, three-fourths of the burden can be released, or three of the preachers can be sent out to preach the gospel in the regions round about, and the expenses of three of the houses can be turned into the channel of the relief of the poor and the sick, or other works of Christian benevolence, and the good accomplished is vastly enhanced.

Now for the practicability of the enterprise. Neither of these denominations will unite under the name of the other. What can be done? Each denomination is but a *fraction* of the religious energy of the place. Represent these fractions to be added thus: $\frac{1}{2} + \frac{2}{3} + \frac{3}{4} + \frac{5}{6} =$ *What?* Add the numerators together, and you have 11-something, but neither eleven halves, or thirds, or fourths, or sixths, but simply eleven *what?* Now any of the school children can tell you that before you can add them, you must reduce them to a common denominator. So these denominations must reduce to a common name before they can be added together for the work of the Lord in this place. The denominator is the name; but what denominator will they all receive? The halves say, we can't reduce to thirds; thirds say, we can't reduce to halves; fourths say, we can't reduce to thirds; and sixths say, we are not reducible to fourths. We find twelfths to be a common denominator. Now, Mr. Halves, can you reduce to twelfths? Yes, readily. How many twelfths will you be? We will be six-twelfths. Will you be of the same value then as now? Yes. And can you do as efficient service under that name? Yes; just the same. In like manner thirds will reduce to twelfths, and two-thirds will be eight-twelfths, and of the same value, and do as efficient work. Three-fourths become nine-twelfths, with unchanged value and efficiency. Then five-sixths adjusts itself to the new name and becomes ten-twelfths, bringing to the work its full value and efficiency. Now as soon as they have accepted the new name they can be added and go to work, and you have thirty-three twelfths, all efficient workmen and represented thus: $\frac{6}{12} + \frac{8}{12} + \frac{9}{12} + \frac{10}{12} = \frac{33}{12}$, ready for efficient service.

Let the following circle represent the vase, and the indices the ducks, in the former illustration.

It belongs to the "Delineation," and is part of the blackboard diagram when there is room for it. Place the name of Christ in the center, with all that clusters around that name, and the story of the cross, as the great central magnet, then the magnetic indices will represent Christians drawn to Christ by the divine magnetism of love in their hearts, as steel turns to the magnet. "And I, if I be lifted up from the earth, will draw all men unto me." (Jno. 12: 32.) In this illustration it is plain to the eye that the nearer they come to Christ the nearer they are to each other.

As four magnets located in different parts of the circle would cluster around themselves the indices within proximate distances, and turn them away from the centre, so sectarian names draw disciples around them in feeble inefficient sectarian circles, and neutralize co-operative energies of the followers of Christ.

Then pull up the local magnets, and all flow to the great centre and be one in Christ. And may God speed the day when the unity of the Savior's prayer may be realized in all its efficiency in the good time coming.

XVIII.
TURNING TO GOD—CONVERSION.

DELINEATION.

Scriptural Order of Steps in Conversion.*

1.	2.	3.	4.	Results:
☞	☞	☞	☞	Healed. Saved. Forgiven. Blotted Out. Remission. Forgiveness.
Hear.	Believe.	Repent.	Turn.	
ακουω	πιστευω	μετανοεω	επιστρεφω	

References Used:

1—Mat. 13:15.	7—Ezek. 33:7–20.	13—Acts 14:15.
2—Jno. 12:40.	8—Gal. 4:9.	14—Acts 15:19.
3—Acts 28:27.	9—2 Cor. 3:16.	15—Acts 26:18.
4—Lk. 8:12.	10—1 Thes. 1:9.	16—Acts 26:19–20.
5—Mk. 4:12.	11—Acts 9:35.	17—Acts 3:19.
6—Isa. 6:10.	12—Acts 11:21.	18—Acts 2:28.

SURVEY.

CONVERSION is one of the most popular terms in the nomenclature of modern revivalism, and yet the word occurs but once in the New Testament. It is said that Paul and Barnabas were "declaring the conversion of the Gentiles," when they reported the good news that from among the Gentiles "a great number believed and turned to the Lord." (See Acts 11: 20, 21, and 15: 3.) But the scriptural meaning of "conversion" we might fail to draw from this one occurrence of the word in the common version. But some thirty-eight times in the Greek New Testament we find *epistrepho* in its various noun and verbal forms,

*Diagram in "Text Book Exposed," by the author.

from which we have convert, conversion, etc. An induction of a sufficient number of these passages will unmistakably reveal the scriptural order of the steps in conversion.

Glancing at the above diagram, while examining the following proof texts, the reader will see that the steps in conversion locate themselves steadily and certainly in the order in which they are placed in the diagram. The Greek verb of the original is placed under the verb that expresses each act in its order.

1. "Lest at any time they should see with their eyes, and hear with their ears, and understand with their hearts, and should *be converted*, and I should heal them." (Mat. 13: 15.)

I emphasize the word under consideration. From the Savior's language here, we learn that seeing or hearing, and understanding, are necessary to conversion or turning, and therefore precede that act. In this and similar passages quoted, *be converted* is in the *active voice* in the original, and should be uniformly translated *turn*, instead of *be converted*. These people's hearts had *become* gross, and they had *closed* their eyes to the evidence, and were therefore responsible for not *turning*, or *converting*.

2. "That they should not see with their eyes, nor understand with their heart, and *be converted*, and I should heal them." (Jno. 12: 40.)

3. "Paul quotes the same. (Acts 28: 27.)

4. "Then cometh the devil and taketh away the word out of their hearts, lest they should believe and be saved." (Lk. 8: 12.)

5. "Lest at any time they should *be converted*, and their sins should be forgiven them." (Mk. 4: 12.

These texts show that *healed*, *saved*, and *sins forgiven*, are used interchangeably. All except the third are in connection with the parable of the sower. They teach us that men must *turn* in order to be saved or forgiven, and that men must believe before they can *turn* and be saved, and that they must understand before they can believe and *turn*, and that they cannot believe without the word. The good ground hearers "are they who, in an *honest* and *good* heart, having heard the word, keep it." To *keep* the word or commandment is to *do* or *practice*.

In all the texts here quoted *be converted* is in the active voice, *turn*, in the original, and are so translated in revised or more recent translations. They are quoted from Isa, 6: 10, where any one can turn and see that it is in the *active voice* in the common version, reading as follows:

6. "Lest they should see with their eyes, and hear with their ears, and understand with their heart, and *convert*, and be healed." (Isa. 6: 10.)

These passages show, to any unbiased mind, that the word *conversion* is the exponent of an act for which man is responsible, and not an act for which God is responsible, and for the performance of which man must wait in long weary suspense. In proof of this position I introduce my next witness.

7. "So thou, O son of man, I have set thee a watchman unto the house of Israel; therefore thou shalt hear the word at my mouth, and warn them for me. ....Nevertheless, if thou warn the wicked of his way to *turn* from it; if he do not *turn* from his way he shall die in his iniquity, but thou hast delivered thy soul.........but that the wicked *turn* from his way and live; *turn* ye, *turn* ye from your evil ways; for why will ye die.........Again, when I say unto the wicked,

thou shalt surely die; if he *turn* from his sin, and do that which is lawful and right......... When the righteous *turneth* from his riguteousness and committeth iniquity, he shall even-die thereby. But if the wicked *turn* from his wickedness, and do that which is lawful and right, he shall surely live thereby.........O, ye house of Israel, I will judge you every one after his way." (Ezek. 33: 7-20.)

It will be seen that *turn* is in the active voice throughout this entire passage from the prophet Ezekiel, from which we learn that God calls upon men *to turn*, not to "be converted," and that the wicked may *turn* to God and be saved, and that the righteous may *turn* from their righteousness and be lost, while God holds each class responsible for the *turning* or *not turning*, by visiting upon them the consequences of their action or persistence.

8. "How *turn* ye again to the weak and beggarly elements, whereunto ye desire again to be in bondage?" (Gal. 4: 9.)

From this we learn that "conversion," or *turning*, may be a good or a bad thing, depending upon the character of the turning, or that *from which* and *to which* we turn.

9. "When it [the heart] shall turn to the Lord, the vail shall be taken away." (2 Cor. 3: 16.)

10. "And how ye *turned* to God from idols to serve the living and true God." (1 Thes. 1: 9.)

Here the conversion of these Thessalonian Greeks, is mentioned with commendation, because the conversion, or turning, was from idolatry to the worship of God. The manner of their conversion was according to apostolic practice, and is recorded as follows:

"They came to Thessalonica, where was a synagogue

of the Jews; and Paul, as his manner was, went in unto them, and three Sabbath days reasoned with them out of the scriptures, opening and alleging that Christ must needs have suffered, and risen again from the dead; and that this Jesus whom I preach unto you is Christ. And some of them believed, and consorted with Paul and Silas; and of the devout Greeks a great multitude, and of the chief women not a few." (Acts 17: 1-4.)

Here the apostolic order of conversion is: 1. They heard. 2. They believed. 3. They turned to God and entered at once into his service.

11. "And all that dwelt at Lydda and Saron saw him, and *turned* to the Lord." (Acts. 9: 35.)

12. "Who, when they were come to Antioch, spake to the Grecians, preaching the Lord Jesus. And the hand of the Lord was with them; and a great number believed and *turned* unto the Lord." (Acts 11: 20, 21.)

Again, the steps mentioned are: they heard, they believed, and turned.

13. "We also are men of like passions with you, and preach unto you that ye should *turn* from these vanities unto the living God. (Acts 14: 15.)

14. "Wherefore, my sentence is, that we trouble not them, who from among the Gentiles are *turned* to God. (Acts. 15: 19.)

These who have *turned* to God from among the Gentiles are the same Grecians mentioned in No. 12, who heard, believed and *turned* at Antioch, and whose conversion, or *turning*, is called "the conversion of the Gentiles." (Acts 15: 3.)

15. "To open their eyes, and to *turn* them from darkness to light, and from the power [authority] of satan unto God, that they may receive forgiveness of

sins, and an inheritance among them who are sanctified by faith that is in me." (Acts 26: 18.)

The Savior here commissions Saul for the conversion of the Gentiles, and sends him to them to effect the following changes: (*a*) to open their eyes; (*b*) to *turn* them from darkness to light; (*c*) to *turn* them from the power [authority] of satan unto God. And all these changes, or turnings, were antecedent to and in order to the forgiveness of sins and the inheritance of the saints.

Now compare this analysis with the diagram and you find a corresponding distribution of the steps. Forgiveness is in the fifth division, as a r*esult* of antecedent steps. The three items here mentioned locate themselves thus: When they *hear* they will "open their eyes" to the truths, and facts, and evidences presented. When they *believe* they will step out into the light, or "turn from darkness to light," and walk in the light of God's word.

These are followed by another step that is to *turn* them from the authority of Satan to the authority of God. What this turning act is we are not told in this connection. The act that *turns* a man from the *authority* of one human government to the *authority* of another, is always a compliance with a *legal form*, the faith, the confidence, the will and determination being antecedent requisites; and short of obedience of legal authority in this form, the citizenship remains unchanged. This legal form is prescribed by the government into whose authority and citizenship the candidate is to be transferred. The kingdom of Christ is no exception to this requirement of a test of loyalty, and the king, through his herald by whom his authority was first proclaimed on earth, prescribed baptism as the act by which the obedience of the subject declares its loyalty to the sovereignty of the " Lord and Christ." This turning act that transfers the authority of one kingdom to another, by the obedience of the subject, is located in Saul's commission, as we have seen, *after* faith, and *before*, and *in order to forgiveness*, and so arranges itself as seen in the diagram.

16. "We have seen that "conversion," or *turning*, is active on man's part; but some one may here say that if Paul was sent to *turn* the Gentiles, they are, after all, to "be converted." Let Paul settle this: "Whereupon, O, king Agrippa, I was not disobedient to the heavenly vision, but showed first to them of Damascus and at Jerusalem, and throughout all the coasts of Judea, and then to the Gentiles, that *they should repent and turn to God*, and do works meet for repentance." (Acts 26: 19, 20.)

Now, with Paul's assistance, we have *all* the steps in the order of the diagram. Repentance not being mentioned in Saul's commission, he supplies it in his report, and says he showed them "that they should *repent and turn* to God." So conversion is man turning to God, and not God miraculously, "converting" him. The entire conversion of a person includes all these acts, or steps. But the turning act, in which the authority is transferred, as now located, immediately follows repentance, and is after faith, and followed by forgiveness.

17. "Repent ye, therefore, and *be converted* [*turn*] that your sins may be blotted out, when the times of refreshing shall come from the presence of the Lord." (Acts 3: 19.)

This is the instruction Peter gave to those who had believed his preaching, briefly presented in the context, verses 12–18, and of whom it is said in the fourth verse of the next chapter: "Howbeit, many of them that heard the word believed; and the number of the men were about five thousand."

From this record we have the following order of facts: *a.* They heard Peter preach the word. *b.* They believed his preaching. *c.* Peter commanded them to *repent.* *d.* He commanded them to *turn*, or "be converted." *e.* This was in order to the blotting out of their sins. This, then, is unquestionably the apostolic and scriptural order of the steps in the conversion of the five thousand converts here reported. And a glance at the diagram will show that Peter locates the steps exactly in the order I have placed them in the diagram, and proves that I have located them in apostolic order.

In this account we have the *second* report of conversions to Christ, given in the authentic history of conversions, showing that the *order* of the steps in conversion had become established in the hands of the inspired apostles, as we shall presently see by an analysis of the prototype, or *first* conversions to Christ, under the gospel. But some may inquire why Peter did not tell what that act was that he commanded them to do after hearing, believing, and repenting, and by which they were to *turn* to God, in order to forgiveness, and in which they were *turned* from the authority of one government to that of another. A sufficient answer will be that he had told them, there at the same place, a few days before, what to do in that fourth step, and for the same purpose, to which attention will now be directed.

18. The time having arrived when the apostles were to commence preaching remission of sins in the name of Jesus for all nations, beginning at Jerusalem, as in-

dicated by the given sign, the descent of the Holy Spirit, Peter stood up with the eleven, and speaking as the Spirit gave him utterance, said: "Hearken to my words;" then, after calling their attention to fulfilled prophecies concerning Christ, he repeated: "Hear these words," (Acts 2: 14, 22), and proceeded to present the testimony, and culminated in that comprehensive and logical conclusion: "Therefore, let all the house of Israel know assuredly that God hath made that same Jesus whom ye have crucified, both Lord and Christ." (Acts 2: 36.) Having heard and believed the facts and testimony, they inquire what they shall do. And Peter, as the Spirit directs him, replies: "Repent and be baptized, every one of you, in the name of Jesus Christ for the remission of sins." (Acts 2: 38.)

Here is the first instruction ever given by divine inspiration, that tells the penitent believer what to do for remission of sins *in the name of Jesus*. And this fourth step, which brings them to the name of Jesus for remission of sins, and which, in subsequent reports, is called *turn*, is here called *be baptized in the name of Jesus Christ*.

Again the steps are located as in the diagram with the fourth step or turning act defined, this being the first time it was ever announced. The order of steps then as here first and permanently arranged by the Holy Spirit, and Peter, and the whole college of apostles, for all nations, and all time, stands thus: 1, hear; 2, believe; 3, repent; 4, be baptized ; 5, remission.

This example, being the prototype, or first practice under the commission, must stand for all time as the model, and being inspired, and never repealed, or altered, or amended, in the word of God, it carries with it the sanction of divine authority.

XIX.
ULTIMATE ELEMENTS AND RESULTANT COMBINATIONS—THE ALPHABET OF THE UNIVERSE.

ULTIMATE elements will be used to represent the last analysis of material and immaterial substances, which I shall call the alphabet. Resultant combinations will represent the audible, visible, and tangible entities wrought out by the significant and definite combinations of the ultimate symbols of this alphabet.

God has given us an alphabet in each of the departments of Nature, addressed to the ear, the eye, and the touch, by which we may spell out his design and action, his plan and operation in the completed, yet ever progressing and moving panorama, in the machine shop of creation. In each of these three alphabets, I shall regard the letters, or ultimate elements, as real, substantial entities, as their results claim the cognition of our physical senses.

I. *Sound.* The phenomena of sound will constitute my first alphabetic lesson, as a basis of analogy for the next. About forty elementary articulate sounds of the human voice, by numerous combinations, are capable of being wrought into more than one hundred and thirty thousand words, even in the English language. Letters are used to represent sounds, the one addressed to the eye, the other to the ear. These combined into words represent thoughts, and the further combination into sentences, paragraphs, essays, etc., presents the reasoning upon these thoughts, until a stream of intelligence, in visible and audible form, is rolled out upon the world.

These letters are substantial entities, visible and tangible, and may not the sounds they represent be also real entities, substantial emanations? We can conceive of them as immaterial substances passing from the sonorous body to the ear. Now conceive of the thoughts conveyed by these sounds, as real entities, the media between real entities and of a "more enduring substance" than mere "modes of motion," and destined to be stored in the department of realism, in the great treasure house of eternity, to the credit of those from whom they emanated. "For by thy words thou shalt be justified, and by thy words thou shalt be condemned." (Mat. 12: 37.)

The department of music furnishes us a fine illustration of a great variety of sonorous sounds combining into melody, rich as the nightingale's, and swelling into harmony as the grand old anthem rolls out upon the enraptured ears of the enchanted multitude in voluptuous praise to the Author of Nature.

We pause in the grove and drink in one rich draught of melody wafted from the throats of the feathered songsters, as each seems to vie with others in vocalizing the air with songs of thanksgiving.

That was rather a beautiful thought, that all the sounds of the world combined would constitute the harmony of Nature.

II. MATERIAL SUBSTANCES AND PHYSICAL ORGANISMS. Decomposing and analyzing the various forms of organic matter, the chemist has discovered about sixty-four primary elements, which, in the present status, may be called the ultimate analysis. Thus God has given us sixty-four letters with which to spell out the visible and tangible forms in the physical universe.

The certainty with which a definite combination of the letters or sounds of the alphabet produce a given word is even excelled by the certainty with which the leters in the physical alphabet, combined in definite proportions, will spell out the required substances. Chemical affinity is very exacting in its demands, and is a very accurate speller. The child just learning to spell must look at every letter separately before he can pronounce the word, but the well trained reader takes in a whole word, and even a whole line, at a glance, and his practical eye will soon detect an error in the chirography of a single word.

So the chemist, having ascertained the definite combination of atoms in a given form or substance, reads the same combination in like forms, the world over.

Take a lesson in the mineral kingdom. The elements that form limestone or marble in one country, will form the same in any other, and so of all the rocks.

The mineralogy of one country compared with that of any other will be spelled out just alike, by the retort and crucible, in the chemical laboratory, and by the present nomenclature will be labeled with the same symbols.

The chemist, lecturing on chemical affinity and chemical equivalents, takes as ultimate elements chlorine and mercury, and says: "Ladies and gentlemen, in this proportion the resultant combination will be calomel." He combines them in that definite proportion, and the fine white powder is forthcoming. The same experiment repeated a thousand times would infallibly show the same results. He changes the proportion of the elements, and says: "Ladies and gentlemen, in this proportion the same elements will produce corrosive sublimate." Though not a prophet, nor the son of a prophet, the result is just as he predicted, because "the law of the Lord is perfect" in chemical affinity.

He next takes two tumblers, and pours nitric acid into one and muriatic acid into the other, and suspends a piece of gold leaf in each, and says: "Ladies and gentlemen, neither of these acids will dissolve gold." After lecturing awhile, he holds up both tumblers to the audience, and the bright gold leaf shows no chemical action. He then pours the contents of one glass into the other, saying: "Ladies and gentlemen, the combination of these two acids will form nitro-muriatic acid, which has the power to dissolve gold, of which you will soon have occular demonstration, by the disappearance of these pieces of gold leaf." After talking awhile, he exhibits the glass, in which the gold leaf has disappeared, having dissolved and mingled with the acid. Thus the letters of the physical alphabet spell accurately.

Water, from the arctics or tropics, from Greenland's icy mountains, or India's coral strand, contains the oxygen and hydrogen in uniform definite proportions. You may freeze it, and melt it, and turn it to steam, and the proportions of hydrogen and oxygen remain unchanged. You may pass the steam through an iron tube heated in a furnace, and decompose it, and fill a balloon with the liberated hydrogen. Then again, you may take the pure hydrogen and burn it in the compound blow pipe with oxygen, and they will combine and form water of the same proportional compound as before. So it would seem that the mutual affection of oxygen and hydrogen is unchanging and undying.

The proportion of oxygen and hydrogen composing

the atmosphere is uniform and unvarying, whether found in specimens brought from the sunny South or the frigid North, from the deepest valleys or Alpine heights, from its compression on ocean's level or its rarefaction at the highest point to which balloon has ever ascended.

We pass to the vegetable kingdom and find the like uniformity. The grass, the shrubs, the trees, in all their varieties, have their uniform plans and measures, and uniform work allotted them. In the absorption and appropriation of his carbon, the majestic oak, though monarch of the forest, never mistakes and appropriates to himself the rule and apportionment by which his neighbor of another species works. In the vegetable culinary department, in the confection of delicious fruits, the apple, pear, peach, etc., compound their confectionaries with as much accuracy and uniformity as does the pastry cook.

And then in the flower garden the proportions for each variety are dealt with unerring skill, that is strongly suggestive of intelligence. The rules for the distribution and appropriation of the ultimate elements in vegetable and floral architecture, are as definite as in the arrangement of letters in written language.

Passing up to the animal kingdom, we find the same constructive alphabet furnishing us some of its letters, with which to spell out all the myriads of forms in animated nature. The thousands of forms with which animal life is clothed, are the resultant combinations of only about one-fourth of the letters of our original physical alphabet, arranged in one endless variety of proportions and organic structures.

Organism is a process that defies the skill of the chemist. He can decompose and recompose inorganic substances. He can deorganize both vegetable and animal organism. but their reorganization, like a coy dame, trusts not herself to the manipulations of the laboratory. Man may combine the same elements, in the same proportion, but organism will not result, and the failure shows that "spontaneous generation" has been all this time pursuing a cold trail.

Coming up to man, we find a beautiful form so "fearfully and wonderfully made," spelled out by the definite arrangement of a few of the letters of our physical alphabet, a resultant combination of ultimate elements in organic union, fit tabernacle for the habitation of human spirit. Then think of the spirit as a real entity, of immaterial substance, inhabiting and superintending the building and repairs of its own material dwelling, by the accurate and definite arrangement of the elements, and the letters strangely spell out, and the mind intuitively pronounces the Godlike thought: "Creative intelligence," and "Nearer my God to Thee," seems transferred from the kingdom of grace into the kingdom of nature.

III. LIGHT. Cognition of external objects by the sense of sight, claims the medium of light. And here again, God has given us an alphabet. The seven prismatic colors, revealed in the analysis of the solar spectrum, furnish us the alphabet. These, by various arrangements and combinations, and comminglings, present to the eye the rainbow, the starry heavens, the beautiful landscape, the variegated foliage, the many tinted flowers, and the human face divine." The artist having studied his luminous alphabet, combines his colors, and shades of colors, and tints and semi-tints, till he feasts the eye with the beautiful harmony of colors; and visual anthems charm the eye, as beauty personified, and artistically arranged in captivating groups, beams down upon you from the ornamented walls of the art gallery. The primary visual alphabet may be studied in the rainbow. And strangely enough, this whole alphabet combined spells white light, or the light of the sun, while their entire absence leaves blackness or darkness, which is no color at all.

We can conceive of light as a real substance, as it emanates from real substances, and is reflected from real substances. The arrangements of physical elements in the flowers causes the reflection of different colors. So the artist uses substances to reflect the tints in the picture on his canvass.

In all these departments we have been recognizing realism, or substantialism. And possibly the nebulous realms of idealism may merge into the golden reservoir of realism, and ideality be swallowed up in reality.—[*Published in Microcosm, Oct.* 1883.

XX.
EQUATION OF LIFE, AND KEYS OF THE KINGDOM.

DELINEATION.

(1.) $a + nb = x$.	(3.) $a + ( ) = x$.
(2.) Faith + Service = Entrance	(4.) $( ) + nb = x$.
	(5.) $nb + a = x$.

SURVEY.

MATHEMATICAL demonstrations and Algebraic equations, in the discussion of Scriptural theses, may possibly, by some good honest souls, be regarded as out of their appropriate sphere and somewhat innovationary, if not revolutionary. At the risk of introducing a new departure, I will venture to throw the question of entering the kingdom of Christ, into the form of an algebraic equation, and find the value of the unknown quantity. Follow me closely in the investigation, and you will find the equation fairly formed and wrought out, and the value of the symbols ascertained, and the keys of the kingdom discovered.

The passage of Scripture for analysis in this lesson is, 2 Pet. 1:5–11. The apostle says: "And beside this, giving all diligence, add to your faith." This is addressed "to them that have obtained like precious faith with us," and is therefore a lesson to Christians. Then, beyond all controversy, the word of God requires of these Christians that they make some additions to the stock they already have on hand. They can not add to nothing. But they have obtained "the like precious faith," and to this they are to make the additions; so he says: "add to your faith." As those addressed were Christians, beyond all peradventure, the faith they had, must include the belief in Christ, and the obedience of the faith, or formal acceptance of Christ.

Now, to commence the equation, let the symbol, (a.) represent the faith they already had. Then as Peter says, add to it, we place the sign plus, ($+$) after it, which says, add to this. Our formula then stands: ($a+$.) Now we are ready for the additions. And let it be born in mind that in proportion as the items added are large or small, the sum or answer sought, will be correspondingly large or small; if, in a bill of goods, you have purchased seven articles, or parcels, and only ten cents worth of each, your bill will amount to seventy cents. But if you purchased a dollar's worth of each, your bill will amount to seven dollars. So in the question before us, if these items added are large, the answer will be large in proportion. This confers upon the subject great practical significance.

ADDITIONS. 1. "Add to your faith, virtue." How much of this item will you add? This is a matter for you to determine. It is a personal matter for each individual to decide by actual practice. The ancient Romans called courage virtue. And here I suppose the term, Christian courage, would approximate its representative value.

2. "And to virtue knowledge." Roaming amidst the ever varying scenes and constantly unfolding beauties, and awe-inspiring grandeur, and soul-stirring sublimity, the Christian philosopher delights to treasure up knowledge from the works of God, and the word of God. If there is one being upon the face of the

earth, whose privilege it is, pre-eminently to acquire knowledge, it is the Christian. He has the advantage of the light of both volumes, and from these resources he can draw the material with which to replenish his store-house of knowledge, and thus add knowledge.

Enchantments and new beauties ever springing up in the pathway of the devoted student of nature and the Bible, may however, so lure him on, as to superinduce an intemperate pursuit of these studies, to the neglect of his personal, family, social, civil, and Christian duties. So just where it is needed, the apostle introduces the next addition.

3. "And to knowledge temperance." Intemperance in drinking does not exhaust the meaning of the term. We are admonished, by an apostle, to be temperate in all things, and we have just seen that even a Christian can be intemperate in study. And in making this addition, his temperance will frequently divert his attention from his enthusiastic pursuit, to attend to some of the practical duties of life. Possibly some of these domestic duties thrust upon him in the midst of intense and exciting studies, may cause him to become restive or impatient at these interruptions. The demand for the occasion, is supplied by the next addition.

4. "And to temperance patience." Possibly this central item is the most difficult of all the additions to be accomplished. Even Christians sometimes lose their patience and say: "I get out of patience." But if they get out of that article, is it not evidence that they had not "added" enough to their stock to last them through "the heated term?" Excitement, getting the upper hand of forbearance, and "Patience on a monument," feeling herself aggrieved and deserted,

steps down and out, leaving, as housekeeper, that unruly member, the tongue, to arrange the bill of fare to suit its own fantastic freaks, though not always to the delectation of the guests. This child of culture, Patience, needs much care and should be cherished.

5. "And to patience godliness." Analyzing this word, we have the base of the word, God, then adding, *ly*, we have, godly, which means like God, or resembling God; then add, *ness*, and we have godliness, which means the state of being like God. Following the instructions of the word of God, and imitating the example of him who "went about doing good," will unquestionably be in the direction of securing that character designated by the term, "godliness."

6. "And to godliness brotherly kindness." Societies and brotherhoods of almost every kind, develop this character in various degrees. And the members of these societies will show special kindness to those of their own brotherhood. But then brotherly kindness has its limitation, and that limit is the particular brotherhood. Our society, our church, our family, our community, our party, our people, etc., mark the boundaries of that characteristic.

7. "And to brotherly kindness charity." Overleaping the circumscribed limits of brotherly kindness, charity [love] goes on missions of mercy to suffering humanity, the wide world over, bringing happiness to the homes of sorrow, and diffusing blessings throughout the universal brotherhood of man.

By apostolic instruction, these seven items are to be added to the one we have in our formula. These seven additions, I will collect into one term, the second term of our equation, and let the symbol (b) represent the things to be added. Then as b, represents *what* is to be added, we will let (n) represent *how much* is to be added, or how many times the quantity b is to be taken. Then nb will be our second term, in which b is a constant quantity, and n, a literal coefficient showing how many times b is taken. Adding this to our first term, the formula stands, $a + nb$. This will constitute the first member of the equation, in which a stands for the faith, and nb for the Christian activities, services, or good works. The practical value of these, is the unknown quantity or answer sought, which may now be represented by the symbol x.

Our equation then stands, $a + nb = x$.

Now hear the apostle's solution and answer, as given in our lesson. "For if these things be in you and abound, they make you that ye shall neither be barren nor unfruitful in the knowledge of our Lord Jesus Christ." Notice the word "abound." These things are not only to be in us, but *abound*. And we shall find the correlative of "abound," in the answer when we come to it. If these abound, the answer will be abundant also. "But he that lacketh these things is blind and can not see afar off and has forgotten that he was purged from his old sins." Here, nearsightedness, and short memory are predicated of those in whom these Christian activities are lacking. A successful speculator must see afar off and know where he can make a present investment that will pay hereafter. To be lacking in "a faithful continuance in well doing," is given as evidence of a short memory, in forgetting that they were cleansed from their alien sins, in accepting the gospel.

"Wherefore, the rather brethren, give diligence to make your calling and election sure, for if you do these things ye shall never fall." Beyond all cavil, the converse of this must be: If you do not practice these things you may fall. Apostolic logic could never have constructed that sentence, if it was impossible for Christians to fall from grace. But diligence is required to make their calling and election sure. And in the first epistle they are addressed as the *elect*. Incongruity, in admonishing the *elect* to make their *election* sure, might be apparent in the minds of some, but it all vanishes when we remember that they had been elected into the present kingdom, and their election into the everlasting kingdom requires personal diligence. Election into some societies, only brings the members elect into a subordinate lodge, and an election from that lodge, is essential to an entrance into a degree lodge, or the grand lodge.

The tabernacle, type of the kingdom of heaven, had its outer court, its holy place, and most holy place, and the way into the most holy place was through the holy place. "For so an entrance shall be ministered unto you abundantly into the everlasting kingdom of our Lord and Savior Jesus Christ."

Now the equation is solved, and the answer found, and the value of the unknown quantity can be substituted. *An entrance into the everlasting kingdom*, is the answer. And it is "so," that is, by doing these things, that it will be ministered to us. You will also notice the word, "abundantly," in the answer, as the correlative of " abound," in the things to be done.

Now substituting the representative values of the symbols in our equation, as a represents the faith; nb, the Christian activities, or service, or good works; and x, the entrance into the everlasting kingdom; the equation, $a + nb = x$, is, by apostolic authority made to read: *Faith + Service = The entrance.*

Remember, these additions furnish a lifetime sum, for each individual Christian, the answer to which, is practically realized on entering the hereafter. Remember, also, that the quality of the answer is contingent upon the second term of the equation. While a and b represent constant quantities, n is contingent upon the activities of a life time, and the value of x, is increased or diminished, with the varying value of n, in the second term, suggestive of which we find "abound," in the elements of the second term, and "abundantly," as its correlative in the answer. In other words, our entrance will be "abundant," or meagre, in proportion to our Christian activities.

Having now solved the equation, I will apply a few tests to settle the presumptive question: "Are the equation, and its conclusions, Scripturally and logically legitimate?" As Peter authorized the additions, and gave the result, I stand behind him as authority for formulating the equation, and proceed to question its relations.

First.—In our equation, $a+nb=x$, may I erase the second term, nb? It would then read: $a+(\ )=x$, or a alone equals x. Then substituting the values of the symbols, we have: Faith alone will give us an entrance. But as $a+nb$ are equal to x, it is certain that a alone can not be equal to the same thing. Therefore *faith alone* can not give us an entrance into the everlasting kingdom.

Second.—May I erase the first term, a, and let the equation stand, $(\ )+nb=x$, or simply $nb=x$. In that form it says that good works alone will save us, and the moralist comes up claiming salvation upon morality without faith in Christ. But as $a+nb=x$, it is clear to a child that nb alone cannot equal the same. Then morality, or good works, without faith in Christ, can not lead us into that kingdom.

Third.—May I reverse the order of the first and second terms? It would then stand: $nb+a=x$. In purely algebraic quantities, that transposition, though in contravention of conventional usage, would not vitiate the equation. But in the hands of an apostle, it is lifted out of that conventional usage. Though, at first blush, it may appear paradoxical, yet it is true, that in the kingdom, as here used, the quantities, $a+nb$, and, $nb+a$, are not convertable, or equivalent terms. Do you ask, why? I answer. 1. Because the apostle said add these to the faith, and not faith to these. 2. Because these works placed after faith, are in the kingdom of Christ, and stand to the credit of the Christian workers. But if they come before faith, they are not of faith, but are in the kingdom of darkness, and not to the credit of the Christian worker, and therefore would not be counted in the Equation of Life. 3. Because the Savior said: " Seek ye first the kingdom of God, and his righteousness and all these things shall be added unto you." (Mat. 6:33.) These are sufficient reasons why the terms in our equation may not be reversed.

Then let the equation stand with the items in the same order the apostle arranged them eighteen hundred years ago. The prestige of apostolic sanction, that gave them potency then, has not been dissipated by the lapse of ages, and they should be as efficient now as they were when they came warm and glowing, from the lips and pen of one who spoke and wrote under the influence of Divine inspiration.

Opportunely, at this juncture, the keys of the kingdom, adjust themselves very nicely to open into the everlasting kingdom, as unquestionably that is where the work in this apostolic lesson opens. And whether called a key or not, we can safely confide in its accuracy and safety, in opening those heavenly doors before us, as we approach the glorious mansions.

The keys were given to Peter, and it will scarcely be questioned that on the day of Pentecost at Jerusalem, he used the one that opens into the present kingdom, admitting the Jews, and teaching them how to work their way in and be safe. And at the house of Cornelius it is equally evident that he used the same key to admit the Gentiles, to whom God had also granted repentance unto life. This first key, admitting into the present kingdom, as used by Peter for Jew and Gentile, is entirely covered by the first term of our equation, represented by the symbol a, by which those addressed in our lesson, had been admitted. Equally certain is it that the work embraced in the second term, represented by the symbol nb, covers the ground of the second key, and beyond all peradventure, opens from the present kingdom, into the kingdom of glory, or as Peter terms it, "the everlasting kingdom of our Lord and Savior Jesus Christ."

Then with infallible keys, and infallible instruction on their adjustments and manipulations, let us be divinely gdided and safely and certainly, "Instructed into the kingdom."—[*Published in Christian Quarterly Review, July*, 1883.

XXI.
CONVERSION OF THE GENTILES.—Acts 10: 1-48.

DELINEATION.

I. *Analysis of Narrative*

a. Devout and Praying Man.
b. Prayed to *God*.
c. Vision and Message.
d. Peter's Vision and Instruction.

e. Gentile Family.
f. Preaching and Believing.
g. Spirit's Mission.
h. Obedience Required.

II. *Miraculous Agencies.*

1.—Angel Visits Cornelius.
2.—Vision of Great Sheet.

3.—Spirit Speaks to Peter.
4.—Spirit on Gentiles.

III. *Design of the Spirit.* What For?

1—To Give Faith? No.
2.—Regenerate? No.
3.—Purify the heart? No.

4.—Purify the Soul? No.
5.—Remission? No.
6.—Gentile Witness? Yes.

SURVEY.

THE conversion of the Gentiles marks an important era in the history of the proclamation of the gospel. For some seven years the gospel had been preached to none but Jews, and the apostles had not yet appreciated the great mystery that the Gentiles were to have the gospel preached to them; and it requires a series of miracles to convince Peter that God will accept them.

A brief analysis of the narrative as recorded in the tenth chapter of Acts, and first eighteen verses of the eleventh, will set the facts before us in their order, and give us the apostolic practice of conversion. This being the first conversion of Gentiles must be a model, and in the hands of Peter, to whom was given the keys of the kingdom, it must correspond in the essential facts with the first introduction of the Jews on the day of Pentecost at Jerusalem. (See Acts 2: 1-42.)

I. *Analysis of The Narrative.*

a. Cornelius, the man divinely selected as the representative of Gentile conversion, is presented before us as a devout or religious man, a praying man, a good man, a charitable man, a man of good reputation, and one who *habitually* prayed to God.

b. He was a Roman officer, stationed in Palestine and making Cesarea his headquarters. Having been in Palestine long enough to learn the Jew's religion, he seems to have been a proselyte to Judaism, for, though a heathen, he prayed to *God*, and not to Jupiter. Here is a religious man, though not a Christian, and not knowing that it was his privilege to be a Christian, living up to the best he knew, and praying *to God*, not having learned how to come to God *through Christ.*

c. While praying to God, in his house, an angel appears to him, and, calling him by name, tells him his prayer was heard. Now would not that be a good experience according to the practice of modern theology? A religious praying man, divinely assured that his prayers are heard. Why modern fanaticism would clap her extatic hands and hail it as an evidence of pardon and acceptance with God. But the angel would correct that error and set him right, for he tells him where to send for Peter, and says: "He shall tell thee what thou oughtest to do," which shows that he ought to do something more than praying, in order to come into the kingdom. Peter expresses it thus: "Who shall tell thee words whereby thou and all thy house shall be saved." Now any one can see that the "words whereby he should *be saved*," are the same words in which he should tell him "what he ought *to do*." Putting these together we see that Peter was to be sent there to tell him what *to do to be saved*. Then it will be safe to watch him and see *what* he tells him to do.

d. Then Cornelius dispatched two of his household servants and one of his body guards, religious men also, on a mission to Joppa to bring Peter. About noon the next day, as the messengers were approaching the city, Peter had retired to the secluded housetop for devotion and meditation. Being hungry, while they were preparing dinner, Peter fell into a trance and saw the vision of a great sheet with a menagerie of all kinds of animals mixed together, and heard a voice inviting him to eat. Regarding that collection as unclean, he declined, as he had always respected the Jewish law that forbid the eating of unclean animals. But the voice replied: "What God hath cleansed call not thou common." The vision thrice repeated is withdrawn, leaving Peter still in doubt as to its meaning. Then the Spirit speaks to him and instructs him to accompany these messengers, for they are divinely sent. He entertains them, and next day accompanies them to visit this Gentile family.

e. The family or household of Cornelius consisted of "his kinsmen and near friends," whom he had called together at the expected hour of Peter's arrival, and of whom it is said: "Now therefore we are all here present before God, to hear all things that are commanded thee of God.'. Here is a religious audience ready to lay aside their religious prejudice and accept all that the apostles are commanded to teach. Then they will all hear, believe, and obey.

f. Then Peter, convinced "that God is no respecter of persons, but that in every nation he that feareth him and worketh righteousness is accepted of him," commenced his discourse. He speaks of Jesus Christ as "Lord of all," of the word sent to the chidren of Israel, of prophecies fulfilled in Christ, of miracles wrought by him, of which the apostles are his witnesses, of his crucifiction, of his resurrection, of which they were also witnesses, and that he had commanded them to preach to the people and to testify that he was ordained of God to be the judge of the living and the dead, and culminates in the following comprehensive conclusion: "To him give all the prophets witness, that through his name, whosoever believeth in him shall receive remission of sins." Notice here that he does not say that those who believe *have* remission of sins, but that they shall *receive* remission of sins *through* his name. Here ends his discourse of teaching, testifying and convincing, and we learn from Peter that they "believed on the Lord Jesus Christ." But Peter has not yet told them "what to do to be saved," for he has not told them to do anything. They are now *believers* with the assurance that those who believe may receive remission of sins "through his name." But they have not yet been informed how they can come to that name for remission.

g. At this point Peter is interrupted by the Holy Spirit coming on these Gentiles, enabling them to speak in other languages, at which phenomenon the Jewish brethren were very much astonished.

h. Now the anxious crowd ready "to hear all things that are commanded thee of God," are waiting to hear him tell them how to come to *his name* for remission of sins, or in other words to tell them *what to do* to be saved, which was the object of his mission to them. Will he tell them, or will he not? Follow him through his mission, and the next thing he says *to them* is, to tell them *what to do.* " And he commanded them to be baptized in the name of the Lord." Now he has told them what to do, and he told them to do the same that he told the Jews to do, when he first preached remission of sins in the name of Jesus at Jerusalem on the day of Pentecost, when he commanded them to "be baptized in the name of Jesus Christ for the remission of sins." Here his mission ended, and their conversion was after the apostolic order.

II. *Miraculous Agencies.*

A little attention to the miraculous agencies connected with this case of Gentile conversion, will now be in order, as some have imagined that the miraculous still inhere organically in conversions.

1. The angel visited Cornelius to tell him where to find Peter, who would come to tell him what to do to be saved. But we know where to find Peter, and what he tells both Jews and Gentiles to do to be saved. So *we* are not required to wait for the angel.

2. The vision of the great sheet, and the voice, came to *Peter* to convince him that the distinction between Jew and Gentile was broken down, and that the uncircumcised were not therefore legally unclean. But that being settled, we do not need to wait for that vision to come to *us* to reveal the same thing over again.

3. The Spirit spoke to *Peter* to convince *him* that he might go to the Gentiles. But we now know that the preacher may go to the Gentiles, and do not need to wait for the spirit to come to *us.* Besides, the Spirit did not go to the man to be converted, but to

the preacher to send him to convert these people by the normal method, the power of the gospel.

4. But the Spirit coming upon the Gentiles is thought to be one of the agencies which should continue to accompany conversions, and therefore demands attention. If God converted these men by the Holy Spirit, then he took the work out of Peter's hands, after he had sent him to lead them to Christ, and tell them what to do to be saved. What was it for?

III. *Design of the Spirit.*

Now three of the four miraculous agencies have been eliminated from the scriptural mode of conversion, their presence having been to bring the preacher of the gospel to a Gentile audience for the first time. Having accomplished that object they disappear as factors in conversion. The fourth miracle, the Spirit on the Gentiles, must in like manner be eliminated or continue as a permanent factor in conversions to the present time. If you claim that it is an exception, and continues as a factor in conversion, you are bound to tell us what it is for, or else withdraw your claim. So you may assume, or guess, the *purpose* of its agency.

1. Some one says: "I think it came to give them faith." Well, no doubt that is your honest opinion: but if my opinion is, that it was not for that purpose, your opinion and mine would just balance each other, and would only be opinions after all. With your consent we will let Peter decide. He was there and knows its purpose. Peter, is that the way they received their faith? Peter decides thus: "You know how that a good while ago God made choice among us, that the Gentiles, by my mouth, should hear the word of the gospel, and believe." (Acts 15: 7.) Thank you,

Peter, for your decision, that these Gentiles believed through your preaching, and not through the miraculous coming of the Holy Spirit, for it forever settles the question that "faith comes by hearing the word of God," as Paul logically proves, and confidently affirms. (Rom. 10: 17.) As the apostolic decision is against your assumption, you may guess again.

2. Another says: "I think it was to regenerate them," or that they were "born again by the Spirit." If your opinion and mine cross each other at this point, Peter again settles it for us thus:

"Being born again [begotten], not of corruptible seed, but of incorruptible, by the word of God." (1 Pet. 1: 23.) From the apostolic court the judgment is rendered against you.

3. A third assumption is that it was to purify their hearts. I appeal this also to the apostolic court, and Peter renders the decision thus:

"And put no difference between us and them, purifying their hearts by faith." (Acts 15: 9.) So the judgment affirmed by Peter is, that their hearts were purified by faith, and that their faith was received through his word.

4. A fourth assumption supposes it to be to purify their souls. An appeal to the apostolic court brings this decision from Peter:

"Seeing ye have purified your souls in obeying the truth through the spirit unto unfeigned love of the brethren." (1 Pet. 1: 22.) Here they received the truth through the apostolic word, and the belief of the truth purified their hearts, while in the obedience of the truth they purified their souls, or lives.

5. Finally, some one makes a guess at a venture, asssuming that it was for remission of sins, or for an

internal evidence that their sins were forgiven. Now Peter, honestly did you teach them that they should receive the evidence of remission, through the Holy Spirit coming upon them? Peter sets us right at this point, by informing us that he taught:

"That, *through his name*, whosoever believeth in him shall receive remission of sins." (Acts 10: 43.) Then beyond all preadventure it is decided that the Spirit did not come upon the Gentiles for any of the five purposes above assumed, and I believe they exhaust the list of assuptions in that direction.

The guesses being exhausted, and all the assumptions ruled out of the apostolic court in deciding what was *not* its object, may we ask the court to decide for what purpose the spirit *was* sent to them. By the same apostle the decisive judgment is thus rendered:

"And God, who knoweth the hearts, bear them witness, giving them the Holy Spirit, even as he did unto us." (Acts 15: 8.)

Then it was God's "witness," or God testifying in their behalf. But to *what* did God testify to them? Surely not to the forgiveness of their sins, for it came upon them before they had even been told how to come to the name of Jesus Christ, to "receive remission of sins through his name." But Peter settles it thus:

"Forasmuch then as God gave them the like gift as he did unto us who believed on the Lord Jesus Christ, what was I that I could withstand God? When they heard these things they held their peace, and glorified God, saying: Then hath God also to the Gentiles granted repentance unto life." (Acts 11: 17, 18.) The apostles and brethren at Jerusalem had called Peter to account for preaching to *the Gentiles*, and Peter here justifies his conduct by presenting this Gentile endowment of the spirit as God's testimony that the Gentiles might be received to the obedience of the gospel, upon the same terms as the Jews, and be saved. The apostles and elders assembled accept the decision, and unanimously decide that by this sign: "Then hath God *also to the Gentiles* granted repentance unto life."

As soon as God bore that testimony that the Gentiles might be saved through the gospel, and all doubt and hesitation in the mind of Peter, and of the six Jewish brethren who accompanied him to the house of Cornelius, was banished, and not before, he completed his mission by telling them what to do to be saved. "And he commanded them to be baptized in the name of the Lord." That Gentile *privilege*, being now assured by divine testimony, it is not necessary for the witness to come again to prove the same thing, as the evidence is recorded in the word of God, and hence the decision is final, and no instance on record of its repetition. The miraculous, being now divinely eliminated from ordinary conversions, this case stands, like all others: They heard, believed, and obeyed, and entered at once into the service.

XXII.
A SCRIPTURAL CONVERSION.—Acts 8:26-40.

DELINEATION.

Agencies and Practices.

1.—The Angel.
2.—The Preacher.
3.—The Road.
4.—The Treasurer.
5.—The Chariot.
6.—The Spirit.
7.—The Prophecy.

8.—The Explanation.
9.—Preach Jesus.
10.—A Certain Water.
11.—The Belief.
12.—The Baptism.
13.—God's Acceptance.
14.—The Rejoicing.

SURVEY.

IN the passage of Scripture indicated above, we have the record of a model conversion, under the apostolic practice. It is a plain narrative, giving the facts as they occurred from its inception to its completion and the sanction of its divine approval. I shall simply call attention to the facts in the order recorded.

The preacher under whom this conversion was effected, had been holding a protracted meeting at Samaria, where he "preached Christ unto them," the report of which is thus placed on record: "But when they believed Philip Preaching the things concerning the kingdom of God, and the name of Jesus Christ, they were baptized, both men and women." (Acts 8:12.)

The subject of this conversion, is a distinguished officer from a far distant country, treasurer to Caudace, queen of Ethiopia, and about to return home from a devotional visit at Jerusalem. God sees in this man a fit instrument to bear the gospel to his home, and plant Christianity in that foreign land, and determines to effect his conversion strictly after the gospel plan.

"And the angel of the Lord spoke unto Philip." Here the first agency is the angel. But the angel did not speak to the man to be converted. So we need not wait for that agency. If it was God's plan to convert men miraculously, he could have sent the angel to the man. But that was not his plan.

The second agency employed is the preacher, and to him the angel spoke and sent him toward the south to the road along which the treasurer would pass from Jerusalem to Gaza. But the preacher knows not yet what service God has for him away down there. Yet he can march under "sealed orders." "And he arose and went." Now in an oral panorama, we may see, in this first section, a man journeying solitary, yet persistent, along the road.

A chariot on the Jerusalem and Gaza road, attracts his attention, as the royal treasurer wends his homeward way. "Then the Spirit said unto Philip, go near, and join thyself to this chariot." Here another agency is introduced, the Spirit, and if it was God's plan to convert men by his Spirit without the gospel, he would have sent the Spirit to the man, but he did not do it; he sent it to Philip the preacher, to indicate that his audience was in that chariot. So we are admonished that we are not to wait for the Spirit. "And Philip ran thither to him," true to the instruction.

Now give the panorama another turn, and the second section reveals a traveler in a chariot, with a pedestrian along side.

Philip has now found his audience in the person of

this Ethiopian officer, who is just reading the text for his sermon on his arrival. He listens and hears him read, in the fifty-third chapter of Isaiah, seventh and eighth verses, a prophecy concerning Christ, uttered more than seven hundred years before. He inquires: Do you understand that? The reply is: "How can I except some man should guide me?" Not that the Scriptures are so mystified as not to be understood without miraculous guidance. But here is a fulfilled prophecy that Philip can explain to the officer who has never heard of its fulfillment. "And he desired Philip that he would come up and sit with him."

Now give the panorama another turn, and the third section reveals a chariot containing two men in earnest conversation. We listen.

"Then Philip opened his mouth, and began at the same Scripture, and preached unto him Jesus." Beginning with the same Scripture: "He was led as a sheep to the slaughter; and like a lamb dumb before his shearer, so opened he not his mouth," he would explain that this was fulfilled when Jesus was led to the Jewish tribunal, and the bar of Pilate, he made no reply to their questions.

"In his humiliation his judgment was taken away," or "extorted from him." This, Philip could explain, was also fulfilled before those tribunals. The humiliation consisted in putting him under oath to testify in his own case, a humiliation to which even criminals are not subjected. When they could not prove the charge of blasphemy against him, the high priest administered the oath to him, saying: "I adjure thee by the living God, that thou tell us whether thou be the Christ the Son of God." (Mat. 26:63.) Under oath he admitted that he was what he had said. The high priest rendered the judgment, thus forcibly "taken" from his own lips, thus: "What further need have we of witnesses? behold, now ye have heard his blasphemy. What think ye? They answered and said he is guilty of death."

But he "preached Jesus." After explaining the prophecy read, he would preach Jesus by explaining many other prophecies concerning him, that had been fulfilled.

He would preach Jesus the babe in the manger, reported by the angels, and admired by the shepherds. He would preach Jesus the babe at home with his parents, receiving the homage, and presents, at the hands of the Eastern Magi. He would preach Jesus the intelligent boy of twelve years old, confounding the learned doctors, and setting an example of obedience to his parents. He would preach Jesus baptized in the river Jordan, and divinely announced to be the Son of God. He would preach Jesus successfully resisting the Satanic temptations. He would preach Jesus working miracles in attestation of the truth of the oracle from heaven. He would present Jesus cleansing the leper, healing all kinds of diseases, casting out demons, expanding a few loaves into a supply for thousands, Jesus standing upon the deck of the vessel in the storm, commanding the elements, while obedient to his voice, winds lull, and waves crouch silently at his feet.

From exhibitions of power over the elements of nature and humanity, he would lead his interested auditor to the confines of the unseen world, and preach Jesus calling departed spirits back to their tenements of clay, to live again amongst their friends.

He would preach Jesus, the man of miracles, the

man of sorrows and acquainted with grief, led from the hall of humiliation and judgment, up the hill of Calvary, expiring on the cross, his heart's blood flowing in healing streams, a crimson tide, a cleansing fountain of potent efficacy to wash away the guilty stains of sin.

He would preach Jesus in the rock-bound, sealed, and guarded sepulchre, bursting the bars of death, and coming forth a triumphant conquerer.

He would preach Jesus, giving his apostles a commission to preach remission of sins in his name, beginning at Jerusalem, after his ascent to heaven and the descent of the Holy Spirit; with the assurance that " he that believeth and is baptized shall be saved."

He preaches Jesus ascending into heaven, and " crowned with glory and honor," and made " both Lord and Christ;" and sending down the Holy Spirit according to promise, to the waiting apostles at Jerusalem, on the day of Pentecost.

He unfolds the teaching of Peter on that day, as he preaches Jesus in prophecy and testimony, to the wondering crowd, and enforces the requirements of the commission, to believe on Jesus the Christ, repent, and be baptized in his name for remission of sins.

He shows him that those who received the word of the apostle, were baptized, and added to the saved, and entered at once upon the practice of the *recurring* duties of Christian citizenship. This far the teaching in the chariot.

"And as they went on their way, they came unto a certain water; and the eunuch said, see,'here is water; what doth hinder me to be baptized?" "And he commanded the chariot to stand still."

Another turn of the panorama, and the fourth section reveals the chariot standing still, with the postilion on his seat, and the two travelers standing by the stream.

Now why did this Ethiopian officer ask to be baptized? Clearly because Philip had informed him that baptism was a requirement in coming to Christ for remission. The eunuch has declared his belief and his purpose to obey.

"And they went down both into the water, both Philip and the eunuch; and he baptized him."

Now give the panorama another turn, and the fifth section shows us two men standing together out in the stream, the one in the act of placing the other under the water, from which he raises him again.

Now why this scene? If baptism did not require a burial in water, they need not go down into the water to perform it. And if sprinkling a little water on a person could be substituted for baptism, the eunuch would not have waited till "they came to a certain water," but would have said, there is plenty of water in the chariot, "what hinders me to be baptized," for they always, on their journeys, carried water in their chariots, in bottles made of skins of animals. But baptism is a burial, for: "So many of us were baptized into Jesus Christ were baptized into his death; therefore we are buried with him by baptism into death." (Rom. 6:3, 4.) "Buried with him in baptism, wherein also ye are risen with him." (Col. 2: 12.) But baptism is also a resurrection, so Philip did not leave his convert under the water.

"And when they were come up out of the water, the Spirit of the Lord caught away Philip, that the eunuch saw him no more."

Another turn of the panorama, and the sixth section

presents us with the chariot still on the shore, but one man has disappeared from the group.

Here the agency that introduced Philip to the stranger, has taken him away. He has finished his work here, and God has a work for him to do along the coast of the Mediterranean Sea. But why is it recorded, that the Spirit caught away Philip? Beyond peradventure, it is the sign manual of the divine acceptance of this conversion. Philip had done the work he was sent to do, and had done it right, and according to the apostolic practice. This record virtually says to Philip: "Well done good and faithful servant," you have finished the work I gave you to do, the service is accepted, and the divine acceptance, will be placed on record that this conversion may stand as a model of apostolic practice for all coming time.

"And he [the eunuch] went on his way rejoicing."

Now give the panorama a final turn, and in the seventh section you see the chariot, with the original proprietor and occupant, in his resumed seat, and homeward bound, wending his way in the direction of Gaza; and rejoicing in the knowledge of "forgiveness of sins, and an inheritance among them who are sanctified by faith that is in Christ."

Now suppose a stranger, from the top of one of those hills, had witnessed this novel scene, what would have been his impressions? And which of all the modern denominational churches would claim that Ethiopian officer as their convert, and endorse the practice? Possibly he might be left out in the cold till he met with those who follow the apostolic practice.

XXIII.
THE NAME CHRISTIAN.

Substance of discourse delivered in Christian Church, at Pleasant Hill, Cass County, Missouri, Oct. 27th, 1878.

DELINEATION.

1.—Family Name.	6.—Chrio.
2—Prophecy.	7.—Christos.
3.—Worthy Name.	8.—Christianos.
4,—My Name.	9.—Chrematizo.
5.—Chrisma.	10.—Kaleo.

SURVEY.

"FOR this cause I bow my knees unto the Father of our Lord Jesus Christ, of whom the whole family in heaven and earth is named." (Eph. 3: 14, 15.)

1. From this text it appears that when Paul wrote the epistle to the Ephesians, about A. D. 64, the whole family had been named, and we may expect to find that family name recorded somewhere in God's book. We wish now to inquire what name was given them, when given, and by whose authority.

We have analyzed, in these discourses, the first three chapters of this letter, and are now prepared to develop and understand this text. We have seen that in the first chapter, and first twelve verses, the apostle speaks of the predestinating, choosing, and qualifying of *us*, the apostles who first trusted in Christ. He then refers to the *ye*, who also trusted, *after* they heard the word of truth, etc. Then of the mighty power of God, in raising Christ from the dead. In the second chapter he addresses the Gentile Christians, reminding them that they were once aliens from the commonwealth of Israel, but that Christ had broken down the middle wall of partition, having abolished the law of commandments, to make of the two, one new man, and reconcile both to God in one body; and that they were no longer strangers and foreigners, but fellow-citizens with the saints. He reminds them that in this is manifested the exceeding riches of God's favor, and in the eighth verse reminds them that it is by the favor of God that these Gentiles are permitted to be saved through the faith, without the law, which had once been imposed on the Jews, but now had been abolished.

Having seen the whole family, Jew and Gentile, united in one body, and built on the one foundation, and "the Gentiles fellow heirs, and of the same body," "according to the eternal purpose," or *plan of the ages*, the apostle breaks forth in the language of the text: "*For this cause,*" etc., and glories in the united family under the new name.

Now what is the new name? and from whence? Is it from heaven, or from men?

2. *Prophecy.* "For the Lord God shall slay thee, and call his servants by another name." (Isa. 65: 15.) "And the Gentiles shall come to thy light, and kings to the brightness of thy rising." (Isa. 60: 3). "And the Gentiles shall see thy righteousness, and all kings thy glory; and thou shalt be called by a new name, which the mouth of the Lord shall name." (Isa. 62:2.)

Here are three passages of Scripture, from the plan

of the ages, uttered near seven hundred years before the birth of Christ. In one it is affirmed that God will call his people by another name; in the next, that the Gentiles and kings shall come to the light; and in the third, that when the Gentiles and kings see the righteousness, they shall be called by the new name, and the presumption is, that it is the one that the mouth of the Lord named.

3. In the year sixty when James wrote his epistle, they were called by a worthy or honorable name, for he says: "Do not they blaspheme the honorable name by which ye are called." (Rev. vers. Jas 2:7.) And what more honorable name than to be named after Christ?

4. About the year ninety-six, the Savior himself, in dictating the epistles to the churches in Asia Minor, uses these expressions: "And for my name's sake hast labored," "and thou holdest fast my name, and hast not denied my faith," "and hast not denied my name." (Rev. 2:3, 13 and 3:8.)

Here a full half century after "the disciples were called Christians first in Antioch," we find Christ himself, the head of the family, commending the churches for still holding fast *his name*, thus further indicating that they were named after Christ Jesus, the one who was dead and is alive again, that it was an honorable name, and some had not denied it, but for it, still labored.

5. But after which name were they called, the name Jesus, or the official name Christ? In other words, will they be called Jesuits, or Christians? We will approximate the answer.

John says: "But ye have an unction from the Holy One and ye know all things." (1 Jno. 2:20.)

And again: "But the anointing which ye have received of him abideth in you, and you need not that any man teach you; but as the same anointing teacheth you of all things." (1 Jno. 2:27.)

Here the apostle uses the word *Chrisma*, which means anointing, or anointing oil, and is translated, *unction*, once, in the 20th verse, and rendered, *anointing*, twice in the 27th verse, and is the noun form of the verb *chrio*, to anoint. Oil is used in the Scriptures as a symbol of the Spirit, sometimes in its sanctifying, and sometimes in its illuminating office. Oil, to illuminate, must be in the lamp. So the Spirit, to illuminate, speaks through the word of God. In these verses, John says, this anointing, this *chrisma*, or Christing, *teaches* you. This points to the official term, Christ. He and his apostles were anointed to teach and preach.

6. The verb *chrio*, occurs five times in the Greek New Testament, and is four times applied to Jesus, and once to the apostles. The following are the passages and translations: "The Spirit of the Lord is upon me, because he hath anointed me to preach the gospel to the poor." (Luke 4:18.) "Thy holy child Jesus, whom thou hast anointed." (Acts 4:27.) "How God anointed Jesus of Nazareth with the Holy Spirit and with power." (Acts 10:38.) "Therefore, God, even thy God hath anointed thee with the oil of gladness above thy fellows." (Heb. 1:9.) "Now he who establisheth us with you in Christ, and hath anointed us, is God." (2 Cor. 1:21.) This last applies to the apostles.

7. The word Christ, or *Christos*, in the Greek, means anointed, or an anointed person, and is a derivative from *chrio*, to anoint, and occurs five hundred and

seventy times, uniformly translated Christ, and applied to Jesus.

8. Thus far we see that there is light all along the line of *chrio* and its derivatives, and we may safely follow it one step farther and see into what it will develop.

Christianos, a derivative from *chrio*, occurs three times in the Greek New Testament, viz: Acts 11: 26, Acts 26: 28, and 1 Peter 4: 16, rendered Christian or Christians, and applied to the disciples of Christ.

(*a*) The Roman court at Cesarea, knew the name by which the disciples of Christ were called, at a period of about nineteen years from the time they received the name. For Paul, in his inimitable address before king Agrippa, was insisting that the king believed the prophets. "Then Agrippa said unto Paul: Almost thou persuadest me to be a Christian." (Acts 26: 28.)

(*b*) Peter, writing to the elect, says: "If ye be reproached for the name of Christ, happy are ye; for the Spirit of glory and of God resteth upon you." (1 Peter 4: 14.) Then, this reproach for the *name of Christ*, is explained in the 16th verse as suffering *as a Christian*, thus: "Yet if any man suffer as a Christian, let him not be ashamed; but let him glorify God in this name." Over twenty years they had now been known to the outside world by the *name Christian*, and had been persecuted under *that name*, brought before tribunals under *that name*, and glorified God *in that name*, by suffering as *Christians*, in " the Spirit of Glory and of God."

(*c*) The name Christian having now been recognized officially and legally for some twenty years, and receiving the sanction of apostolic benediction, we will visit Antioch about the year 43 and witness the naming of the family, the record of which is found in the eleventh chapter of Acts.

In verse 18, the apostles and brethren in Judea, having heard Peter's report of the conversion of the Gentiles, and their divine acceptance, at the house of Cornelius, withdrew their objections, and "glorified God, saying: Then hath God also to the Gentiles granted repentance unto life." Hitherto the light of the gospel had remained with the Jews, but is now about to shine to the Gentiles. About this time some of the brethren went to Antioch and commenced preaching the Lord Jesus Christ to the Gentiles, or Grecians. "And the hand of the Lord was with them; and a great number believed and turned to the Lord." (Verse 21.) The light of the gospel, and God's righteousness, which had hitherto remained among the Jews, we find now going forth to the Gentiles, according to prophecy, and for the first time, Jews and Gentiles, are builded together in Christ in one congregation, significantly pointing to the arrival of the time when they should be called by the new name for which God's people had been waiting over 700 years. And now we are prepared to look for the calling of the new name, which, according to the plan of the ages, (Isa. 62: 2) the mouth of the Lord shall name.

When the church at Jerusalem heard of these proceedings at Antioch, they appointed Barnabas, as an apostle from the church to go and look after that matter, who, pleased with this new missionary feature of their work, saw at once that there was a field of labor for his old friend Saul, whom Jesus had already called to go to the Gentiles, "to open their eyes and turn them from darkness to light." He goes immediately to Tarsus in search of Saul, and brings him to Antioch. "And it came to pass that a whole year they assembled themselves with the church, and taught much people. And the disciples were called Christians first in Antioch." (Acts 11: 26.)

Now the family has received the long looked for name, and that name is *Christian*, and recorded in the Bible. It is given at the right time, when the Gentiles had come in, and under the superintendence of Saul, an apostle of *Jesus*, and Barnabas, an apostle of *the church*, so that the *head* and the *body*, the *bridegroom* and the *bride*, are mutually represented at the naming of the family, and recorded as the result of a year's labor of these special apostles.

We have now learned *what* the name of the united family is, and that it was given *when* the family was united, and that it was by them accepted, that they suffered persecution under that name, and were encouraged by an inspired apostle to persevere and to glorify God in that name; and that the name has come down through the ages, we are well aware, as the only name that can unite the whole family.

But was the name given by divine authority? Some say it was given by their enemies; but that is only an assumption, as there is not even a hint in that direction. Three things are represented as being done in connection with that mission, *assembling*, *teaching*, and naming or *calling*. These three verbs being *infinitive* in the Greek, their subjects are not expressed. Simply, it was to them, or happened to them; or belonged to them, as a part of their mission, *to assemble*, *to teach*, and *to call* the disciples Christians. And then the words for *disciples* and *Christians*, are both in the accusative case, which corresponds to the object of a transitive verb in the English, the one as the object of the transitive verb *call*, and the other in same case by apposition. But the translators do not hesitate to give "they," as the subject of *assembled* and *taught*. Is it not then as clearly the implied subject of *called?* Though for technical or other reasons, the last clause is rendered, in the passive voice: "The disciples were called Christians," the truth will crop out that Paul and Barnabas were responsible for the naming, as well as the teaching.

9. A still stronger witness will now be summoned, in the word itself, which is used, and rendered *called* in Acts 11: 26, where they were first called Christians. The word in the Greek is *chrematizo*, and occurs in noun and verbal forms ten times in the New Testament, to which I will call attention, that the reader may see that the word itself is an expression of divine authority, meaning to give a divine admonition, or in the Greek mythology, to announce an oracle.

(1.) "And *being warned of God* in a dream." (Mat. 2: 12.) The words in *italics* are the translation of the one word under consideration.

(2.) "Notwithstanding, *being warned of God* in a dream, he turned aside." (Mat. 2: 22.)

(3.) "And it was *revealed* unto him by the Holy Ghost." (Luke 2: 26.)

(4.) "*Was warned from God* by a holy angel." (Acts 10: 22.)

(5.) "She *shall be called* an adulteress." (Rom. 7: 8.)

(6.) "But what saith the *answer of God* to him?" (Rom. 11: 4.)

(7.) "As Moses *was admonished of God* when he was about to make the tabernacle." (Heb. 8: 5.)

(8.) "By faith Noah *being warned of God* of things not seen as yet." (Heb. 11: 7.)

(9.) "For if they escaped not who refused him *that spake* on earth." (Heb. 12: 25.)

(10.) "And the disciples *were called* Christians first in Antioch." (Acts 11: 26, the passage under consideration.) If the word carries *divine authority* in it, as all these examples show, were not the disciples, *by divine authority*, called Christians? Then they were called by the name that the mouth of the Lord named.

10. There is another word, *kaleo*, which occurs 146 times in the New Testament, and is the word for *call*, when not by divine authority, and which would have been used here, if they had been called Christians by their enemies, or even by their friends, if not by divine authority called. But by divine authority they were *chrematized.*

XXIV.
GOD'S BUILDING.—1 Cor. 3: 9–17.

DELINEATION.

Elements Classified.	*Material Classified.*
1. Proprietor. ⎫	1. Gold. ⎫
2. Architect. ⎬ Co-operants.	2. Silver. ⎬ Durable.
3. Workmen. ⎭	3. Precious Stones. ⎭
4. Foundation. ⎫	4. Wood. ⎫
5. Material. ⎬ Means.	5. Hay. ⎬ Combustible.
6. Plan. ⎭	6. Stubble. ⎭

SURVEY.

ILLUSTRATIONS of the kingdom of heaven, and the Churches of Christ, drawn from familiar objects, abound in the scriptures. In the passage before us, the inspired apostle gives a graphic delineation of the structure of the divine temple, "the Church of God at Corinth," in particular, and the churches of Christ," in general, "with all that in every place, call upon the name of Jesus Christ our Lord."

This building had been the subject of prophecy, long ages before the foundation was laid. Seven hundred and twenty-five years before Christ, Isaiah had written concerning its foundation, thus: "Therefore thus saith the Lord God, behold I lay in Zion for a foundation, a stone, a tried stone, a precious corner stone, a sure foundation." (Isa. 28: 16.)

B. C. 519, Zechariah was divinely instructed to typify and illustrate Christ on his throne, as the builder of the temple of God, by crowning the high priest, in contravention of Jewish ritual, where priests wear mitres, and kings wear crowns; and with crown on the high priest to proclaim: "Thus speaketh the Lord of hosts, saying, behold the man whose name is the BRANCH..........Even he shall build the temple of the Lord,..........and he shall be a priest upon his throne." (Zech. 6: 11-13.)

Ages rolled on, and this child of prophecy came at the appointed time, and inaugurated the building of "the temple of the Lord," of which building we will now sit at the feet of the apostle, and learn a lesson of practical application.

Requisite to the building of a temple, palace, or edifice, are the following six classes of elements, which I have diagrammed in the delineation, viz.: 1. Proprietor; 2. Architect; 3. Workmen; 4. Foundation; 5. material; 6. Plan. The first three are co-operants, and the next three I call means.

The co-operants, working in harmony with the means at their command, carry on the building to its completion.

Contemplating the erection of an edifice, the proprietor selects an architect to draw up plan and specifications of such a building as he desires, and employs workmen to build according to the plan of the architect, supplying them with foundation, building material, and a copy of the plan.

All these elements are recognized in the lesson before us.

1. *Proprietor.* 9th verse. "Ye are God's building." This settles the question that God is the proprietor.

2. *Architect.* Who are the architects of God's building? Is there hesitation at this point? The 10th verse settles it. The apostle says: "According to the grace of God which is given to me, as a wise master-builder

[architect], I have laid the foundation, and another buildeth thereupon." In this case Paul is the architect, and he represents the class of apostles.

3. *Workmen.* 9th verse. "For we are laborers together with God." Here, the "we," who are co-operants, or co-workers with God, are Paul and Apollos, who had been co-laborers, when Paul planted and Apollos watered; the first representing the class of apostles, the second that of preachers or workmen. That they do thus represent the two classes, see the sixth verse of the next chapter, where the apostle says: "And these things, brethren, I have in a figure transferred to myself and to Apollos, for your sakes."

4. *Foundation.* 11th verse. "For other foundation can no man lay than that is laid, which is Jesus Christ." The foundation then is Jesus Christ, the same referred to above in Isa. 28: 16, and quoted and applied by Peter. (1 Pet. 2: 4-6.)

5. *Material.* Now comes the work. Material of two classes, and three grades in each class, are mentioned as possible in this building. The one class may be compared: good, better, best; the other: bad, worse, worst. These I diagram and classify, as in the delineation, thus: 1. Gold; 2. Silver; 3. Precious Stones; 4. Wood; 5. Hay; 6. Stubble. Of these, the first three are durable material, the next three combustible material.

Tested in the fiery ordeal through which these material must pass, the durable will assay at a high premium, while the combustible, in dissolving elements, reduced to dross, become a worthless mass.

But what these materials represent, is a practical question demanding a solution, upon which hangs much of the significance of the whole figure.

Confronting us at this point are three theories demanding our attention.

First. One theory assumes that the materials represent the conduct or character of men and women in this life, the gold, silver, and precious stones, representing the good conduct, or good works, while the wood, hay, and stubble represent the bad works or wickedness. If any one's work stands the fiery ordeal, the builder receives a reward; but if the work is burned, the builder suffers loss, but he himself shall be saved. Upon this is predicated universal salvation.

This view, however, is obnoxious to the objection that it makes no provision for the salvation of infidels; for these works are all built upon the foundation Jesus the Christ, and as the wickedness of unbelievers is not built upon that foundation, they are not included in the term, "he himself shall be saved."

Second. Another theory claims that the materials represent the doctrines that men have followed in this life, that gold, silver and precious stones represent the true doctrines, while the wood, hay, and stubble represent false doctrines.

This view also squints strongly in the direction of universal salvation, teaching that men may maintain and propagate the most pernicious and destructive doctrines through life, and yet be saved themselves.

The universal feature of this view, however, is open to the objection that it looks not to the salvation of unbelievers, as all these doctrines are built upon the one foundation Jesus the Christ.

Third. A third theory makes the material represent living human beings, men and women, who have been built into the church, God's building, by co-operant workmen, preachers, and those who labor in word and doctrine.

What most concerns us at this point, is to ascertain which is the scriptural theory, and cut off debate, for an apostolic decision is not a debatable question. Our course then is brief, for Paul settles the question in our lesson. The wonder is that the different theories should ever have become popular.

Apostolic decision, verses 9, 16, and 17, "Ye are God's building." "Know ye not that ye are the temple of God?" "For the temple of God is holy, which temple ye are."

With this inspired decision, we have plain sailing, and need not wrangle over the opinions of uninspired men. Preachers and other Christian workers, with the apostolic plan in their hands, go forth and build, upon the foundation, Jesus the Christ, living material, men and women.

Another inspired apostle renders the same decision. Addressing the elect, he says: "To whom coming, as unto a living stone, disallowed indeed of men, but chosen of God, and precious, ye also as lively [living] stones, are built up a spiritual house, a holy priesthood, to offer up spiritual sacrifices, acceptable to God by Jesus Christ." (1 Pet. 2: 4, 5.)

In the light of the decision of both these apostles, personal accountability, terribly in earnest, stares us in the face. "The fire shall try every man's work," and "the day shall declare it." "The day of judgment and perdition of ungodly men," when, according to John's vision, "whosoever was not found written in the book of life was cast into the lake of fire."

"If any man's work abide which he hath built thereupon, he shall receive a reward." Here, if the work,

Christians, built into the church, hold out faithful and stand the fiery ordeal, the workman who built them in will receive a reward. They will be stars in his crown of rejoicing, present and ready to answer to their names at the roll call of eternity. For the glorified Savior has said: "He that overcometh, the same shall be clothed in white raiment; and I will not blot his name out of the book of life." (Rev. 3: 5.)

"If any man's work shall be burned, he shall suffer loss; but he himself shall be saved; yet so as by fire." If some of those living stones, men and women, turn out to be combustible material, apostatize, their names are "blotted out of the book of life," at the fiery ordeal and are "not found written in the book of life," and they are "cast into the lake of fire," and, being "burned," the workman, preacher, who built them in, "suffers loss."

Personal responsibility of those who apostatize and are lost, being admitted, the question arises, will the preacher who built them in, be responsible for their unfaithfulness, and be lost because they are lost? This the apostle anticipates, and answers by saying: "But he himself shall be saved."

But this springs another question: "Will every preacher who ever built any living material into the Church, be saved unconditionally?" Paul anticipates this, and responds: "Yet so as by fire" [through fire]. That is, he will not be lost because of the apostacy of some of his converts, but will be held responsible for his own conduct, and be tried by the same fiery ordeal, and thus, if found faithful, be saved, "yet so as through fire." Though not responsible for the ultimate outcome of bad material, he will be held accountable for the manner of working it into the building, which brings us to the sixth and last class of elements.

6. *The Plan.* We have seen that the apostles were the architects, therefore we look for the plan at their hands. And they have given us a divinely inspired plan.

Twelve architects were selected at first, and Paul was afterwards added to the architectural college. After more than three years apprenticeship, Jesus charged them not to even lay the foundation till after his resurrection, and then not till after his ascension and the descent of the Holy Spirit, which occurred on the day of Pentecost, when they commenced, as recorded in the second chapter of Acts.

In the building of Solomon's temple, stones were not permitted to take position in the edifice, till dressed in all their dimensions to fit the place they were intended to occupy. So in the antitype, the church or temple of God, with a living stone as the foundation, the living stones must be dressed according to the plan of the architect, before they can occupy places in the building.

Every one knows that solids have three dimensions, length, breadth, and thickness, and stones prepared for a building must be dressed in these three dimensions. In like manner we may expect the living stones to be dressed in three dimensions, preparatory to being placed in the building.

But does the apostle recognize a plan in our lesson? All the other elements have been found, and we look for this. Here it is in verse 10: "But let every man take heed how he buildeth thereupon." The "how," calls for a plan, and herein lies the responsibility of the workman.

Does the plan of the apostles require the living

stones to be dressed in three dimensions? Beyond all peradventure it does.

Now go to the Pentecost (Acts 2d), where God had providentially assembled representative men, "Jews, devout men out of every nation under heaven," to witness the laying of the corner stone of God's temple, the Church of Christ, and the dressing and building in, of the first living stones.

The architects being all present, by divine appointment, the celestial telegraph announces from heaven the signal for commencing, and Peter, Grand Master Architect, "standing up with the eleven," commences the work, and lays the foundation (verses 14-36).

Next comes the dressing of material: Verse 36, faith is required as the first dimension dressed. Verse 38 requires repentance as the next dimension to be dressed. The dressing of the third dimension is required in the same verse, in these words: "Be baptized every one of you in the name of Jesus Christ for the remission of sins."

Here are the three dimensions in the apostolic plan. And none of them asked to be put in, without dressing, for "they that gladly received his word were baptized, and the same day were added about three thousand souls."

To show that these dressed stones were now in the building, it is added: "And they continued steadfastly in the apostles doctrine and fellowship, and in breaking of bread, and in prayers." These latter are Christian duties, and consequently *recurring* duties.

Now should any modern builder think he can get living stones into God's building, without dressing in the three dimensions, let him "take heed how he buildeth."—[*Published in Christian Quarterly Review, January* 1885.

XXV.
BY GRACE YE ARE SAVED.—Eph. 2: 8.*

DELINEATION.

PROPOSITION: YE ARE SAVED.
Adjuncts: 1. By Grace. [τη χαριτι.] Feminine.
2. Through Faith. [της πιστεως.] Feminine.
3. And that (?) [και τουτο.] Neuter.
4. The Gift. [το δωρον.] Neuter.

SURVEY.

"FOR by grace ye are saved through faith; and that not of yourselves; it is the gift of God." (Eph. 2: 8.)

Here we find a proposition affirmed, with four adjuncts, to the full understanding of which, we must give attention to the scope of the apostle's teaching in this epistle. Want of attention to this scope has caused much confusion in the popular teachings of modern theology.

Some will take the first adjunct, *grace*, and carry it away into some solitary place *alone*, and by some secret and unauthorized ceremony declare the nuptials of "Salvation by *Grace* alone."

Others will decoy the second adjunct *faith* into solitary confinement, to feed upon the same thin gruel, imagining that justification by *faith alone* is a wholesome diet and very full of comfort, though feebleness follows its footsteps.

Thus the ghosts of "faith alone," and "grace alone," stalk abroad alone, yet always together, like a husband and wife living together, yet alone. I have never been able to learn what crime faith or grace has

*Diagram in "Text Book Exposed," by the author.

committed, that they should each be stripped naked and turned out into the world alone.

The apostle had been speaking in the first chapter of the choosing, predestinating, qualifying, and inspiring, of *us*, the apostles who *first* trusted in Christ. (Verses 3-12.) Then in the 13th and 14th verses, he refers to the *ye*, the Gentile Christians, who *also* trusted in him, after they had heard the word of truth, the gospel of their salvation, as preached by the *us*, the predestinated, called, and inspired apostles.

Through the remainder of the chapter, verses 15-23, he calls attention to the mighty power of God, "which he wrought in Christ when he raised him from the dead, and set him at his own right hand in the heavenly places, far above all principality, and power, and might, and dominion, and every name that is named, not only in this world, but also in that which is to come; and hath put all things under his feet, and gave him to be the head over all things to the church, which is his body, the fullness of him that filleth all in all."

Addressing the same Gentile Christians in the next chapter, verses 11-22, he reminds them that formerly they were Gentiles, aliens, without Christ, without hope, without God, and destitute of any claim upon which to rest a hope; and that it was therefore entirely through grace, or favor, that Christ had broken down the middle wall of partition between them and the Jews who had the covenants and promises, that he might reconcile both to God through the cross. Having done this he says: He "came and preached peace to you that were afar off, [the Gentiles] and to them that were nigh." [The Jews.] Now they have been built in with the Jews, and are of the same family and household, and no longer strangers and foreigners. Here are the three classes: *we* the apostles, *ye* Gentile Christians, and *them* the Jews.

Now we are prepared to appreciate the apostle in the text when he reminds these Gentiles that they had no claim to plead, but that it was entirely through the *grace*, or favor of God, that *they* were permitted to be saved through the faith, that is, through the gospel, without the works of the law, the burden of which had been for so long a time on the shoulders of the Jews.

A brief analysis of the sentence as outlined in the delineation, will make this plain and clear as day light.

The simple proposition, addressed to these Gentile Christians, reads: *Ye are saved*, or as the Revised Version renders it: "have been saved." The unlimited proposition simply affirms that these Gentiles had been saved.

But this proposition is limited by the adjunctive phrase: *by grace*, and thus limited, would read "you have been saved by grace."

The proposition is also limited by the phrase: *through faith*, literally *through the faith*, which is equivalent to saying through the gospel. Take this limitation separately, and we read: "Ye have been saved through the faith."

Now take both limitations and read: By grace ye have been saved through the faith.

The next limitation adds: "And that not of yourselves." That (something) is not of themselves. But what is that something?

The next limitation says: "it is the gift of God." That (something) that is not of themselves, is the *thing* declared to be *the gift of God*. Then clearly that *thing* that is the gift of God, may be placed in the third adjunct, in the parenthesis after *that*, as any one can see, whether he can read the Greek phrases in the brackets or not. Some claim that faith is the thing that is here declared to be the gift of God. If that assumption is true, faith can be put where the parenthesis is, in place of the interrogation point, and we will read: And that *faith* not of yourselves, it is the gift of God. The English scholar, though a grammarian might fail to detect the error in that construction, though the eye of the Greek scholar, will at a glance see that it is inadmissible, for *that*, [*touto*] in the Greek, is neuter gender, and *faith* [*pisteos*] is feminine gender, and cannot be limited by *touto*. So *that faith*, in the above sentence is inadmissible.

Again, *gift*, [*doron*] in the Greek is neuter gender, and faith being feminine cannot be the gift. Grace, [*chariti*] in the Greek is also feminine, and cannot be the gift. Then, since neither *faith* nor *grace* can possibly be what is called the gift of God, in the text, what is it that Paul here calls the gift of God? Beyond all dispute, the *gracious gift* of God is, that the Gentiles may be saved through the faith of the gospel, without the burden of the works of the law, under which the Jews had so long labored. In strict accord with which the apostles and elders at Jerusalem decided not to burden with circumcision and the law, "those who from among the Gentiles are turned to God."

XXVI.
SUBSTANTIALISM.

AN ADDRESS ON THE SUBSTANTIAL PHILOSOPHY.—BY PROF. G. R. HAND.

[Delivered before the annual State meeting of the Churches of Christ in California, September 26th, 1884, and by unanimous vote requested for publication in the Microcosm and Christian Church News.]

"IN the beginning was the Word, and the Word was with God, and the Word was God." (John 1: 1.)

Seeing, by the programme sent me, that the committee have appointed me to address the State Meeting, on the new Science of Substantialism, without indicating whether an oral address or a written essay was expected, I deemed it prudent to prepare a written discourse. I say the *new* science, for I believe its name is not yet recorded in any dictionary.

I purpose commencing at "the beginning," as beyond, or anterior to that period, possibly there might not be found *substance* for a *foundation* upon which to build.

Here the λογος, translated, "the Word," is affirmed to have existed at "the beginning," beyond which our research does not penetrate. This Logos, it is affirmed, existed in connection with the Θεος, translated "God," and it affirms that the *Theos* was *Logos*, or, as transposed, that *Logos* was *Theos*.

Clearly, then, *something* was coexistent with God, and that something, is called the *Logos*, whatever that may be, and by which, or with which "all things were made" and without which, "was not any thing made that was made."

We are anxious to know what this Logos is, which was coexistent with God, and a co-operant, or means, by which God created the heavens and the earth.

Pickering's Greek Lexicon defines *Logos*: "The outward form by which the inward thought is expressed." The same Lexicon defines *Theos:* "A causer, or maker, a god." Then God is "the inward thought," or self-existing intelligence, "the I am," and "the maker," or creator. But with him, existed "the outward form," and that, or any outward form, must be a *substance*, and not a *nothing*, or nonentity.

Webster defines *substance:* "That which underlies all outward manifestations." But, "the outward form," the *Logos*, must be one of the "outward manifestations," and substance must have existed underlying the *Logos*, else there could have been no "outward manifestation;" and *Theos*, the intelligent actor, is represented as existing in connection with "the outward form," the *Logos*, and a basic underlying *substance*.

Under apostolic and lexical guidance, we are now entering the frontier regions of Substantialism.

We interview Moses on the subject of "the beginning," and he responds: "In the beginning God created the heaven and the earth. And the earth was without form, and void; and darkness was upon the face of the deep; and the Spirit of God moved upon the face of the waters. And God said let there be light, and there was light." (Gen. 1: 1–3.,

Here Moses informs us that God, the original intelligent actor, "created the heaven and the earth." But he does not say that he made it out of "nothing." Neither is it a necessary inference that he was driven to that extremity, for John testifies, as we have already seen, that there was an abundance of *something* at hand, a *substantial* entity, and a much more available material than *nothing*, out of which to create the earth and atmosphere.

In the last quotation, it is said: "The Spirit of God moved upon the face of the waters." This introduces us to another entity called "the Spirit of God," the πνευμα, which seems to be not included in the things created, but coexistent with God, and co-operant with him in creation.

The same Greek Lexicon gives, among other definitions of *Pneuma*: "Breath," "breath of life," "life," "soul or mind," "the Holy Spirit," "a spirit," "a spiritual being." So *Theos*, *Logos*, and *Pneuma*, with the underlying *substance*, were present at the beginning. And John testifies that "God is a Spirit." (John 4: 24.)

To avoid running into materialism, we must classify. *Substance* is primarily divisible into two grand divisions. 1. *Immaterial* substances. 2. *Material* substances.

I. *Immaterial Substances* will include three classes. *a. Intelligent* entities, or forces, as Spirit. *b. Vital* forces, including both animal and vegetable life. *c. Physical* forces without life, as gravity, magnetism, electricity, heat, light, sound, etc.

II. *Material Substances* will include those of which we may take cognizance by our physical senses, and by the appliances of philosophy and chemistry, and the other sciences, and will appear in the solid, liquid, fluid, semifluid, aeriform, gaseous, and other more or less attenuated forms.

The underlying substance, with the *Logos*, at the beginning, may be regarded as including the *immate-*

rial substances, which are invisible separately, and with which *Theos* clothed himself in "outward manifestation," without the charge of materialism. Then, if by combination, analysis, condensation, rarefaction, or attenuation, he clothes himself with garments of visible "outward manifestations," it surely can detract nothing from his "eternal power and Godhead."

Here Substantialism drives down its initial stake, and takes its bearings, admitting, as per necessity from the foregoing definitions and revelations, the existence of immaterial substance in the active co-operants in creation, the *Theos*, the *Logos*, and *Pneuma*, with the essential underlying *substance*, which may include all the immaterial substances above named.

Substantialism sees *Theos*, the intelligent actor, in his vast laboratory, the machine shop of creation, prescribing the compounding of invisible elements of immaterial substance, to form *matter*, or material substance of which he made the heaven and the earth. In this way Substantialism can admit that God created the *matter* out of which he made the heaven and the earth, but that he created it out of the pre-existing immaterial *substance* "underlying all outward manifestations," and which "was in the beginning with God."

Thus the thinking mind is not required to stultify itself by attempting to swallow the human dogma, nowhere affirmed in the Scriptures, that he created it out of nothing, the logical scientific axium, *ex nihilo nihil fit* to the contrary notwithstanding.

Under the supervision of intelligent force, and the obedient action of the physical and vital forces, material substance is seen merging into visibility and tangibility. Even some of the *material* elements are still invisible, as hydrogen, oxygen, nitrogen, and carbonic acid gases; but when, by the prescription of the great chemist, they are compounded, they assume the form of visible and tangible material entities. At the command of God we see the elements in motion. Invisible carbon and oxygen, pair off in chemical affinity, and rocks in huge proportions stand before us. Oxygen and hydrogen, silently and unseen, approach the hymenial altar, and by the divine ceremony prescribed in elective affinity, in definite proportions, are made one, and the name assumed in the now visible marriage relation, is *water*, which God spreads as a garment over the underlying rocks.

Then, obedient to the divine behest, oxygen and nitrogen, in definite proportions, form a mechanical copartnership to perform service in atmospheric meteorology, and the aerial ocean encircles the earth in its loving embrace, and fans it with its zephyrs.

Another edict goes forth, and vegetable vital forces draw elements from the mineral kingdom, and arrange them in thousands of organic forms, and the multifarious phenomena of vegetable life, announce the birth of the vegetable kingdom.

He issues from headquarters another order, and vital forces of animal life, draw materials from the vegetable kingdom, arranging them in myriads of organic forms, heralding the birth of animated nature.

One step nearer divinity, calls forth the grand edict that combines the immaterial with the material, and connects divinity with humanity. Spirit, or breath of life from the divine reservoir of spiritual existence, is placed in the human form divine, from material substance made, and man becomes a living soul; and the era of human intellectual existences, is inaugurated, and to man is given dominion over the works of creation inferior to himself, and the enthronement of mind affirmed.

Intelligence dwelling in, and looking out upon, and controlling the material world, must needs have some media through which spirit can cognize material as well as immaterial substances, to which end, the great designer furnishes him an outfit in what are known as "the five senses," enabling him to feel, taste, smell, hear, and see, external objects; all which senses or media, are, by Substantialism, regarded as real substances, or substantial entities.

1. In the sense of touch, or feeling, we are individually cognizant of the fact that material substance comes in actual contact with our tactile nerves.

2. In taste we are also conscious of actual contact, of material substance, in more or less diluted form, with our gustatory nerves.

3. In smell, philosophy admits that the sensation produced upon the olfactory nerves, is communicated by direct contact of infinitesimal particles of highly attenuated material substance, with the nasal organs.

4. The sense of hearing, or sound, is by the popular philosophy, regarded as produced by the contact of vibrations of air, with the tympanum, or ear drum. But Substantial philosophy recognizes sound as a real immaterial substance, or substantial entity, emanating from the sonorous body, conducted by the atmosphere or any other conductor, and coming in contact with the auditory nerve.

5. Sight is also regarded as the result of the actual contact of an immaterial substance, light, with the visual organs and optic nerve, entering the eye at various angles from external objects of visual recognition.

Thus invisible objects, by change of consistency, or by combination, may become visible.

The department of sound is the field where the main battle of Substantialism has been fought, and the wave theory of sound demoralized.

The popular theory as taught in the school books, presents us with waves of air, a material substance, in alternate condensation and rarefaction, driven from vibrating strings, or resonant instruments, and hurled against the ear drum, causing it to move physically, in and out, in vibrations synchronizing with those of the sounding instrument.

The slowest vibration producing an audible sound, I believe is sixteen per second, and producing the lowest pitch of sound. Then higher pitches of sound require more rapid vibrations, until they run up into the hundreds and even thousands of vibrations in a second.

A full seven octave piano has strings of over eighty different rates of vibration, producing more than eighty different pitches of sound, each of which to be audible, must pelt and beat the ear drum into tremulous agitation of more than four score different rates of pulsations, simultaneously, or in instantaneous succession of changing rates.

Then a full orchestra will present some hundreds of different rates of tympanic vibration, and we begin to feel a rising sympathy for our polite little gentleman, the ear drum, acting as doorkeeper to our auditorium, and compelled to make a different style of bow to every pitch of sound that demands admittance. That is putting on style, and changing the style with wonderful rapidity.

A grave deputation from the lowest bass, demands

a hearing, and Mr. Ear Drum bows sixteen times per second to admit them to the audience room.

But here comes an airy deputation from the "upper class" of notes, arrayed in twinkling robes, demanding an entrance, and our little friend dons an extra suit of super-subservient agility and nimbleness, and makes about half a thousand polite bows every second of time while admitting them.

But here comes representatives of a hundred different pitches of tones and semi-tones between these, and all demanding simultaneous admittance; and the politeness of our delicate membrane, is taxed to an eruptive tension when called upon to perform the impossible physical feat of bowing sixteen times per second, and five hundred times per second, and at all the intermediate rates between these, and all at the same time.

The wonder is that the ear drum has stood the wear and tear of impossible performances, for so many centuries, without going to pieces. It should have raised a rebellion long ago. The skill of equestrianism would be severely taxed to so train a horse that he could trot, and pace, and canter, and gallop, and lope, and amble, and run, and walk, all at the same time, and pass round the training ring, in all these gaits at once, and at all the different rates of speed known to the turf. And yet the execution of the unreasonable demand, would fall short of the task imposed upon the ear drum by the wave theory of sound.

Physical *impossibilities*, as well as possibilities, exist in the material world. It is sometimes said that nothing is impossible with God, and yet possibly it would not be a breach of reverential courtesy to say that there may be physical impossibilities with him. But whether the impossible feat of tympanic vibration imposed upon the ear drum by the wave theory of sound, is one of the divine impossibilities, I leave open for discussion.

But space in this address will not permit me to discuss this feature of our subject. I simply lead you to the battle-field, and ask you to survey the reeking remnants on the gory field, strewn with killed and wounded, dead and dying.

Dissolving views of captured prisoners and retreating combatants, occasionally turning back to fire a farewell shot, may give variety. Prominent in that conflict, figured the shrill notes of the locust, as by its rapid stridulations, it threw the surrounding atmosphere into multitudinous vibrations.

Tremulous tones of tuning forks figured fantastically in the fray. Small arms rattle and canon roar amid the blare of trumpet notes, while, from the melancholy siren sounds of the distant fog horn, a soothing influence steals over the conflicting belligerents.

Dense volumes of smoke from exploding powder magazines, impelled by the elastic force of liberated gas, roll in accumulating masses, borne onward and upward in steadily unfolding convolutions, and wreath a sulphurous canopy over the tragic scene.

Having commenced with "the beginning," in what I may be permitted to call Theistic Substantialism, I do not purpose extending its ramifications far beyond the limits of that field, and will therefore return, from this excursion.

We read that "things which are seen were not made of things which do appear." (Heb. 11: 3.)

Here the visible things were made from the *invisible*, and not from *nothing*.

Paul says: "For the invisible things from the creation of the world are clearly seen, being understood by the things that are made." (Rom. 1: 20.)

While we cannot see the invisible things, not even the immaterial substances, yet we can see invisibility merging into visibility, in "outward manifestation" of his "eternal power and Godhead," thus revealing the "invisible God," who "stretcheth out the heavens as a curtain and spreadeth them out as a tent to dwell in." (Isa. 40: 22.)

Here the prophet seems to lead us into the penetralia of Substantialism, where, in the presence chamber of the invisible God, we may gaze upon his environments.

From a photograph taken, by the inspired poet laureate of Israel, some three hundred years before the pen of Isaiah drew the foregoing picture, we take the following view: "O Lord, my God, thou art great; and art clothed in majesty." Then peering through this majestic, though invisible clothing, into the dwelling place of Deity, and home of Substantialism, he proceeds: "Who coverest thyself with light as with a garment; who stretchest out the heavens like a curtain; who layeth the beams of his chambers in the waters; who maketh the clouds his chariot; who walketh upon the wings of the wind * * * who laid the foundations of the earth. * * * Thou coveredst it with the deep as with a garment." (Psalm 104: 1-6.)

This carries us back to the creation, where the infant earth lay wrapped in swaddling clothes of water, and "darkness was upon the face of the deep." Exterior to the clouds and mists of darkness, was God himself, clothed in garments of light, beholding the darkness that enveloped the earth.

His voice is heard for the first time in the realms of space. and the sublime sentence that pioneered the pathway of thought, from the source of all intelligence in "outward form," to greet the new creation, called for LIGHT.

God said, let light be, and light was there, where the darkness was before, that is, on the face of the deep, and the smiling waters greet the light, in sparkling recognition.

Another photograph bears this sublime view: " He bowed the heavens also and came down; and darkness was under his feet. And he rode upon a cherub and did fly; yea he did fly upon the wings of the wind. He made darkness his secret place; his pavilion round about him, dark waters and thick clouds of the skies." (Psalm 18: 9–11.)

In all these sublime manifestations of the entities and activities of *Theos*, and *Logos*, and *Pneuma*, so beautifully portrayed by inspired prophets and apostles, can there be any valid objection to regarding all these actors as real substantial entities? And is it degrading to the character of God, to accord to him the ability to utilize the immaterial substances that "underlie all outward manifestations," in framing and bringing forth all these grand outward manifestations, in earth and air and sea?

Is it any stain upon his originality, that he, who is clothed with light, should have enjoyed companionship with light from "the beginning," beyond which " the memory of man runneth not to the contrary," and of which the ken of prophet, taketh not cognizance?

We can regard gravity, magnetism, electricity, caloric, etc., as immaterial substances existing through all the realms where God existed, as his accompaniments, or clothing, or external nature, subject to his intelligent control, and ready at any time, at his bidding, to become "the outward form by which the inward thought" of deity would be expressed, and God be honored thereby.

Then if the great chemist of the universe, should compound some of these immaterial substances, and form material and visible substances, it would be but the visible made from the invisible, and becoming "manifest;" and we have seen by the definition, that substance "underlies all outward manifestations."

John, having informed us that the *logos* was in the beginning, says: "And the Word was made [or became] flesh and dwelt among us." (Jno. 1: 14.)

Now the *logos* which was the "outward form," in creation, becomes the outward form—and that form is flesh—in which the invisible God is made "manifest" to men.

May not this throw some light on Rev. 3: 14, where the same writer calls Jesus Christ "the faithful and true witness, the beginning of the creation of God." Some have thought this passage makes Christ a *created* being. It need not so imply. Understand "creation" here to mean the *work* or performance, and not the *things created*, and *archee*, beginning, will refer to the beginning of the *work*. And *logos* is represented as being a co-operant with God in the beginning of creation.

The "manifestation" is expressed in another place, thus: "That which was from the beginning, which we have heard, which we have seen with our eyes, which we have looked upon, and our hands have handled, of the Word of life; for the life was manifested and we have seen it." (1 John 1: 1.)

Here an invisible substance, the life, the *logos*, was made "manifest" and visible.

Again, he says: "And ye know that he was manifested to take away our sins.........For this purpose the Son of God was manifested that he might destroy the works of the devil." (1 Jno. 3: 5, 8.)

In this manifestation, the *logos* has become the Son of God, a new relationship, and different from that sustained " in the beginning."

Referring to this manifestation, Paul says: "God was manifest in the flesh." (1 Tim. 3: 16.)

Thus we see Substantialism multiplying before us in the Scriptures, and invisible substances coming into new relationships and visible manifestations.

Spirit is immaterial substance, and spirits are substantial entities. After immaterial substance and invisibility had put on visible manifestations, in the physical universe, it pleased God to connect the visible and invisible, the material and immaterial, the physical and the spiritual, and give the unseen spirit a visible " manifestation " in man. So God made man of *material* substance, and breathed into him the *immaterial*, the " breath of life," spirit, the *pneuma*, and man became a living soul.

In the microcosm man, we have a combination of two worlds, the material, and immaterial, the physical and spiritual.

The spirit of man, then, is an emanation from God, who is also Spirit, and the great fountain of spirit. Hence God is said to be the father, the maker, the giver, the owner of our spirits. And we find such expressions as the following: " O God, the God of the spirits of all flesh." (Nu. 16: 22.) "The God of the spirits of all flesh." (Nu. 27: 16.). "The Lord, who stretcheth forth the heavens, and layeth the foundation of the earth, and formeth the spirit of man within him." (Zech. 12: 1.) "Shall we not rather be in subjection to the Father of spirits, and live?" (Heb. 12: 9.)

This substantial relationship of material and immaterial substance, spirit and body, must be separated in death, but a more substantial reunion is promised. The apostle says: "Knowing in yourselves [or for yourselves] that ye have in heaven a better and an enduring substance." (Heb. 10: 34.)

The Psalmist says, in view of the silent and unseen coming together of material and immaterial substance, in the embryo man: "Thine eyes did see my substance, yet being imperfect; and in thy book all my members were written, which in continuance were fashioned, when as yet there was none of them." (Psalm 139: 16.)

With an eye to the dissolution of this corporeal frame, Solomon wrote: "Then shall the dust return to the earth as it was, and the spirit shall return to God who gave it." (Ec. 12: 7.)

Peter, looking to the same dissolution, says: "Yea, I think it meet, as long as I am in this tabernacle, to stir you up by putting you in remembrance; knowing that shortly I must put of this my tabernacle, even as our Lord Jesus Christ hath showed me." (2 Pet. 1: 13–14.)

Watching the same vanishing relation, Paul says: "But though our outward man perish, yet the inward man is renewed day by day. * * * While we look not at the things which are seen, but at the things which are not seen; for the things which are seen are temporal; but the things which are not seen are eternal." (2 Cor. 4: 16, 18.)

Here the substantial inner man is renewing strength daily, while the material outward man, is wasting away; and the bodies, the *seen*, are declared to be mortal, temporal, and the spirit, the *unseen*, eternal.

But the *separation* is not eternal. The spirit leaves the mortal clay for a while. "But if the Spirit of him that raised up Jesus from the dead, dwell in you, he that raised up Christ from the dead, shall also quicken your mortal bodies by his Spirit that dwelleth in you." (Rom. 8: 11.)

The difference between the material and immaterial in man, is aptly illustrated by the Savior, when he suddenly appeared to his disciples after his resurrection. "But they were terrified and affrighted, and supposed that they had seen a spirit. And he said to them * * behold my hands and my feet, that it is I myself; handle me, and see; for a spirit hath not flesh and bones as you see me have." (Luke 24: 37, 39.)

So a disembodied spirit, being immaterial, is, according to the great teacher, an intangible entity, not having flesh and bones.

But Paul, speaking of the incarnation, says: "Who is the image of the invisible God, the first born of every creature." (See Col. 1: 15-18.)

The image of the invisible, required *substance* to make a visible "outward manifestation," as we have seen, and the *logos* was there in the beginning, who, with the underlying substance, became "the outward form by which the inward thought is expressed," and the "manifest" image of God. But he is "the first born of every creature," the first born from the dead, or as John says: "The first begotten of the dead." Revised version reads, "the first-born of the dead." (Rev. 1: 5.)

He has pioneered the pathway through the dark regions of the tomb, and conquered death in his own dominions, and bids us follow, trusting in him to lead us safely out into the bright realms of eternal day beyond the dark confines of the charnal house of the mortal remains of Adam's race.

In full confidence of this glorious deliverance, let us in conclusion, join with the apostle, in the triumphant culmination of visions of the seen and unseen, the temporal and eternal, and "light afflictions" placed in antithetical counterpoise with "a far more exceeding and eternal weight of glory," as the announcement of the triumph of "glory," breaks forth in the sublime language. (2 Cor. 5: 1.) For we know that if our earthly house of this tabernacle were dissolved, we have a building of God, a house not made with hands eternal in the heavens."—[*Published in Microcosm, February and March*, 1885.]

XXVII.
CLEANSING FROM SIN.—1 Jno. 1: 6-10, and 2: 1-5.

'The blood of Jesus Christ his Son cleanseth us from all sin.''—1 Jno. 1 : 7.

DELINEATION.

1.—Walk in the Light.	5.—Propitiation,
2.—No Sin?	6.—How Know Him.
3.—Confess Sin.	7.—Know we are in Him.
4.—Advocate.	8.—The 3 Relations to Sin.

SURVEY.

READ the entire passage indicated at the heading, and then attend to the analysis.

1. The apostle says: The blood of Jesus Christ cleanses from all sin. But is this cleansing conditional or unconditional? Does it cleanse everybody indiscriminately, or only those who comply with the conditions or terms of cleansing? This is a basic question, and must be kept in view and answered, not by our opinions of the fitness of things, but only in the *light* of the scriptures.

(*a*). Now turn the light on, as we have it before us, and read. John says: The blood "cleanses *us* from all sin." But who are included in the "us?" Does it include all alien sinners? If so, is it right certain that all mankind are cleansed? The twelfth verse will answer that question. "I write unto you little children, because your sins are forgiven you for his name's sake;" or literally rendered, "through his name." This identifies those whose sins, the blood cleanses, with those whose sins are forgiven "through his name." But the first time forgiveness, or remission "through his name" was ever offered to the world was to penitent believers on the day of Pentecost, and they were commanded to be baptized "in his name" for remission. (Acts, 2: 38.) These were Jews, but the Gentiles were also commanded to be baptized in his name, after they had been instructed that those who believe on him should receive remission of sins "through his name." Then clearly, baptized penitent believers constituted the class addressed whose sins the blood of Jesus Christ cleanses.

(*b*.) Read again: "If we walk in the light......the blood of Jesus Christ cleanses us from all sin." (Verse 7.) Here the condition of this cleansing is, walking in the light. Of course it is the light of God's word. The Psalmist says: "Thy word is a lamp to my feet and a light to my path." (Ps. 119: 105.) And Paul endorses it thus: "Among whom ye shine as lights in the world, holding forth the word of life." (Phil. 2: 15, 16.) And the light of that word as we have just seen, leads us to obedience for the cleansing, as required of both Jews and Gentiles. Let us walk in the light.

2. We are not to assume that we are cleansed without obedience, or that we do not sin, and so deceive ourselves. For the apostle adds: "If we say that we have no sin, we deceive ourselves, and the truth is not in us." Then our self-assumed sanctification and perfection from sin, should put on a little modesty in the light of this apostolic admonition.

3. We stand corrected, and inquire, since all are liable to sin, what are we to do? The answer is forthcoming: "If we confess our sins, he is faithful and just to forgive us our sins, and cleanse us from all unrighteousness."

4 We do not approach God, for forgiveness, except through the advocate, for: "If any one sin, we have an advocate with the Father, Jesus Christ, the righteous." To have an advocate at court, we trust our cause in the hands of an advocate, and he presents our cause for us. Those of whom John says "we have an advocate," had placed their cause in the hands of our advocate as we have already seen.

5. Not only is he our advocate, but our mercyseat, or propitiation. [*Hilasterion*, here rendered propitiation, is the word for mercyseat.] "And he is the propitiation for our sins." The mercyseat covered the ark in which were the tables of the law, and above which was the luminous presence of God. So Christ our mercyseat, stands between the law, and God's execution of justice. Law knows no mercy. It says that man has violated the law and deserves to die, while mercy pleads and says, "spare him." Thus justice and mercy meet together. And this mercyseat is broad enough to cover "the sins of the whole world," on the same conditions of "Walking in the light."

6. Since Christ our mercyseat is in heaven, and we cannot come literally to the mercyseat for remission, or cleansing from sin, how are we to *know him* in the forgiveness of sins? The apostle answers: "And hereby we do know that we know him, if we keep his commandments."

That is clearly apostolic teaching. But suppose modern theology should teach that we should have a feeling sense of forgiveness, or know God in the pardon of our sins, before we obey his command: "to be baptized in the name of the Lord:" and some in the extacy of spasmodic excitement, protest earnestly and honestly that they *know him*, before obedience, while modern fanaticism claps her hands, in apparent triumph over the apostolic decision. What will the apostle say to that procedure? He answers in the next verse. "He that saith I know him, and keepeth not his commandments, is a liar, and the truth is not in him." The apostle's answer is rather blunt, but very incisive in a deadly thrust to the vitals of fanaticism.

7. As this remission, or cleansing from sin, is in Christ, how can we know that we are in him? The apostle answers in this next verse: "But whoso keepeth his word, in him verily is the love of God perfected; hereby know we that we are in him." Then we are not left to guess, or imagine, or think, or hope that we are in him, but it is our privilege to "*know* that we are in him." At this point, the fanaticism of modern conversions, turns pale, and stands aghast in holly horror.

8. The fantastic vagaries, and wild fanaticism, in endless varieties of visible and audible manifestations, supposed to be seen and heard and felt under highly excited conditions of emotional natures, in connection with supposed conversions, may be traced to the fact that modern revivalism has ignored the three relations to sin, and taught the sinner to look for the evidence of remission, where the word of God, or apostolic practice has never located it.

Man sustains three relations to sin, and to be cleansed from sin by the blood of Christ, or to enjoy the remission of sins in Christ, he must be separated from sin in each of these relations, and in the following order: First, the love of sin; second, the practice of sin; third, the guilt or stain of past sins.

First—The love of sin. As long as the sinner loves sin, he will continue to practice it. But faith in Christ as a loving Savior, separates him from the love of sin, and transfers his affections to another object. He now loves God and Christ, and the people of God, while he hates sin. This transfer of the affections to a new object, is the scriptural change of heart. And the subject of this change now rejoices in believing. But it is a mistake to teach the sinner that this joy or love is an evidence of pardon, and of his acceptance in Christ. To teach him thus would be to lead him into the error of getting off at a way station. He is on the right track, but has only been separated from one relation to sin. We are all together thus far, and if you get off at this station we must leave you behind.

Second—The practice of sin. The sinner from whose heart the love of sin has been removed will no longer desire to practice it. He will change his mind or will, and resolve to practice or live a new life. This determination that changes his practice is known as repentance. He now has faith and repentance. But if you tell him that he now has remission of sins, you deceive him, and bid him get off at another way station, and we leave you behind and proceed to next station.

Third—Guilt or stain of past sins. Separated from sin in two relations, there remains one more from which to be separated, and that is to be cleansed from the gutlt or 'stain of past sins, which introduces the subject into the enjoyment of "remission of sins." We have an internal consciousness of the change that took place in our hearts when we were separated from the *love* of sin, as that took place within us. But what is to be our evidence of the change that frees us from the guilt or stain of our past sins? The sin to be be cleansed or forgiven is not in our hearts; then where is it? It is not on our bodies that it may be cast off like a burden from the shoulder, with a sense of relief.

What is sin? The apostle says: Sin is transgression of law. Then sins are acts, and past sins are *past actions*. These stand against us on God's book in heaven, and their cleansing, or blotting out, or canceling, in the mind of God, will constitute forgiveness. As that takes place in heaven, for us, and not in us, or by us, how are we to know when it is accomplished? This is, perhaps, the most important question to be decided in a man's whole life. Nebulous hypotheses, and jubilant sensationalism, called to the witness stand, give dubious and unreliable testimony on this vital question. Angels are not permitted to bring the required answer from heaven. We cannot ascend into heaven and look on God's book for ourselves to see how the account stands, and we are forbidden to ask others to ascend up into heaven for us, to bring Christ down. (Rom. 10: 6.)

Are we then left in despair? Why may not Christ be brought down from above to cleans us from sin? Clearly because that cleansing takes place in heaven, where God is, where the cleansing blood is, and where Christ the mediator officiates. The apostle says of the mediator of the new covenant, that "by his own blood he entered in once into the holy place.", Not holy places, made with hands, "but into heaven itself, now to appear in the presence of God for us." (See Heb. 9: 12, 24.)

Then nothing short of the infallible word of God can teach us how to come to Christ and enjoy the assurance that our past sins recorded in heaven have been "cleansed" by the blood of Christ also in heaven, and "blotted out" from God's book of remembrance.

The blood of Christ was shed in his death. Then how do we come to his death? The apostle answers: "Know ye not that so many of us as were baptized into Jesus Christ were baptized into his death? Therefore we are buried with him by baptism into death." (Rom. 6: 3, 4.) "In whom we have redemption through his blood, the forgiveness of sins." (Col. 1: 14.) Notice these points. *a*. Forgiveness of sins, is in Christ, not out of him. *b*. We are baptized into Christ. *c*. If in Christ before baptism we could not be baptized into him. *d*. Those baptized into him are then in him. *e*. Then they enjoy that forgiveness which is in him. *f*. His blood was shed in his death. *g*. Those baptized into him were baptized into his death. *h*. Therefore a baptism into death is a burial. So the final act of faith that brings us into Christ, for remission of sins through his blood, is a burial in baptism and a resurrection, symbolizing his death, burial, and resurrection.

We are now prepared to appreciate the force of the Savior's language in the commission: "He that believeth and is baptized shall be saved;" and Peter's command to those who believed his preaching, upon the first proclamation under that commission: "Repent and be baptized every one of you in the name of Jesus Christ, for the remission of sins."

Those who have come to this test, "walk in the light" and have the sure word of the Lord as evidence of the forgiveness of their sins. Claims of evidence of forgiveness, short of this, are based upon human testimony, and may be very deceptive.

In proof of the correctness of this last statement, I present a single example which came under my own observation. An aged brother, of highly emotional nature, and raised under the exciting influences of modern revivalism, had recently become a member of the Church of Christ. In a long conversation with him, on religious topics, upon which it was ever his delight to converse, he made the statement that he was convinced that the Lord gave him the evidence that his sins were forgiven before he obeyed the gospel in baptism. I asked him upon what he predicated his evidence of forgiveness, or in what way the Lord told him he was pardoned. He replied that he could tell it best by giving his experience. I said all right, and listened to a long experience, without once interrupting or questioning him, for I wanted to know all there was in it. I mentally and silently noted every point that would be likely to have any connection with his evidence.

He had gone through the usual mourners bench excitement, with agony and prayer at meetings, or alone, at home or in the forest. And the noticeable points were as follows:

1. After long protracted, and almost hopeless agony, he saw a little star up in the heavens, the first glimmer of light.

2. At another time, when praying, he saw heaven opened, and saw that God was paying attention to his prayers.

3. At a subsequent time, when at home standing on the porch, and looking across the field to the woods, he saw the trees praising God.

4. He next saw a luminous cloud ascending from the trees.

5. At another time, he saw around his head a circle of light, apparently about six feet in diameter.

6. At another time, when he had been earnestly

praying, he felt full of love all over—loved God, loved Christ, loved the people of God—and everything around appeared more lovely than ever before. This ended his evidential experience.

I then desired to ask a few questions for information, which he answered.

1. Did you really see a star in the heavens, and could others have seen it; or did it only seem so to you in your excited state of mind, and with your eyes shut? Answer. "Of course there was no star there. It only seemed that way to me with my eyes shut."

2. Did you really see heaven opened and see God? Answer. "No; I did not see God. It only seemed so."

3. How were those trees praising God? Were they clapping their hands and singing? Did your family see them? Answer. "Of course the trees were not doing anything unusual, but it seemed that way to me."

4. How about that luminous cloud? Did you call the attention of your family to it, and could they see it too? Answer. "Of course there was no cloud there, but that is the way it seemed to me."

5. Was that circle of light visible with your eyes open, and could others see it? Answer. "Of course there was no circle of light there, but I seemed to see it with my eyes shut."

6. I shall not ask you if that love was a reality. I take it for granted that you felt that love. We all know when we love, and we all love when we believe on Jesus Christ. But I wish to know upon which of these six points you predicate your evidence of pardon, as you have admitted that five of them were *deceptions*. Or do you base it upon all of them together? If that is the evidence of pardon, am I to teach the sinner to look for those steps? That he must see a little star,

then see heaven opened and see God; then see the trees praising God; then see a luminous cloud ascending from the trees; then see a circle of light around his head, and finally feel full of love, and take it for granted that God has forgiven his sins? His answer was: I predicate my evidence only on the last one—the love. Then said I, the other five, being *spurious*, may be dismissed, as having nothing to do with your experience as an evidence of acceptance. While the reality of that love is not questioned, your mistake is in accepting it as an evidence of your forgiveness and acceptance with God, while it is not so regarded in the word of God or the apostolic practice. But this error, which is the result of the teaching and and practice of modern theology, ignores or disregards the three relations to sin as above explained. We should rely upon the sure word of God for his forgiveness and acceptance, and not on the fluctuating phenomena of an excited emotional nature. Let us walk in the light.

XXVIII.
THE VICTORY, TYPICAL AND ANTITYPICAL.—1 Cor. 10: 1–12.

DELINEATION.

Type.	Antitype.
1—Bond Men.	1—Sinners.
2—Bondage.	2—Sin.
3—Moses.	3—Christ.
4—Signs.	4—Miracles.
5—Message.	5—Gospel.
6—Believe.	6—Faith.
7—Turn away.	7—Repentance.
8—Sea.	8—Baptism.
9—Song.	9—Rejoicing.
10—Journey.	10—Christian life.
11—Fall.	11—Apostacy.
12—Jordan.	12—Death.
13—Canaan.	13—Heaven.

SURVEY.

OPPRESSION, with cruel and relentless hand, bearing heavily upon the wearied lives of over half a million bond men of Israel's race, toiling in the national brick-yards of Egypt, had long been calling for deliverance and national retribution, when God sent deliverance by the hands of a deliverer. This great deliverance is used as an illustrative lesson by the apostle Paul, in the text above indicated. The distinction between the present salvation, and the future or eternal salvation, is made to stand out in sharply defined features, through the illustrative examples herein presented.

By the present salvation is meant the salvation from sin, in the kingdom of Christ, and enjoyed in the present life. The future salvation refers to that enjoyed by the faithful, in the eternal life after the resurrection from the dead. The first is entered into, through faith and obedience of the gospel; the second, after a faithful "continuance in well doing," concerning which Paul says: "Work out your own salvation with fear and trembling," and to which Peter refers, when he admonishes the faithful Christians to: "Give diligence to make your calling and election sure; for if ye do these things, ye shall never fall; for so an entrance shall be ministered to you abundantly into the everlasting kingdom of our Lord and Savior Jesus Christ." (See Rom. 2: 7, Phil. 2: 12, 2 Pet. 1: 10.)

Our lesson is introduced in the previous verses, by the illustration of the races in the Olympic games in which some obtain the crown, and some fail. He then introduces the example of the Israelites saved from their bondage in Egypt, many of whom never entered Canaan.

He says: "All our fathers were under the cloud, and all passed through the sea; and were all baptized unto [εις, into] Moses in the cloud and in the sea." Notwithstanding they were all saved out of Egypt, and started for Canaan, yet many of them fell by the way and failed to reach the promised land. He then tells us that these were examples, [τυποι] literally types, for us, in verses six and eleven, and says, "they are written for our admonition." He then enforces the admonition thus: "Wherefore let him that thinketh he standeth take heed lest he fall."

Let us then examine these examples or types, both typically and antitypically, by placing type and antitype side by side, as in the Delineation, and learn their significance, and heed their admonition.

1. In the type we find Israelites in bondage to the Egyptians, groaning for deliverance. In the antitype, are sinners in bondage to sin.

2. Involuntary servitude under national authority, typifying the service of sin, fast bound by Satan at his will.

3. God sends the offer of deliverance through Moses, to the Israelites. He offers deliverance to the sinner, through Christ.

4. In order to convince the Israelites of his divine mission, Moses was enabled to show them signs. Christ confirmed his divine mission by "signs and wonders and divers miracles."

5. The message proclaiming to the captives, deliverance from bondage, to all who are willing to accept the offer. The message of the gospel proclaiming to the sinner, deliverance from the bondage of sin, is brought from heaven by Christ, offering remission of sins in his name, to all who accept the terms.

6. Belief in the messenger and message, was required to induce the Israelites to trust their new leader and follow him. So faith in Christ, our Moses, is required before the sinner will put his trust in him and obey and follow him.

7. The Israelites having believed, turned away from their life of toil and bondage, and resolved to walk in a new life under Moses. So the sinner, having believed, resolves to turn away from his past sinful life, and walk in a new life under Christ.

8. The Israelites placed the sea between them and their oppressors, by being baptized into Moses, in the cloud and sea.

9. In this baptism, they were separated forever from that which held them in bondage, and with jubilant ecstacy they sing the song of rejoicing. So the sinner who by faith in Christ comes to the obedience of faith in baptism, has the assurance that his past sins are forever blotted out, and he is now prepared to sing the songs of redeeming grace, and rejoice with joy unspeakable and full of glory.

10. Having sung the song of rejoicing, they start for the land of Canaan, under the leadership of Moses. So the converted sinner, rejoicing in his deliverance, now starts for the heavenly Canaan, under the leadership of Christ.

11. But many of them apostatized and fell by the way and never entered Canaan. So in the antitype, those who have been saved in Christ, and enjoyed the present salvation, may apostatize and fail to secure the eternal salvation. Hence the admonition in our lesson: "Let him that thinketh he standeth take heed lest he fall."

12. The Jordan stood between Israel and the Canaan. So the jordan of death stands between the Christian and the heavenly Canaan.

13. The land of Canaan was to Israel the promised land to which they journeyed. So the heavenly Canaan, or "Home over There," is the promised land to which the followers of Christ are journeying, and in which they expect to enjoy the eternal salvation.

Having the stakes set along the two lines, let us take some of the bearings, with an eye to the apostolic admonition.

As Moses stands with unsandaled feet before the luminous presence of God, in the burning bush, listening to the voice that commissions him to go and lead the Israelites up out of Egyptian bondage, he hesitatingly responds: "But, behold they will not believe me, nor hearken to my voice." But his confidence is reassured, when, panoplied with the signs of the serpent rod, the leprous hand restored, and water turned to blood, he was assured that these signs would challenge their belief. When these signs were done in the sight of the people, the record says: "And the people believed." (Ex. 4: 31.)

Now they have heard the message, seen the miraculous confirmation of the divine mission of the messenger, and believed. Note the bearing. Are they now saved? And as these are our types, is the sinner saved when he has believed the gospel upon the confirmed testimony? In other words, will his faith alone save him? If so, our type fails. But the history shows that the believing Israelites were not yet saved.

They resolve to act out the convictions of their faith, and turn away from their tasks and task-masters, and start for the promised land. Encamped on the shore of the Red Sea, they present us another bearing point. Are they now saved? They now clearly have in type, what may typify faith and repentance. But their further encounters show that they were not yet saved. Then if the sinner with faith and repentance, can be pronounced saved without another step, the type fails again.

Now take the bearings of the next step. Pharaoh with his host, pursues these partially escaped but unsaved fugitives, causing the utmost consternation. "And Moses said unto the people, Fear ye not, stand still and see the salvation of the Lord, which he will show to you to-day." Then they are not yet saved, and the way of salvation not yet revealed, and for the revealing of which they stand still and wait. The "stand still" part, is the command of Moses, not the Lord. There is no divine command to stand still after the way is made known.

"And the Lord said unto Moses, wherefore criest thou unto me? Speak to the children of Israel, that they go forward." This is the Lord's instruction, tell the people to go forward. So in the antitype. Instead of speaking to the Lord for hesitating penitent believers, the Lord's plan is: "Speak to the people that *they go forward.*" Tell them what to do to be saved.

But the sea is before them, how can they go forward? Never mind that. The command is to go forward. God will take care of the sea. The power of God is able to manipulate the elements, for when, at the divine command, the rod is stretched out over the sea, pointing the direction of the march, a strong wind causes the waters to recede all that night. And the record shows that it was the same night during which the children of Israel marched through the sea. So the waters just receded before them fast enough to keep out of their way. And the water stood as a wall on the right hand and the left. The next chapter says the waters were congealed. (Ex. 15: 8.) The pillar of cloud went up from before them and stood behind them, illuminating their pathway through the deep, while radiating darkness from its negative side, into the camp of the Egyptians. In our lesson Paul says they were all under the cloud. Then the cloud was over them.

We now look into this brilliantly illuminated tunnel through the sea, the first specimen of divine submarine civil engineering, that pioneered the pathway of light, through the gloomy depths of an improvised national thoroughfare. On the right and on the left, walls of congealed water all brilliant with luminous rays from the fiery cloud; in front a receding breastwork of water sparkling with cloud-lit rays; underfoot solid ground; in the rear the luminous cloud; overhead a luminous canopy of cloud in lurid splendor looking down upon their onward march.

In this magnificent national burial the fugitive Israelites "were all baptized unto Moses in the cloud and in the sea." In this baptism their relation was changed, and from being bond-servants of Pharaoh, they became God's free men, and servants of God under Moses, while that which had held them in bondage, is utterly swept away.

So in the antitype, Paul addressing the Christians at Rome, who had been buried in baptism, and risen to walk in newness of life, says they had obeyed from the heart that form of doctrine delivered them, and recognizes it as the transition act thus: "Being then made free from sin ye became the servants of righteousness." The analogy here holds good. As the Israelites, after the baptism, could rejoice in freedom from Egyptian bondage, so the penitent believer, after baptism, is pronounced free from sin, and classed among the people of God.

Freed from bondage, the Israelites start on their memorable journey, from the Red Sea to the Jordan. So the sinner saved by grace, and redeemed from the bondage of sin, starts on his journey, the Christian life, from baptism till death.

In this journey are incidents to which Paul refers in our lesson, as among the things which are "types for us," and written for our admonition. Among these are the spiritual drink, the spiritual meat, the smitten rock, the fleshly lusts, the idolatrous dance, the destructive fornication, the temptation and serpent scourge, and the death-involving murmurings.

Just here, the significant and plausible question may arise: If this journey is typical of the life and experience of the Christian, how came the Israelites to wander forty years in the wilderness? Not all Christians spend forty years probation.

Now read the thirteenth and fourteenth chapters of Numbers, and find that the forty years' journey was not on God's original programme. While encamped near the southern border of Palestine, Moses, by divine instruction, sent twelve men to spy out the land and make a report. They spend forty days in going, searching and returning, bringing specimens of the fruit of Canaan, and reporting it as a land flowing with milk and honey, and the people dwelling in walled cities, and giants among them, the sons of Anak. Ten of the spies in the majority report, say: "And there we saw the giants, * * * and we were in our own sight as grasshoppers, and so we were in their sight." Their report disheartened the people. But Caleb and Joshua brought in a minority report favorable to going up and possessing the land. They say that with the help of God we are able to go up and take possession. The multitude take counsel of their fears, accept the majority report and refuse to go up. Now they have taken the responsibility. God's plan was for them to enter into their inheritance. But their will was opposed to God's will, and they rejected God's offer.

Then God changed his plan, and decreed that they should wander in the wilderness forty years, till their bodies should fall in the journey, and their children should grow up and enter in. He assigned them a year for a day, thus: "After the number of the days in which ye searched the land, even forty days, each day for a year, shall ye bear your iniquities, even forty years, and ye shall know my breach of promise." (Num. 14: 34.) So the altering of the plan inaugurated the forty years' journey, and the elimination of the disobedient element before entering Canaan.

Again, some may inquire why Moses and Aaron did not enter Canaan, as they were not in the disobedient element eliminated by the above decision.

That question is settled by reference to Ex. 17: 1–7 and Nu. 20: 1–12. In their early travel towards Canaan, the Israelites came to a place where there was "no water for the people to drink." And God told Moses to lead them out to the rock in Horeb, and smite the rock, and it should yield them a supply of water. "And Moses did so in the sight of the elders of Israel."

About thirty-eight years later in their journeyings, they again come to a place where "there was no water for the congregation." And the Lord told Moses, with Aaron, to lead them out to the rock, and "speak to the rock before their eyes." But Moses rendered an imperfect obedience. He took the rod, and took Aaron, and led the people to the rock, as commanded. But instead of speaking to the rock as commanded, he smote the rock twice, as not commanded. The supply of water flowed abundantly for the innocent people, but for this disobedience, were Moses and Aaron debarred from entering Canaan.

That rock had been smitten thirty-eight years before, and the fountain opened, and now it was their privilege to speak to the smitten rock. In our lesson, Paul says: "That rock was Christ." As "these things were types for us," we may pass from this rock type, to Christ the antitype, and learn that Christ once smitten, and the fountain opened, is not to be smitten again. Or that the sinner who has by faith and obedience, accepted the smitten rock, the crucified Savior, having been buried with him by baptism into death, is not required to repeat the initial step, but is thenceforth privileged to "speak to the rock," and ask for the forgiveness of daily sins through his name.

XXIX.
MINISTRY OF THE NEW COVENANT.

DELINEATION.

I. *Antitheses*—2 Cor. 3: 6.

First Cov.	Second Cov.
1.—Old.	1.—New.
2.—Letter.	2.—Spirit.
3.—Kills.	3.—Gives Life.
4.—Done Away.	4.—Remains.

II. *Specialties*—Heb. 8: 6-13.

First Cov.	Second Cov.
1.—Engraved.	1.—Understood.
2.—On Stone.	2.—On Hearts.
3.—National.	3.—Personal.
4.—Teach.	4.—Not Teach.
5.—Not all Know.	5.—All Know.
6.—No Mercy.	6.—Merciful.
7.—Sin Remembered.	7.—Not Remembered.

SURVEY.

READ the Old Covenant (Deut. 5:1-22), where Moses says: "The Lord our God made a covenant with us in Horeb. The Lord made not this covenant with our fathers." He then recites the language of the covenant, the ten commandments, and says: "These words the Lord spake unto all your assembly in the mount.........and he wrote them on two tables of stone, and delivered them unto me."

Here the Old Covenant is identified, as the law of the ten commandments, on tables of stone, and the fact is revealed that it was made with Israel, and not with the fathers of the Patriarchal age. For more than twenty-five centuries the race had been without "this covenant" on tables of stone. Then it was given to Moses "in Horeb, for all Israel, with the statutes and judgments." (Mal. 4: 4.) Not given to Gentiles. And only added to the Abrahamic promise, "till the seed should come," "Thy seed, which is Christ." (Gal. 3: 19, 16.) This covenant then was limited to one nation, and expired by limitation at the coming of Christ, and gave way to the new covenant, of which the apostles were ministers.

Paul says: "Who also hath made us able ministers of the New Covenant; not of the letter, but of the spirit; for the letter killeth, but the spirit giveth life." (2 Cor. 3: 6.)

I. In this, our text, stand out the *antitheses*, placed in the Delineation. The "covenant of the *Spirit*," given and accepted on the day of Pentecost, when the Spirit came down, is *new* in contrast with the "covenant of the *letter*" "engraven in stones," on Mt. Sinai more than fifteen hundred years before. The first executed the death penalty, *killing* the wilfully disobedient; the second offers *life*, and calls to repentance. Three thousand were *killed* at the giving of the first; three thousand were *made alive* at the giving of the second.

Through the remainder of the chapter, the apostle contrasts the ministration of the new with that of the old, and in the eleventh verse says: "For if that which is done away was glorious, much more that which remaineth is glorious." And in the 18th verse he rises to sublimity in the graphic photograph, "But we all, with unveiled face, beholding as in a glass, the glory of the Lord, are changed into the same image from glory to glory."

II. *Specialities.* The second diagram in the delineation presents the special points in which the new covenant differs from the old, as given by Paul. (Heb. 8: 6-13.

Having premised that: "We have such an high priest who is set on the right hand of the throne of the Majesty, in the heavens," and that: "He is the mediator of a better covenant, which was established upon better promises," of which covenant the Lord says by Jeremiah, 31: 31, "I will make a new covenant with the house of Israel and with the house of Judah, not according to the covenant that I made with their fathers in the day when I took them by the hand to lead them out of the land of Egypt," the apostle quotes from Jeremiah the antithetical points of superiority of this *new covenant*, of which Jesus "is the mediator," in the following prophetic language: "For this is the covenant that I will make with the house of Israel after those days, saith the Lord; I will put my laws into their minds, and write them in their hearts; and I will be to them a God, and they shall be to me a people; and they shall not teach every man his neighbor [fellow-citizen], and every man his brother, saying: Know the Lord; for all shall know me from the least to the greatest. For I will be merciful to their unrighteousness, and their sins and their iniquities will I remember no more. In that he saith a new covenant he hath made the first old." (Heb. 8: 10-13.)

The specialties may be weighed thus: 1. The first was put on tables of *stone*, as infants were in that covenant, in whose *minds* it could not be placed; the second is placed in the *minds* of intelligence. 2. The old not being *understood* by infants, could not be written in their hearts; and the old was enforced by authority;

the new draws by the affections. 3. The old was a *national* covenant, into which infants were born without any will of their own; the new is a *personal* covenant, into which *individuals* enter voluntarily and understandingly. 4. The old required infants, already in the covenant by virtue of a Jewish birth, to be *taught* to "know the Lord," as soon as they were old enough to understand; the new requires intelligent persons to "know the Lord" before they can come into the new covenant, and therefore a *brother* or fellow *citizen*, is not to be taught that which he knows already. But he must be taught Christian duties, or duties of citizenship, while those not in the covenant are to be taught to "know the Lord." 5. The reason given for the above is, that all in the new covenant, from the least to the greatest of them, *know the Lord*; while many under the old did not, and many could not, know him. 6. Under the old: "He that despised Moses' law died *without mercy*" (Heb. 10: 28), while the new says: "I will be merciful to their unrighteousness;" and now, righteousness, or justification, is offered through Christ's righteousness. 7. Under the old there was a remembrance again made of sins every year, (Heb. 10: 3), while in the new God says: "Their sins and their iniquities will I remember no more." On becoming citizens, in compliance with the terms of citizenship in Christ's kingdom, all alien sins are blotted out and remembered no more forever. They enter the kingdom with a clean record, and are held responsible for a "faithful continuance in well doing."

It is as requisite for us to know the terms of citizenship under the the new covenant, as it is for the citizens of the state to know the laws under the New Constitution. The lawyer who would ignore the New

Constitution, and conduct his client's suit according to the requirements of an abrogated law under the Old Constitution, would not be deemed trustworthy, while his counterpart, the preacher, who directs the inquiring sinner to terms of salvation, under the Old Covenant, should be esteemed equally untrustworthy.

The unveiled gospel is placed in the hands of men, and the apostle says: "We have this treasure in earthen vessels [the apostles], that the excellency of the power may be of God, and not of us." It is not confided to the ministry of angels. They are not permitted to preach the gospel. But to these earthen vessels, the ably qualified ministers of the new covenant, have been committed the terms of reconciliation.

XXX.
WRITING ON THE HEART—2 Cor. 3: 3.

DELINEATION.

I. *Epistolary Elements.*	II. *Textual Order.*
1.—Writer.	1.—Epistle....Christians.
2.—Tablet.	2.—Writer....Christ.
3.—Pen.	3.—Pens....Apostles.
4.—Ink.	4.—Ink....Spirit.
5.—Epistle.	5.—Tablet....Hearts.

SURVEY.

"FORASMUCH as ye are manifestly declared to be the epistle of Christ ministered by us, written not with ink, but with the Spirit of the living God; not on tables of stone, but in fleshly tables of the heart." (2 Cor. 3: 3.)

In this text the apostle has summarized the work and result of the writing on the heart, under the new covenant, in making Christians. The figure of epistolary writing, being used by the apostle as an illustration, I call attention to the delineation.

I. *Elements.* Familiarity with epistolary correspondence will enable us to notice the process of writing a letter or epistle. You see the gentleman take his seat by the writing desk; he places before him the tablet or paper, but he does not write with his bare fingers, nor pour the ink on the paper, nor smear it on with his fingers; he takes a pen and dips it into the inkstand to get it filled with ink. He is now ready for work. See how carefully he traces characters on the paper, connecting them in such a manner as to form letters, and words, and sentences that convey intelligence.

II. *Application.* The purpose of the writing is to produce an epistle. In the text the *Christians* addressed are the *epistle*, and Christ, the *writer*. "Ye are manifestly declared to be the epistle of Christ." The writing was done on their *hearts*. "Not in tables of stone, but in fleshly tables of the heart." The *ink* with which it was written was the Holy *Spirit*. "Not with ink, but with the spirit of the living God." But how did Christ write with the spirit on their hearts? Did he do it abstractly, by direct impact of the Spirit, without any instrumentality? Is that the way they were made disciples of Christ? If so, then Paul's figure is inappropriate, for the writer does not write with ink abstractly, but with a pen. Then the figure is incomplete without the *pen.* But the apostle was not so thoughtless as to omit the pen. Here it is: "Ministered by us." Then it was ministered, or served, by "us." the *apostles*, and thus written on their hearts to make them Christians, and they thus became the epistle of Christ.

It then stands as delineated, Christ the *writer* through the apostles as *pens*, filled with the Holy Spirit, as *ink*, wrote upon the tablets of the *hearts* of these Corinthians, and produced an *epistle*, the *saints* or church at Corinth. Now the figure is complete.

For satisfactory evidence that the figure as now completed, is *true to the facts*, we turn to the sacred record, (Acts. 18: 5, 8), where the writing was done on these hearts, and these Corinthians were made disciples of Christ. It is there recorded that Paul labored to convince them "that Jesus was the Christ," and the result was that "many of the Corinthians hearing believed and were baptized." The facts in the case then sustain the figure.

III. *The model example.* The first practice in writing

on hearts by the Spirit, under the new covenant, will throw floods of light on the apostle's figure of living epistles. The Savior, the model writer, came on his mission of salvation, and selected twelve pens with which to do the writing. These he prepared and trained during some three years and a half, teaching them how to write, what to write, where to write, and when to write. Before his ascension, he told them he was going away, and as pens cannot write without the ink, they must wait for power from on high, which would be when he sent down the Holy Spirit. They waited, and on the day of Pentecost the Spirit came, "and they were all filled with the Holy Spirit," and could speak in all the languages. Now the pens are filled with ink, the Spirit, and endued with the power from on high, and "qualified as able ministers of the new covenant," ready to commence writing on the hearts of the children of men. Filled with the Spirit, the pens begin to write, and "words" are traced out upon the hearts of that great audience, till convinced that Jesus is now "both Lord and Christ," and pierced in their hearts, they cry out to know what to do. Now Christ as *writer*, through Apostles as *pens*, has written with the *Spirit* upon the *hearts* of thousands, and the writing has affected their hearts and moved them to action, for as many as "gladly received the word were baptized, and the same day there were added to them about three thousand souls." This is the first practice, and consequently the *model practice*, in writing on hearts to turn them to the Lord, and the first day's practice rolls out a large *epistle*, of some three thousand pages of human hearts, on which has been indelibly written the glory of the Lord.

XXXI.
PHYSICAL AND SPIRITUAL GYMNASIA.

BY G. R. HAND.

"FOR bodily exercise profiteth little; but godliness is profitable unto all things." (1 Tim. 4: 8.)

Providentially, the light of science is permitted to throw its radiant beams over the face of nature, unfolding, in panoramic view, the entities and activities, of the ceaseless ongoings in the great machine shop of Creation, enabling the lover of truth to cull his specimens for analysis in the laboratory of the Great Chemist of the universe, under the calcium light of divine revelation. Possibly the casual reading of the text at the head of this paper might reveal to the untrained mind nothing more than the disparagement of bodily exercise, and the degrading of the human body, to a low rank as an object of Christian estimation. Fanatical enthusiasm may carry this sentiment to extremes, and lead to the "neglecting of the body," as a kind of burdensome appendage, to be endured for a while, as a necessary evil.

But such an idea is neither scriptural, nor philosophical, and the analysis of our text will yield no such ingredients. But on the contrary, the combined light of science and revelation, will tend to elevate the body to the position it is entitled to occupy in our affections. While it is true that, in the text, the physical and the spiritual are placed in antithesis, it is not to degrade the physical, but to elevate the spiritual, or, as the Roman orator expressed it: "Not that I loved Caesar less but that I loved Rome more."

The apostle had just instructed Timothy to avoid common and silly fables, "and exercise thyself rather unto godliness." Then as a basic reason for exercising godliness, he adds: "For bodily exercise profits little; but godliness is profitable unto all things." The noun "exercise," in the text is *gymnasia*, in the Greek, and the verb, "exercise," in the previous verse, is the verbal form of the same *gymnasia*, in the Greek. So the status of the entities and activities, placed in antithetical counterpoise may be labeled: PHYSICAL GYMNASIA *versus* SPIRITUAL GYMNASIA. The first member of this antithesis, will be placed in the focus of the light of science, and the second in that of the light of revelation, that the combined brilliancy may photograph, upon our mental canvas, distinctly outlined, their intrinsic and relative importance.

The apostle does not say that bodily exercise is of but little profit, but that bodily exercise [gymnasia] is profitable *for a little*, [pros oligon] that is, for a little while; but the godliness *for all*, [pros panta] for all things, or all time. As if to place it beyond peradventure, that *duration* is in contrast, he adds: "Having the promise of the life that now is and of that which is to come."

Physical gymnasia, then, is located in this life, and is profitable only in this life, but is profitable nevertheless. "The spirit of the man that is in him," and lives and moves and controls, and superintends the activities and growth and repairs, of the physical organism, during this life, is destined to leave this tenement of clay behind, and step out into the unseen, leaving behind "the life that now is," in which bodily gymnasia is profitable, and entering the border land of the life "that is to come," with the promise of the benefits of the spiritual gymnasia, to minister aid and comfort, when the cycles of time have merged into the golden cycles of eternity.

Peter speaks of being "in this tabernacle," and of "putting off this my tabernacle," which he calls his "decease." (2 Pet. 1: 13-15.) This shows that Peter recognized the spirit of man as an entitative being, an immaterial substance, dwelling in a tent or tabernacle of material substance, which he must put off at his decease.

Paul recognizes the same inner man, and outer man, and tabernacle dissolved, etc., and has the inward man "renewed day by day, while the outward man is perishing, and says: "The things that are seen are temporal, but the things that are not seen are eternal." [Aionia.] Now in this case, the things seen are the bodies, and the things not seen are the spirits, making the bodies temporal, and the spirits eternal, which again limits the valuation of physical gymnasia to this life, and passes the spiritual, with apostolic benedictions through the portals of eternity. (See 2 Cor. 4: 16-18.)

But, though invisibility to mortal eyes, may be predicated of the spirit man, yet visible exhibitions of its presence and power in the physical organism are abundantly manifest. From the invisibility, of the entity, and visibility of its activities, as to man's spirit, Paul makes an excursion into the realms of nature, and draws a similar lesson from the attributes of the invisible God, and the visible manifestation of his power and immanence in the works of Creation. "For the invisible things of him from the creation of the world are clearly seen, being understood by the things that are made, even his eternal power and Godhead." (Rom. 1: 20.)

Physiology opens its portals before us, inviting our attention to numerous examples, and practical illustrations of the truth affirmed in the statement: "Bodily exercise profits," though limited to this life. A few of these must suffice for the present.

The apostle, being familiar with Grecian philosophy, knew well the status of the gymnasia in the national system of Grecian education, and was prepared to affirm an admitted truth in saying that "bodily exercise profits." The Grecian youth, trained in the gymnasia, were monuments of its truth. The bodily exercise, or gymnasia, developed their physical organism, expanded and strengthened their muscles, promoted a free circulation of the blood, and a healthy action of the whole corporeal system, and thus it "profited" the young men, by endowing them with health and strength and power of endurance, to go forth as soldiers, and fight the battles of their country.

Other nations besides the Greeks had their gymnasia. Most of the modern nations recognize the value of the gymnasia, and have some kind of gymnastic exercises either in their public or private systems of education.

Prussia gives the training of the body a prominent position in her national system of education, and some of the most perfect specimens of well formed limbs, finely developed muscles, with wonderful strength and power of endurance, that I ever saw, were trained and moulded in the Prussian Gymnasia.

In the United States, where "Young America" comes to the front so constantly, there is perhaps, not so systematic a recognition of gymnastic exercises, or physical training in our national education. Yet, in nearly every city will be found a gymnasium, or some place of physical training, either public or private. They are sometimes called *turn* halls, and *turn* exercises, referring to the fact that these exercises turn out finely developed and rounded forms, in body and limb, like a turning lathe, turning out beautifully rounded forms in wood and metal.

In a thoroughly furnished gymnasium, with apparatus and well appointed outfit, there are various appliances, adapted to all the muscles of the body, so that each part of the human form so "fearfully and wonderfully made," can receive its share of exercise in turn, and " profit for a little " thereby.

The advanced systems of education in some of our large cities have, incorporated in their workings, a gymnasia especially arranged for the young ladies of the schools, and known under the new nomenclature as *calisthenic* exercises; the change in the name being suggested by the etymology of the word, *gymnos*, meaning naked, and the Grecian youths sometimes practicing without the encumbrance of clothing. Modified and introduced into our mixed schools of young ladies and young gentlemen, and practiced by both sexes in the school-room together, it must needs change its name. So *calisthenics*, having *beauty* and *strength* in its etymology, the very qualities to be cultivated, very appropriately and very politely bows *gymnastics* out, and gracefully occupies his vacated seat.

Would you have a visible illustration of bodily exercise profiting a little, then compare the robust farmer with the pale emaciated form of the sedentary student, who, with but little exercise, has spent years in racking his brain over the occult mysteries of science, and has "burnt the midnight oil" in extracting the roots of highly involved powers of algebraic quantities, and exhuming the abstruse and hidden roots of Greek and Latin verbs, until "his shadow has grown less," and it will not be necessary to place the specimens on a Fairbanks' platform to determine where the bodily exercise has profited, even a little, in their relative avoirdupoise.

Now try the blacksmith, the muscles of whose arm have been exercised in wielding the hammer. Trust your hand in his, and allow him to give you a good fraternal squeeze, of persistent duration, until the vise-like pressure elicits from you a note of admiration! and you have a feeling sense of the truth that "bodily exercise profits a little," if not more.

Development of brawn and power in the blacksmith's arm being now assured, just change the programme a little and compare his *right* arm with his *left*. That arm that swings the hammer day by day, and year by year, brings to its muscles a stronger flow of blood, with a larger supply of nutriment, and fuller development than is ministered to the other arm; and the superior development of the dexter muscles, over the sinister, is susceptible of occular demonstration, and *Dextra* and *Sinistra* declared unequal competitors.

Bodily gymnasia being one of the activities essential to healthy physical development, the Author of Nature has wisely implanted in the young a desire for muscular activity. Watch the little babe as it lies upon its back, with pedal extremities elevated, and feet and hands actively engaged in a fantastic game of juvenile gymnastics. The growth of its little limbs and muscles, will soon present them as living witnesses to testify that in its case, "bodily exercise is profitable for a little" child.

Physical gymnasia is now sufficiently sustained, and

its status vindicated, and our obligation to "present our bodies a living sacrifice" shown to be "our reasonable service."

The transition to *spiritual gymnasia* will now be quite easy. Peter says: "As new born babes desire the sincere milk of the word that ye may grow thereby." (1 Pet. 2: 2.) As exercise and food are necessary for growth, God has implanted in the infant a desire for both. With this as the basis of analogy, the apostle transfers the teaching into the realms of the spiritual. As the child desires the natural physical pabulum, its mother's milk, so the spiritual wants of the new born babe in Christ, desire the milk of the word, which, with the spiritual exercise, or gymnasia, is in order to *growth*. The preparation and panoply and drill exercise in the spiritual gymnasium, we find in the apostolic instructions, in their epistles to the churches.

As this has the promise of the life that now is, and of that which is to come; after enjoying all its benefits here, we launch into the unseen hereafter. Hence the leader, or "Captain of our salvation," passed through the portals of death into the unseen world and returned. He has given us a guide book, and those who practice godliness, according to its instruction, through this life, have his promise, not only here but hereafter. While those who ignore the guide book, the word of God, will be like the man who despised the use of the guide book in traveling in a new country, and trusted to his genius and was lost.

Peter gives a list, or brief curriculum of the Christian activities in the spiritual gymnasium, in which "godliness" is a prominent factor, and intimates that the diplomas of those who graduate in the full course of that curriculum, will be a passport into the everlasting kingdom, or as Paul sxpresses it in our text, a promise of the life that is to come.

But Peter's curriculum is not an optional course, in which each student may select or neglect at pleasure. It is very explicit; and after enumerating the activities, he says: "For if ye do these things ye shall never fall; for so an entrance shall be ministered unto you abundantly into the everlasting kingdom of our Lord and Savior Jesus Christ." (2 Pet. 1: 11.)

In this, the *do*, or practice, stands out in unmistakable prominence. Let it be borne in mind that these activities are all located in this life, and to be performed while in the body; but their accumulated interest stands on deposite to our account in that "promise of the life to come"—"that we may lay hold on eternal life."—[*Published in Microcosm, August*, 1888.

XXXII.
MISSION OF THE SPIRIT.—Exegesis of Jno. 16: 8.

DELINEATION.

1.—Who. 16: 8, 7, 13. and 15: 26.
2.—What. 16: 8.
3.—When. 16: 8, 7; Lk. 24: 49; Acts 1: 4, 8; 2; 1-4.
4.—Where. Lk. 24: 49; Acts 1: 4, 8.
5.—With what aids. 15: 27; Lk: 24: 48; Acts 1: 8; 2: 1-4.
6.—Why. 16: 9, 10. 11.
7.—How. 16: 13, 14; 15: 26, 27; 14: 26.

SURVEY.

"AND when he is come, he will convince the world of sin, and of righteousness, and of judgment." (John 16: 8.)

Based upon this passage of scripture, the religious world has been treated to a dogma, representing the Holy Spirit as going out into the world and abstractly, or immediately, acting upon the hearts of sinners to convince them of sin. A careful, logical and scriptural exegesis of the passage may be of service to the thoughtful and honest inquirer.

A forthcoming fact, or transaction, is predicted by the Savior to his apostles; but the full scope and meaning of the fact may not at the first glance flash upon the mind of the casual reader.

A fact is an action, and there are certain circumstances surrounding, or connected with every action, from which, as standpoints, we may examine the action, and learn what may be known concerning it. These refer to agent, action, place, aids, cause, manner and time; and by logicians have been formulated into a line of Latin pentameter verse, thus: "*Quis, quid, ubi, quibus auxiliis, cur, quomodo, quando,*" which in plain English, ask, or answer the questions: who? what? where? with what aids? why? how? when?

To know an object well, we must view it from different standpoints. If you have seen a house only from one view, you may not recognize it when approached from a different direction.

I purpose examining this theme from the seven standpoints above named, and in the same logical order, except to let *time* follow the *act*. It will be seen that Jesus answers all these questions, and I present his answers in his own language.

I. FROM STANDPOINTS ANTECEDENT TO THE FACT.

a. Who? "When he is come, he will convince the world of sin," etc., verse 8. But who is "he?" "If I go not away the Comforter will not come to you; but if I depart I will send him to you," verse 7. But who is "the Comforter?" "But when the Comforter is come whom I will sent unto you from the Father, even the Spirit of truth [of *the* truth] which proceeds from the Father." (John 15: 26.) Then "he" is the Comforter, the spirit of the truth, or the Holy Spirit. So far we have plain sailing. The Holy Spirit is to do this work of convincing.

b. What? The Holy Spirit as agent, will do what? "He will convince the world of [*peri*] sin, and of [*peri*] righteousness, and of [*peri*] judgment," verse 8. Here the subject of the proposition is "he," with the simple predicate "will convince." The word for "convince" is rendered "reprove" in the common version; but the scholarship of the world endorses *convince* as a better rendering. If a man is convinced of sin, he is convicted of sin, and stands reproved *for* sin. But "he" is to convince the world of (*peri*, *concerning*), three things, viz: concerning sin, concerning righteousness, and concerning judgment. While the rendering, "reprove," might do in relation to *sin*, to "reprove the world of righteousness," would scarcely be admissable. "Convict," as used in the revised version, may express its relation to *sin*, but *convince* covers the whole ground, and is preferable.

The "sin" is the sin of unbelief in rejecting Jesus as the Messiah. The "righteousness" is not that of men, but the righteousness or justification of Jesus from the charge upon which he was condemned to death. The "judgment" is not a judgment to come, but the unjust judgment of the court below, set aside and reversed by the supreme court above. All which will appear more fully under the "why."

c. When? Now that we have the subject and predicate, "He will convince," our first and very important and inquisitive adjunct steps to the front and demands: When will he do this convincing? The answer is in the text: "When he is come," or having come he will convince, etc. But when will he come? "If I go not away, the comforter will not come unto you; but if I depart I will send him unto you," verse 7. Then he cannot come till after Jesus goes away, which places this "convincing" after the ascension. But what wait they for? "Tarry ye in the city of Jerusalem, until ye be endued with power from on high." (Lk. 24: 49.) But when may they look for that power? "But ye shall receive power after that the Holy Spirit is come upon you." (Acts 1: 8.) Then the power is connected with the coming of the Holy Spirit. And when shall we look for that? "But ye shall be baptized with [*en, in*] the Holy Spirit not many days hence." (Acts 1: 5.) Now the time is approaching, and we are within ten days of it. The risen Jesus has now been with them forty days, and after this interview he is "taken up." We now step forward ten days to the Pentecost, or fiftieth day from the resurrection. "And when the day of Pentecost was fully come * * they were all filled with the Holy Spirit and began to speak with other tongues as the Spirit gave them utterance." (Acts 2: 1-4.) Now the Spirit has come, and has conferred on them the power they were awaiting for, and every restraint is removed, and every "until" taking out of the way. As he was to do the convincing when he came, and he came on the first Pentecost after the resurrection, clearly this convincing was to be done on that day, beyond all peradventure; and the record of the events of that day will show its fulfillment.

d. Where? Now that the "when" is settled, the "where" will almost settle itself, for in the passage in which he tells them to wait for the Spirit and power, and to first commence preaching remission in his name, he also tells them *where* to wait—*at Jerusalem.* (See Luke 24: 46-49; Acts 1: 4-8, and 2: 1-4.) And they were waiting at Jerusalem when the Spirit came, and did commence then and there.

e. With what aids? What a question, you say. As if the Holy Spirit needed aid in doing this convincing! Never mind what the Holy Spirit *needs*, or what he *can* do without aid. I promised to let the Savior answer all these questions. So listen to his answer: "But when the Comforter is come, whom I will send unto you from the Father, even the Spirit of truth, which proceedeth from the Father, he shall testify of [*peri*, *concerning*] me. And ye also shall bear witness, because ye have been with me from the beginning." (John 15: 26-27. Here the testimony is *concerning Jesus*, and is clearly *with the aid of the apostles.* "And ye are witnesses of these things." (Luke 24: 48.) And ye shall be witnesses unto me, both in Jerusalem and in all Judea, and in Samaria, and unto the uttermost part of the earth." (Acts 1: 8.) And that is just the order in which their testimony, as witnesses for Jesus, did go out. According to the Savior's own statement then the Spirit was to *testify*, and to do this convincing with the aid *of the apostles*. He was to testify, and they "also" were to testify.

f. Why? This question is answered in the 9th, 10th, and 11th verses. As there are *three things* of which he is to convince the world, so there are *three whys* in the answer.

1st. "Of sin, because they believe not on me." verse 9. Here the Spirit, with the aid of the apostles, is to present the testimony to convince the world of the *sin* of unbelief, in rejecting Jesus as the Messiah, as the Spirit was to testify *concerning Jesus*, and the apostles were *also* to testify and be *his* witnesses.

2d. "Of righteousness, because I go to my Father, and ye see me no more," verse 10. Not of *men*, but of Jesus, is this justification predicated, because *I*, the one to be justified, go away and ye see *me* no more. The concurrent testimony is to convince the world of the justification of *Jesus* from the charge on which he was condemned by the Jewish Sanhedrim, and before the bar of Pilate. Having been condemned as an imposter, by the highest ecclesiastical tribunal on earth, and at the bar of the highest civil court condemed to death and executed, Jesus, after his resurrection, ascends to heaven, and carries an appeal from the decision of the court below, to the Supreme court of the Universe. His appeal is sustained, and he stands justified in full from the iniquitous charge, and the justification placed on record in the archives of heaven, by the recording angel, clerk of the Supreme court of the Universe. But as the other witnesses, the apostles, cannot go into heaven to examine the record, and Jesus goes away, and they "see him no more," and can not, as original witnesses, testify to that fact, the concurrent testimony of the Spirit is required; and from the court of heaven, the Holy Spirit is dispatched, as a swift-winged messenger, to bear the news to earth, and convince the world of his justification.

3d. "Of judgment, because the prince of this world is judged," verse 11. This is not a judgment *to come*, as we sometimes hear it quoted, but a judgment that had been rendered. The prince of this world *is judged*, or *has been judged*. The appeal from the judgment of the court below had been sustained and the judgment reversed, and thus the prince of this world had been judged when the Spirit came down on the day of Pentecost, and brought the testimony to "convince the world of judgment." All this the Savior foretold to his apostles.

g. How? Here we enter the disputed territory. Some have assumed that the Holy Spirit enters the hearts of sinners, and abstractly, and immediately, that is, independent of instrumentalities, does this testifying and convincing; but is this even a necessary inference? It is not safe to jump at conclusions. How then is this convincing to be done, mediately or immediately? If a man tells you that your neighbor A had cut down a lot of forest trees without an ax, you might question his veracity. But you question his knowledge, thus: Did you see him cut them down? No, sir. Did he tell you? He did not. Then how do you know? Neighbor B told me that he had cut them down, and never said a word about an ax, and I inferred that he did it without an ax! Now would this be a necessary inference? You say, no, it would not; for the ax being the ordinary instrument for such work, the inference would be that he used the ax, unless it was otherwise distinctly stated. If the Savior had told the apostles that the Spirit would convince the world of sin, without telling them how it was to be done, would it be a necessary inference that he would do it abstractly? Certainly not. As language is the normal medium of communication between spirit and spirit, the inference should be that language would be the medium used in giving the testimony to convince the world of these facts. But Jesus did not leave them to guess. He told them how; and inference is ruled out. Here we have it from his own lips:

First *How*. "Howbeit when he, the Spirit of truth, is come, he will guide you [the apostles] into all truth," [all *the* truth] verse 13.

Second *How*. "Whatsoever he shall hear, that shall he speak," verse 13.

Third *How*. "And he shall show you things to come," verse 13.

Fourth *How*. "He shall glorify me," verse 14.

Fifth *How*. "For he shall receive of mine, and shall show it unto you," verse 14.

Sixth *How*. "He shall testify of me." (15: 26.)

Seventh *How*. "And ye also shall bear witness, because ye have been with me from the beginning." (15: 27.)

Eighth *How.* He shall teach you [the apostles] all things, and bring all things to your remembrance, whatsoever I have said unto you." (14: 26.]

Here are eight "hows" given by the Savior himself. Surely that is enough to estop the wildest imagination from running off into inference for the how.

These facts and this testimony were in the future when Jesus made the promise to his apostles, but were accomplished, all and singular, on the day of Pentecost.

II. FROM STANDPOINT SUBSEQUENT TO THE FACT.

Now turn to Acts 2: 1–42, and see the accomplishment of all the testifying and convincing, to which the Savior had pledged the Holy Spirit, in the language of our text.

(a.) Verse 1. "And when the day of Pentecost was fully come, they were all with one accord [unanimously] in one place."

Here we find the apostles at the designated place, Jerusalem, and waiting for the Spirit and power Jesus had promised.

(b) Verses 2-4. And they were all filled with the Holy Spirit." Now the Spirit has come as promised.

(c.) Verse 4. "And began to speak with other tongus, as the Spirit gave them utterance." Now they have received the power from on high.

(d.) Verse 5. Jews, representative men from all nations, providentially assembled to witness the laying of the corner stone of the Church of Christ, are present.

(e.) Verses 6-12. "How hear we every man in our own tongue, etc." Here the representatives of many nationalities admit that they hear their own vernacular dialects spoken understandingly by these illiterate Galileans.

(*f.*) Verse 13. Even skeptics witness the effects of the Spirit upon the speech of the apostles, but attribute it to the spirit of wine.

(*g.*) Verses 14-31. Now the Spirit is "guiding them into the truth;" and they are unfolding the significance of prophecy of a thousand years standing, now made "more sure" (2 Pet. 1: 19) in its recent triumphant fulfilment.

(*h.*) Verse 32. "This Jesus hath God raised up, whereof we are all witnesses." Now they are "bearing witness" *also*, or concurrent with the testimony of the Spirit.

(*i.*) Verses 33-35. "Therefore being by the right hand of God exalted, etc." The Spirit's testimony that day brought down from heaven.

(*j.*) Verse 36. "Therefore let all the house of Israel know assuredly that God hath made that same Jesus whom ye have crucified, both Lord and Christ." Now he has glorified Jesus, or testified to his glorification, as Jesus had said: "He shall glorify me."

(*k.*) Verse 37. "Now when they heard this, they were pierced in their hearts, and said to Peter and the rest of the apostles, men and brethren, what shall we do? "Now they are *convinced* of the sin of rejecting Jesus, of his justification, and the judgment rendered in the court above. Righteousness and justification are translations of the same word in the Greek. As convicted sinners they now inquire what they shall do.

(*l.*) Verses 38-40. "Then Peter said to them, repent, and be baptized every one of you in the name of Jesus Christ for the remission of sins." The Holy Spirit, through Peter, the whole college of apostles standing by and assenting, now for the first time on earth, makes known authoritatively, what convicted sinners shall do for remission of sins in the name of Jesus; and the oracle reads as quoted at the head of this paragraph. This is in strict accordance with what Jesus had said to them in his commission: "And that repentance and remission of sins should be preached in his name among all nations, beginning at Jerusalem." (Luke 24: 47.)

(*m.*) Verse 41. "Then they that gladly received his word were baptized." Those that were convinced on that day, complied with the terms of citizenship, in the new kingdom, in which is enjoyed the remission of sins in the name of Jesus.

(*n.*) Verse 42. "And they continued steadfastly in the apostles' doctrine and fellowship, and in breaking of bread, and in prayers." Now they are in the enjoyment of the privileges and immunities of citizenship, and in the practice of Christian duties.

In view of these facts, well may Paul exclaim: "So then faith comes by hearing, and hearing by the word of God." (Rom. 10: 17.)

Thus the Holy Spirit did, at Jerusalem, with the aid of the apostles, for reasons given, in manner described, on the appointed day, furnish the testimony to convince the world of sin, of righteousness, and of judgment. And in like manner he continues to convince those who give earnest heed to his testimony, which has been "written that we might believe that Jesus is the Christ, the son of God, and that believing we might have life through his name." (John 20: 31.) Let us not resist the Spirit by rejecting his testimony.

[*Published in Christian Quarterly Review, October*, 1882.

XXXIII.
THE BALANCES OF CREATION.

Delineation--Packages Weighed.

1—Material. Isa. 40: 12, 15, 17. 4—A King. Dan. 5: 27.
2—Immaterial. Prov. 16: 2. 5—Grief. Job, 6: 2-3
3—Man. Job, 31: 6. Ps. 62: 9. 6—Affliction. 2 Cor. 4: 17.

SURVEY.

MATERIAL substances are placed in antithetical counterpoise upon human balances, and their relative avoirdupois determined in view of barter or sale. and the commercial value of the commodities thus weighed, is estimated by the force of gravity exerted upon the scale beam, at a standard money value. Who has not heard of the "Philosophers' Scales?" But God's scales will transcend these by how much the finite is excelled by infinity.

In God's scales. material and immaterial entities are placed in antithetical counterpoise. We shall go to the Scriptures for examples, illustrations, and estimates.

1. MATERIAL. " Who hath measured the waters in the hollow of his hand, and meted out heaven with a span, and comprehended the dust of the earth in a measure, and weighed the mountains in scales, and the hills in a balance?......Behold the nations are as a drop of a bucket and are counted as the small dust of the balance; behold, he taketh up the isles as a very little thing......All nations before him are as nothing." Isa. 40; 12, 15, 17.

These specimens of God's weighing completely cast in the shade the mightiest efforts of man, to weigh even a portion of a mountain by piling it upon a human platform.

The weigh master divides up a herd of cattle to be driven in squads upon his platform to be weighed by piecemeal. But here come mountains and hills, and islands, trooping to the proprietor of worlds, to be weighed on the balances of creation, while the water is measured and the heavens [the atmosphere] is spanned. Even the nations may remain upon the mountains while poised in the balance, as their presence will have no more influence than the dust on the balance, that the merchant would not think necessary to brush off.

But perhaps you begin to say, this is all figurative exageration. Has God really weighed the mountains and measured the water, etc.?

That is the very thing I purpose inquiring into for our edification. The chemist goes to the mountains, and the hills, and the water, and atmosphere, and brings home specimens, and subjects them to a chemical analysis in the laboratory. Every specimen of rock from the mountains turns out to be composed of certain elements in definite proportions by weight; showing that every portion of the mountains and solid substances of the earth, have been weighed by the Great Chemist in the balances of creation. Every specimen of water from the mountain torrent, flowing river, or placid lake, is composed of definite proportions of oxygen and hydrogen by weight and measure, showing that the Great Chemist had weighed and measured the waters long ages before the chemist undertook the contract on a small scale in his laboratory. The specimens of atmosphere, in like manner, present a uniform proportion of oxygen and nitrogen, re-proclaiming to the intelligent chemist, that the hand of the Creator has been along there before him, and meted out heaven [the atmosphere] in its expansion and proportions.

Light from the chemical laboratory thus reveals, in all material compounds, a definite law of proportion in each, whether in the mineral, vegetable, or animal kingdoms, and shows that the inspired word of God, in advance of chemistry, proclaimed literal and physical facts in regard to the divine weighing and measuring.

II. IMMATERIAL. Thus far our weighing and measuring have been limited to the material. We are next led into the immaterial, in which more delicate balances are required. I recognize substance in the material and immaterial. In other words, there are material substances and entities, and immaterial substances and entities. In weighing the latter our material balances are of no avail.

"All the ways of man are clear in his own eyes; but the Lord weigheth the spirits." Prov. 16: 2.

Here we encounter the fact that, while man may weigh his own ways, by balances of his own construction, yet the weighing of spirits is entirely too ethereal for his material scales, and must be submitted to God's weighing. The weight of a spirit and its estimated value, will not be tested by the stock scales, and the table of commercial currency.

The spirits of men are evidently the entities contemplated in the text, and the textual connection is strongly suggestive of the intimate connection between the ways of men and the estimated value of the spirits when weighed. But the weighing of disembodied spirits, or of inanimated bodies, is not the practical work before us in this lesson. I pass on to the weighing of man, who is composed of both body and spirit, or in whose material organism, the body, resides the immaterial organism, "the spirit of man that is in him."

III. MAN. With body, soul, and spirit, man steps upon the scales to be weighed and valued by the Lord's appraisal, which cognizes the activities and sufferings of these combined physical and spiritual entities.

More than fifteen centuries before the Christian era, the patient man of Uz, when sorely tried, gave vent to his feelings, thus: "Let me be weighed in an even balance, that God may know mine integrity." Job 31: 6.

Here the standard accuracy of God's balance is invoked, not to test the avoirdupoise of the physical organism of this man whose flesh is wasting away by persistent disease, but that his integrity might be established before God. Driven almost to despair by his sufferings, and the keen sarcasm of his "miserable comforters," he is willing to place his integrity upon God's even balance.

The sweet singer, and King of Israel, weighs two classes of men thus: "Surely men of low degree are vanity, and men of high degree are a lie; to be laid in the balance they are altogether lighter than vanity." Ps. 62: 9.

The integrity of these characters is so light that they kick the beam with nothing but "vanity" as a weight in the scale.

IV. A KING. Next we shall see a king placed upon the scales; for God's scales will weigh kings just as easily as "men of low degree." The profligate king sits in his banqueting hall, amid the voluptuous feasting and bacchanalian revelry of a thousand lords and princes, with his wives and concubines. All unseen, the balances are adjusted and the king weighed. Quick as the lightning's flash, the unseen hand keeping tally of the weighing, is suddenly disclosed and writes hpon the plaster of the wall, the terrible result: "Thou art weighed in the balances and art found wanting." Dan. 5: 27. And proud Belshazzar, with all his pomp and splendor, and with a thousand lords thrown in for good measure, kicks the beam and is pronounced light weight, in such precipitate haste, that loosened joints and smiting knees, but heralded his dire destruction at the hands of the approaching foe, as king and kingdom sunk to rise no more.

V. GRIEF. Next comes heart-broken sorrow to weigh its grief and calamity: "Oh, that my grief were thoroughly weighed, and my calamity laid in the balance together! for now it would be heavier than the sand of the sea." Job 6: 2-3.

Here, in the estimation of Job, we seem to have heavy weight, although the counterbalance is the sand of the sea. But this estimation is from the standpoint of suffering humanity.

VI. AFFLICTION. Take one more weighing, and let the light of eternity shine upon the unseen scale. "For our light affliction, which is but for a moment, worketh for us a far more execeding and eternal weight of glory." 2 Cor. 4: 17.

Here *affliction* is placed in the scale as seen and felt by us; and *glory* as the weight in the scale to us unseen. But when, with the light of eternity shining upon it, we look at the unseen, our affliction seems light and brief, while the glory in the other scale, becomes "a far more exceeding and eternal weight." The seen to us is temporal, the unseen is eternal. Let us endeavor to bring our Christian activities up to the *full-weight* standard.—[*Published in Pacific Church News, August* 15, 1883.

XXXIV.
THE TABERNACLE.

DELINEATION.

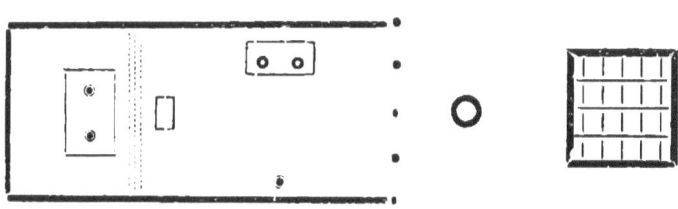

SURVEY.

"AFTER this I will return, and will build again the tabernacle of David, which is fallen down; and I will build again the ruins thereof, and I will set it up; that the residue of men might seek after the Lord, and all the Gentiles upon whom my name is called, saith the Lord." (Acts 15: 16–17.

This is a prophecy from Amos 9: 11–12, here quoted by James as agreeing with Peter's report of the conversion of the Gentiles at the house of Cornelius, wherein he had "declared how God at the first did visit the Gentiles, to take out of them a people for his name." (Acts 15: 14.) The tabernacle of David had fallen down, and the reconstruction had taken place according to prophecy and God had taken from the Gentiles "a people for his name."

The diagram represents the plan of the tabernacle with the location of the furniture, showing the location of God's luminous presence, and the steps by which those, who "might seek after the Lord," were taught to *draw nigh.* For size, form and location of most of these. (See Ex. 25:) Read also the eighth and ninth chapters of Hebrews.

Paul says: "Then verily the first covenant had also ordinances of divine service, and a worldly sanctuary. For there was a tabernacle made, the first, wherein was the candlestick, and the table, and the shew bread, which is called the sanctuary. And after the second vail, the tabernacle, which is called the holiest of all; which had the golden censer and the ark of the covenant overlaid round about with gold, wherein was the golden pot that had manna, and Aaron's rod that budded and the tables of the covenant; and over it the cherubim of glory, shadowing the mercy seat, * * * a figure for the time then present. * * * But Christ being come a high priest of good things to come, by a greater and more perfect tabernacle, not made with hands, that is to say, not of this building; neither by the blood of goats and calves, but by his own blood, he entered in once into the holy place, having obtained eternal redemption for us." (Heb. 9: 1-5, 11-12.)

These being "types," or "paterus," or "figures," or "shadows" of the things of the "true tabernacle," into the holy place of which Christ has entered, will help us to recognize the steps by which we are taught to draw nigh to God, for remission of sins in the name of Jesus.

The tabernacle, located in the west part of the outer court, was 30 cubits long, 10 cubits wide, and 10 cubits high, with door or entrance facing to the east, the entire east end being open, with five pillars, represented by the dots in the diagram, on which was hung a curtain covering the whole front, but thrown back in time of service, exposing to view the whole interior of the first apartment. The second curtain, or vail, drawn across the tabernacle 10 cubits from the west end, inclosed the sanctum sanctorum, or holy of holies, being 10 cubits in length, breadth, and height, in which was placed the ark of the covenant, two and a half cubits long, by one and a half cubits wide and high, covered with the mercy seat, a lid of pure gold, of same length and breadth of the ark, with a cherub, or angel on each end, between which angels, or cherubim, was the luminous appearance of the presence of God, where the high priest went to make atonement for the people.

The other apartment of the tabernacle was twenty cubits long, and contained the lamp-stand on the south side; the table of the show bread, or bread of the presence on the north, two cubits long and one cubit wide, and a cubit and a half high, on which were placed weekly, twelve fresh loaves of bread, in two piles of six loaves each; and the altar of incense at the extreme west end in front of the vail. In this apartment, the common priests performed their daily service.

To the extreme east, see diagram, was the altar of sacrifice, five cubits square, and three cubits high, covered with a brazen grate, on which the sacrifices were consumed by fire. Between this and the tabernacle, just in front of the door, was placed the laver, supposed to be about two and a half cubits in diameter, containing water in which priests were washed all over, upon their consecration to the office, and at which also they ever after washed their hands before entering the tabernacle.

The outer court, for which we have not room in the

diagram, was one hundred cubits long, and fifty cubits wide, and represents the world; first the Jewish world out of which God took the apostles and gave them to his Son (Jno. 17: 6), and afterward the Gentile world, whom God visited "to take out of them a people for his name." (Acts 15: 14.)

Now notice that God's presence is in the most holy place at the *extreme west*, while the people who have sinned and seek forgiveness, are *far from God*, and commence at the *extreme east*, at the altar of sacrifice. All this is significant, and all the intervening steps are significant, and have an antitypical significance in the new institution, " the true tabernacle which the Lord pitched and not man."

With the types before us, we now go to "the beginning" of the new institution, as Peter calls it (Acts 11: 15), and see if the Holy Spirit, guiding the twelve architects, on the day of Pentecost, arranged the steps of approach in the new tabernacle, in the order of the types.

Convicted of sin, the Jew brought the lamb to the altar, in the outer court, confessing, and repenting of his sin, lays his hands on the head of the lamb, kills it, and the priest presents the offering. In the antitype, the sinner, convicted of sin in rejecting the Messiah, and now convinced that God has made that same Jesus both Lord and Christ, accepts Jesus as the lamb of God, confesses him, repents and determines to change his conduct, and trust in Christ. Thus far we are at the altar of sacrifice, have accepted the great sacrifice, and resolved to give our own bodies, not to be burned, but to be presented as a "living sacrifice." As the common priests were typical of Christians, we must follow them in the types through the steps antecedent to their entering in, and performing divine service. The next step is at the laver, just outside the door, where the candidate is washed all over, clothed in priestly robes, and anointed with the holy oil, which completes his sanctification, or consecration to the service. He is now entitled to walk into the sanctuary (there being no steps between those pillars), and participate in all the service indicated by the articles of furniture in that apartment. In the antitype, the laver can find its significance only in baptism, that being the only institution in which water is used. Here the sinner having believed, and confessed Christ, and repented, is baptized, and robed, "put on Christ" (Gal. 3: 27), and anointed, "because ye are sons God hath sent forth the spirit of his Son into your hearts, crying, Abba, Father." (Gal. 4: 6.) Now the sinner is fairly initiated, and entitled to enter upon the practice, and into the enjoyment of Christian duties and Church privileges.

Now turn to Acts 2: 14–41, and you find that the steps in drawing near to God, in the new tabernacle were arranged in the same order as indicated in the outer court furniture, until the three thousand were made disciples and added. First, they were called upon to hear the testimony upon which they were convicted of sin in rejecting Jesus as the Christ. Then they were informed that the lamb was already provided, and slain, and the great high priest was ready to officiate for them; "That God hath made that same Jesus whom ye have crucified, both Lord and Christ." Believing this they inquire what to do, and the answer carries them from the altar, through all the steps to the door of the tabernacle, "repent and be baptized every one of you in the name of Jesus Christ for the remission of sins." (Acts 2: 38.) Here, belief follows the hearing of testimony, conviction of sin follows the belief, repentance follows the conviction, and carries them right on from the altar of sacrifice to the laver, and they are commanded to be baptized. "Then they that gladly received his word were baptized, and the same day there were added to them about three thousand souls." (2: 41.) Any one can see that these steps are all outside and initiatory, and antecedent to the enjoyment of Church privileges and blessings, as no priest in the type, could pass into the tabernacle who had not taken all these steps. They that gladly received his word were baptized, and his word was the word of the Holy Spirit. Then those that gladly receive the word of the Holy Spirit, will be baptized, and such are "led by the Spirit of God," and Paul says: "They are the Sons of God." (Rom. 8: 14.)

That those who were baptized, were then admitted to Christian fellowship and all the Christian duties and privileges we learn from the next verse. "And they continued steadfastly in the apostles' doctrine and fellowship and the breaking of bread, and in prayers." (2: 42.) These are all Christian duties, to which all are entitled who have come through the introductory steps, indicated by the furniture in the outer court. All Christian duties are *recurring* duties, in which they *continue steadfastly*. Then if baptism were a Christian duty, and a person could become a Christian without baptism, and then be baptized because he was a Christian, it would be necessary to find out from the "apostles' doctrine," how often he must be baptized in order to be *steadfast* in that duty. But it is not mentioned among the things to be continued, but those baptized were admitted to these practical duties.

Now look at the diagram and see if the Christian activities to which the baptized believers are admitted includes all indicated by the furniture in the sanctuary. (42d verse.) "And they continued steadfastly in." 1. "The apostles' doctrine." The doctrine or teaching is typified in the lamp-stand, on the south side, and on which were seven golden lamps. These were trimmed and kept burning by the priests, and shined out into the outer court. So the Christian should keep the word of God as taught by the inspired apostles, shining brightly, and let the light shine out into the world. 2. The "fellowship." No one visible article of furniture in the tabernacle represents that. Fellowship, is partnership, and the partnership contributions of the whole congregation, supplied the treasury from which was furnished the bread, the oil for the lamps, the costly incense, and the support of the priests who waited upon the service. So the fellowship was fitly represented by all the furniture, and the service. 3. "Breaking of bread." This has its type in the table of show bread. Twelve loaves, corresponding to the twelve tribes, reduced to one loaf in the one body, of which the many members of the one body partake. 4. "And in Prayers." The prayers are represented at the altar of incense, located in front of the vail, and nearest the mercy seat, of all the furniture of the sanctuary. The location indicates the sacredness of prayer in the Christian institution, and shows that in prayer the Christian draws nearer to God, where Christ our mercy seat is, than in any other part of the worship. The order of steps in drawing near to God in the types, is thus seen to be maintained with fidelity, by the inspired apostles in presenting the plan of the new tabernacle.

Now return to our text, and notice, that while none but Jews could draw near to God in the old tabernacle; the new one is so modified, "that the residue of men might seek after the Lord, and all the Gentiles upon whom my name is called." The "residue of men" or rest of mankind, would include all Gentiles, but the restriction, "upon whom my name is called," limits the privilege of "seeking after the Lord," in the new tabernacle, to those of them, who are made eligible by having the name of the Lord called upon them. The name of the Lord is called upon them in baptism. So with the first Gentile converts. Peter taught them that Jesus Christ is "Lord of all;" and that those who believe, shall receive remission of sins "through his name;" "and he commanded them to be baptized in the name of the Lord." (See Acts 10: 36, 43, 48.) This case of first Gentile conversion is reported by Peter to the council of apostles and elders at Jerusalem, and by them recognized as: "How God at the first did visit the Gentiles to take out of them a people for his name." That *how* of God's plan settled the question under discussion. There were some who maintained that circumcision must be required of the Gentiles to render them eligible to the new salvation and worship, as it was essential to their approach in the old tabernacle. But God's *how* as reported by Peter in his practice, and James' confirmation of the same, by applying the prophecy in our text, carried the decision of the council, that circumcision was not required of *the Gentiles*, but that all believers "upon whom the name of the Lord was called," were entitled to come in and "might seek after the Lord," in the new tabernacle, which the Lord pitched.

Recognizing these prerequisites to drawing near,

Paul exhorts the Hebrew Christians: "Let us draw near with a true heart in full assurance of faith, having our hearts sprinkled from an evil conscience, and our bodies washed with pure water." (Heb. 10: 22.)

Having now seen that type answers to antitype, as the image in the mirror answers to the face before it, are we at liberty to change the order of these steps?

a. Suppose I remove the table from the sanctuary, and place it between the laver and the altar of sacrifice in the outer court. You correctly say it would be a derangement of the order. But while the types are in that order, we strike off a proof sheet. And it reads that the unbaptized are invited to the Lord's supper.

b. Remove it a little further, and place it beyond the altar of sacrifice; and your proof sheet will read that you are inviting unbelievers to the Lord's table. Better return it where the Lord put it.

c. Remove the altar of incense and place it between the laver and altar of sacrifice in the outer court, and your proof sheet charges you with lowering the dignity and sacredness of prayer by carrying it out into the world, and teaching the unbaptized that they can draw near to the mercy seat acceptably while in disobedience.

d. Remove it still further and place it beyond the altar of sacrifice; and your proof sheet charges you with profaning the sacredness of prayer, by inviting unbelievers to the altar of prayer. Then put it back in its appointed place.

e. Remove the laver from its position, and bring it inside the sanctuary, and strike off a proof sheet. Do you like its reading? It says you are trying to make Christians first, and baptize them afterwards. One objection to that change is that the laver could not be removed inside without taking away at least one of the pillars. Another objection is that the Lord told Moses to place it outside and between the door and the altar of incense.

f. Remove it in the other direction and place it beyond the altar of sacrifice, and a proof sheet taken while in that position, will read that you are baptizing persons without faith and repentance, even infants who are not capable of believing. And as without faith it is impossible to please God, it is safe to conclude that neither infants nor unbelievers can render an obedience in baptism that is pleasing to God. Return it to its place.

Then it will be safe to let the types remain as the Lord placed them by the hand of Moses; and rest satisfied with the order of the corresponding steps in the New Institution, the true tabernacle which the Lord pitched, and not man.

XXXV.
SCRIPTURAL FORMS.

DELINEATION.

I. *Forms.* II. *Stand Points.*

1—The Truth.
 Rom. 2 : 20.

2—Knowledge.
 Rom. 2 : 20.

3—Doctrine.
 Rom. 6 : 17.

4—Sound Words.
 2 Tim. 1 : 13.

5—Godliness.
 2 Tim. 3 : 5.

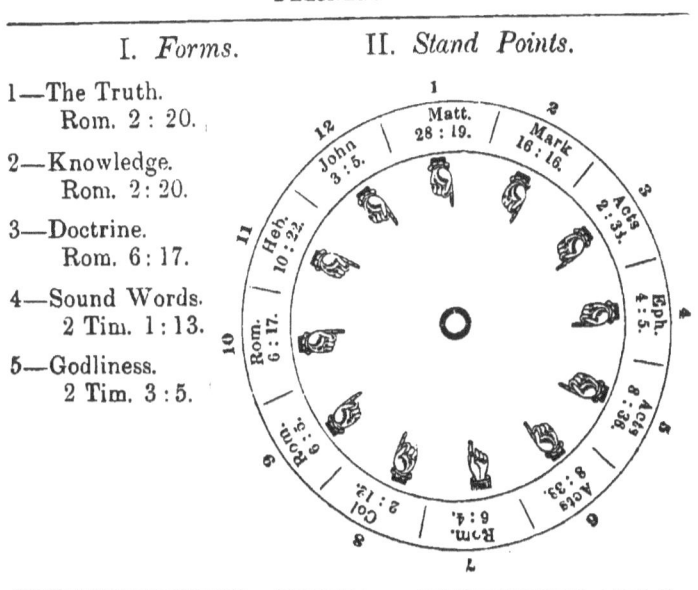

SURVEY.

SCIENCE and Christianity present us with various forms whether material, immaterial, or logical. All entities assume some form, in space or in our minds. Nature develops many forms in the great machine shop of the universe. Developing forms in the kingdom of nature are seen in endless variety, yet in harmonious uniformity. Animal life is done up in myriads of forms, in harmony with the laws of the animal kingdom. And even the mineral kingdom develops its varied forms in harmony with the laws of aggregation and crystalization.

In the realm of mind we have forms of thought. Ideas flitting through the mind in panoramic vision, take on the varied forms of imaginary reality.

With this introduction to forms in general, we are prepared to see the Scriptural forms floating into shape before our mental vision. The things waiting to be photographed into visible or mental forms, in this picture, are these: 1. *The Truth.* 2. *Knowledge.* 3. *Doctrine.* 4. *Sound Words.* 5. *Godliness.*

1. *The Truth.* Facts and truths concerning Jesus the Christ, and the law of God, cluster around an entity, and crystalize into a form, the conception of which, in sacred nomenclature, is, called "the truth;" and those who posess it are said to have "the form of the truth." Rom. 2: 20.

2. *Knowledge.* When the truth is received, understood, known, it assumes the form of knowledge, and is appropriately and Scripturally called "The form of knowledge." Rom. 2: 20.

3. *Doctrine.* When this knowledge is taught to others it becomes teaching or "doctrine," for doctrine means teaching. In that form it appropriately receives the Scriptural appellation: "Form of doctrine." Rom. 6: 17.

4. *Sound Words.* Teaching this doctrine, or communicating this knowledge, necessitated the use of some form of words. And, as the apostles spoke in the words which the Holly Spirit taught, (1 Cor. 2: 13,) they present the form of doctrine in "a form of sound words," and we hear the apostle instructing one of his pupils, thus: "Hold fast the form of sound words which thou hast heard of me." 2 Tim. 1: 13.

5. *Godliness.* The truth and knowledge taught in the form of sound words, received, obeyed and

practiced, becomes practical godliness, or assumes the form of godliness. The activities of Christianity, in obeying God's teaching, and imitating the example of Him "who went about doing good," will superinduce that state of being like God, expressed by the term "godliness," and having assumed this form, may very appropriately be termed, "the form of godliness." Paul speaks of some pseudo Christians, as "having a form of godliness." 2 Tim. 3: 5. From this we see that the obedience, and the activities, have their appropriate forms, and that it is possible for persons to have "*a* form" not "*the* form," while remaining oblivious to its power. They may call it "a mere form," which would be a useless or powerless form, thus robbing it of all significant potency.

We see then that *the truth* known becomes *knowledge*, and taught becomes *doctrine*, and is conveyed in *sound words*, and obeyed and practiced in the *form of godliness*.

What particular feature or form of practice, these "lovers of pleasure more than lovers of God," that Paul said would come "in the last days," would hold as *a form* without power, or *a mere form*, the apostle does not designate. But among all the forms of Christianity, there is perhaps none more significantly subjected to this crucial test, in these last days, than that of baptism. Some do call that act of obedience, "a mere form," or a "non essential," and yet practice it.

As this lesson is on forms, I next inquire into the form of baptism, for it has a form. And whether a mere form or not, it is a *legal form* prescribed by the law giver of the new kingdom, for those who would become citizens.

You recognize a physical object by its form. And

you are not sure you know it till you have seen it from different standpoints. So we will place the object under examination, baptism, in the center of a circle, as in the Delineation, and examine it from the different standpoints. As baptism is an action, we shall know its form, when we have ascertained what the action is.

STAND POINTS. 1. Mat. 28: 19. "Go ye therefore and teach all nations, baptizing them into the name of the Father, and of the Son, and of the Holy Spirit." Here we learn that baptizing is an *act* to be performed by those discipling the people. But, unless we know the meaning of the word, we have not learned what the act is.

2. Mark 16: 16, "He that believeth and is baptized shall be saved." Here we learn that it is an *act*, to be submitted to by those who believe the gospel, but what that act is, is left for further inquiry.

3. Acts 2: 38. "Repent and be baptized every one of you in the name of Jesus Christ for the remission of sins." Again we learn that it is an *act*, to be submitted to by penitent believers, for remission of sins, but the act is not yet defined.

4. Eph. 4: 5. "One Lord, one faith, one baptism." If there is *one* baptism to be practiced in the church, and baptism is an *act*, then there is *one act*, whatever that may be, and it will exclude all other *acts* for that purpose.

5. Acts 8: 36. "And the eunuch said, see here is water; what doth hinder me to be baptized?" From this standpoint we learn that *water* is the element, whatever the act.

6. Acts 8: 38. "And they went down both into the water, both Philip and the eunuch; and he baptized him." From this standpoint we learn, not only that

water is the element, but that the act requires both to go down *into the water*, in which the baptism is performed.

7. Rom. 6: 4. "Therefore we are buried with him by baptism into death." Here we learn that baptism is a *burial*, and can now understand why the act requires Philip to go down into he water, in order to *bury* the eunuch in baptism.

8. Col. 2: 12. "Buried with him in baptism, wherein also ye are risen with him." From this standpoint we learn that the form, or act of baptism, not only buries the subject, but *raises* him again.

9. Rom. 6: 5. "For if we have been planted together in the likeness of his death, we shall be also in the likeness of his resurrection." In the previous verse, the apostle had said they were buried by baptism, and here he uses the figure of *planting* and coming up, of seed of vines, with that of a stalk, that they may grow up together.

10. Rom. 6: 17. "But you have obeyed from the heart that form of doctrine which was delivered you." The "form" they had obeyed, is in the fourth verse called a *burial*. So we have now found the "form,' and it is here called a "form" which they had obeyed, and that form was a burial in baptism. So the "form" of baptism is an *act*, and that act is a *burial*. But the apostle does not call it a "mere form," but a form in the obedience of which, they were freed from sin.

11. Heb. 10: 22. "Let us draw near with a true heart in full assurance of faith, having our hearts sprinkled from an evil conscience, and our bodies washed with pure water." Here the sprinkling is of the *heart*, and can have no reference to baptism. But *bodies washed*, is admitted to refer to baptism, and here given as one of the conditions antecedent to drawing near.

12. John 3. 5. "Except a man be born of water and of the Spirit he cannot enter into the kingdom of God." Creeds and commentaries generally, apply this "born of water," to baptism. For a man to be born of water, he must be in the water and come out of the water.

From these stand points we learn that the form of baptism is an action, active on the part of the administrator, and passive on the part of the subject, that water is the element, that the act leads the parties into the water, and buries the subject and raises him again, thus by faith pointing with significant potency to the burial and resurrection of Christ to whom the penitent believer with unreserved loyalty, yields the "obedience of faith,—for His name.

XXXVI.
TRUE DEVELOPMENT—MILK OF THE WORD.

DELINEATION.

1.—Physical Nature.	4.—Moral.
2.—Intellectual.	5.—Devotional.
3.—Social.	6.—Word Pictures.

SURVEY.

"AS new born babes desire the sincere milk of the word, that ye may grow thereby." (1 Pet. 2: 2.) Possibilities of development, and means of growth, are clearly implied in this text, to which our attention is now invited. The subject of this development is man, and I use the term man in its generic sense to include the race—men, women and children—but especially the children. The term development will be used, not in the Darwinian sense of evolving a man from a monkey, or moneron, but as developing manhood from childhood, maturity from infancy. For the healthy development of a new born babe in Christ, into a full grown man or woman in Christ, a perfect Christian, the pabulum prescribed in the text, is "the sincere milk of the word," pure, unadulterated, undiluted, by humanisms.

Development is education, and true education implies the harmonious development of the whole being. Instruction and education are not identical, but in their action are antipodal, the former acting *ab extra*, the latter *ab intra*. To instruct is to *build in*. To educate is to lead or *bring out*. But we build in, in order to bring out; we instruct in order to educate, instruction being the *means*, and education the *end*, to be accomplished.

From an educational standpoint, man is sometimes regarded as a two fold being, having body and mind, involving physical and intellectual education. From a religious point, he is sometimes regarded as a threefold being, with body, soul and spirit, all which are significantly presented to the service of the Lord. But I purpose considering him as a five-fold being, or as having five natures to be educated, or developed, and in the following order; 1. The physical nature. 2. The intellectual nature. 3. The social nature. 4. The moral nature. 5. The devotional or religious nature.

These are properly called *natures*, from *natus*, born, and being native, or born with the child, are developed by the appropriate training. Education is not a creation. Its province is not to create one of these natures, but to reach them in their feeble nativity and strengthen them, and bring them out in beautiful harmony.

1. *The Physical Nature.* The new born babe is introduced into the family with a physical organism, a body, demanding primary attention; and for awhile exclusive attention. If those other natures are born with it, they will call for attention after a while, but not now. Among the urgent demands of this incipient development, are the breath of life, the bread of life, and the activities of life, in appropriate exercise. priate exercise.

a. The lungs are imperious in the demand for plenty of pure air to breathe, for if the child breathes not, it eats not, neither does it live.

b. Along with the *necessity*, God has implanted the *desire* for food, and wisely too, a desire for the *ap-*

propriate food, the mother's milk, the pabulum adapted by nature to its digestion. The solid food of the family it desires not, neither can it digest. But through exercise the digestive organs are strengthened and acquire the ability to appropriate and assimilate the stronger diets of adults. Then food is required in small quantities, and at short intervals, no oftener and no more at a time than can be digested. The attempt to feed the children but once a week, gorging them with enough at once to last them a week, will most assuredly result in failure in the anticipated growth, and possibly stir up an incipient rebellion in the region of the stomach.

c. Exercise of the muscular system is essential to healthy development, and the God of nature has wisely implanted in the child a *desire* for the exercise and activities of limbs and muscles adapted to the promotion of the desired object. To be convinced of this, you have but to look at the healthy infant, lying upon its back, in loose robes, or in a state of nudity, with elevated feet and hands flying in every direction, as if engaged in a fantastic game of juvenile gymnastics, or infantile calisthenics.

2. *The Intellectual Nature.* Anxious mothers have spent weary hours watching for incipient signs of intellect in the child, to be assured that the child will not be an idiot. But the little manifestations come at length, and then the intellectual training commences by degrees. Here again the growth is gradual, and the intellectual food, like the physical, must be served in small quantitis, and such only as can be digested. But as the digestive organs acquire strength by exercise, the quantity and quality can be gradually increased.

When the boy first goes to school, he is not sent to the blackboard to demonstrate a proposition in Geometry. But by a persistent course of training in mental arithmetic, with progressive problems, from the most simple to the more complex, his mind grows stronger and more vigorous, till after a while he can grasp and hold as in a vise, the most complex problem, while he analyzes and examines its parts, and puts them together again, and announces the result upon the conditions of the problem.

At this point may also apply the illustration of setting the table but once a week. It would be worse than useless to attempt to cram into the head of a child enough at one lesson to last a week; the intellectual digestion would break down under the load.

3. *The Social Nature.* Man is a social being, and to some extent gregarious. The social nature is susceptible of cultivation. The sociabilities, the courtesies of life, the manners of refined society, are the result of training. And this also commences in the family, and extends to society. The child that has never been in polite society, may be *taught* the civilities and usages, but will be awkward, nevertheless, if it has not been *trained* and practiced in them.

4. *The Moral Nature.* Morality has reference to the rules of right and wrong. But a series of lectures on morality, weekly or monthly, will not educate the moral nature. That process may enlighten, but not educate or develop. It will require training, persistent, constant, daily training. Instruction may teach them what is right, but *training* requires them to *walk in* the right, and avoid the wrong way, day by day and continually, until it becomes second nature, and verifies the saying of the wise man: "Train up a child in

the way he should go, and when he is old he will not depart from it."

5. *The Devotional Nature.* That man has a devotional or religious nature will here be taken for granted, not discussed. But its development in harmony with the other natures is what concerns us here. The family, the school, the Sunday-school, the church, society, all exert an influence along this line. But towering above all these influences, is that of the mother. Reaching out for some object or being, above us and stronger, upon which we may take hold and rely, and trust with confiding faith, the devotional nature is ever looking up and is therefore elevating.

The child learns to confide in its mother as a superior being, who loves it, and is able and willing to take care of it and provide for its wants, and whom it can trust in all dangers and under all possible circumstances. Here the first dawnings of the devotional nature are manifested and called into activity, and the tendrils of the little heart cluster around and take hold on one single object, and that object is expressed by that endearing term, *mother.*

But gradually guiding these tendrils, the mother trains them to extend their grasp and entwine around another, who co-operates with her in furnishing for it all the nice delicacies of food and drink, and providing the rich, comfortable clothing, and ministering to its wants, and the father becomes to it an object of devotion.

A sister, like a ministering angel, daily caring for its litle wants and pleasures, perhaps becomes the next object around which its little tendrils of affection are entwined. Thus, one by one, are additional objects above it, included in its affectionate grasp, and it seems borne upon the arms of love.

Still higher upon the trellis work, are those little tendrils trained by the delicate hand of the mother, as she teaches the child of one still greater and more powerful than its father, who cares for it, and who furnishes the seed, and soil, and water, and warm sunshine, by means of which its father has been able to raise all the grain, and vegetables, and fruit, from which all its little delicacies have been supplied, and who is the author and giver of every good and perfect gift. The devotional nature has been thus trained upward, like a vine reaching to heaven, till the tendrils, now above the skies, take hold upon God who sits upon the circle of the heavens and provides for the wants of his creatures. The heart now glowing with gratitude to one so great and powerful, and yet so good and kind, is in condition to receive impressions of him through whom we may draw near to that God whose throne seems to be so far away.

6. *Word Pictures.* The mother, beyond all others, can teach the child by word pictures. A sketch of a few of these, in brief outline specimens, must suffice for our present purpose.

a. The mother draws one of those beautiful inimitable word pictures, in which the tongue excels the pencil and brush, for execution, and the tender heart excels the canvas for reception. The scene is laid in Palestine, on a beautiful clear night, when the stars are beaming in sparkling splendor, like the eyes of heaven looking down in smiles upon the earth below. Calm and serene are the surroundings of the lovely pasture in which the sheep lie down satiated, while their guardian shepherds linger near to protect from possible danger. Conversing upon the pure atmosphere, and the star-lit sky, the same heavens into which the poet laureate of Israel, the Psalmist king, when a boy, had gazed, from those same plains of Bethlehem, more than a thousand years before; and gathering new inspiration from their surroundings and associations, the stillness of the atmosphere is broken by their soft, murmuring voices, as in subdued tones they commence chanting that memorable and appropriate Psalm of Bethlehem's Bard: "The heavens declare the glory of the Lord, and the firmament showeth his handy work." All at once the appreciating heavens glow with additional splendor, and the dulcet tones of their incipient song are supplemented by a reinforcement of heavenly choristers. "And, lo, the angel of the Lord came upon them, and the glory of the Lord shone round about them." The heavenly messenger informs them of the birth of a remarkable child in Bethlehem, and says: "Ye shall find the babe wrapped in swaddling clothes lying in a manger." The interest of the scene is heightened by the sudden appearance of a multitude of the heavenly host singing loud anthems of praise. To complete the picture on Bethlehem's plains, the shepherds did not even wait till morning to go and see the babe, but went immediately to Bethlehem, and in great haste found and saw that babe.

The picture, ornamented and beautified, captivates the children, and they want to see that beautiful babe. All children love babies, and if there is a new baby in the neighborhood they want to go and see it. The mother promises to go and take them, in word picture, to see that babe, for which visit they anxiously wait till next lesson.

b. The promised picture developes a scene in Bethlehem, in which the central figure of deep interest is that beautiful babe, a babe of promise, born to be king, and yet presented under such strange circumstances, and in the midst of such incongruous surroundings. No richly ornamented cradle, or costly silks and satins, compose the princely paraphernalia of the regal natal outfit. But there, in the presence of Mary and Joseph, they find "the babe lying in a manger." The babe finds a place in the hearts of the children.

c. Another picture will present a child at home with its parents, in the presence of a company of wise men from the far away eastern country, who have come a thousand miles to see the babe, and make it some rich presents, the original Christmas presents. When, with its ornamental drapery, this picture has charmed the hearts of the children, they are informed that this babe is the same that they saw in the last picture, though not in the same unique companionship.

d. A boy twelve years old, in the midst of the learned doctors, in the temple at Jerusalem, asking and answering difficult questions, and returning with his mother, setting an example of obedience to his parents, will furnish for another picture a fine group. Though the questions and answers may not be represented by the brush in an ordinary painting, they can be thrown into the word picture, and the wonderful intelligence of that boy will increase the admiration of the children when they learn that this is the babe with whom they had become familiar in former pictures, and whom they had learned to love.

e. Another fine picture will interest them in which a little ship on the sea of Galilee is represented as driven by the storm, and riding upon the raging billows, tempest-tossed, and perilous shipwreck staring them in the face. In despair, the terror-stricken sailors wake a sleeping passenger, who steps upon the rolling deck, and as one born to rule the storm, commands the winds and the waves to be still, and they obey him at once, and all is calm, the disturbed equilibrium of gravitation in the waves, yielding to an immediate adjustment, in contravention of the laws of undulatory oscillation, at the command of the master.

The assurance that the babe in the manger, the child with the wise men, and the boy with the doctors, stands before them in this picture, strengthens the tendrils of their little hearts, that have already taken hold of the personage in these pictures. But the transition since the last picture is so great. What has transpired? This natural and child-like inquiry calls for another picture of an antecedent event.

f. A vast crowd on the banks of the river Jordan comes into the picture, with a man by the stream who has been teaching and baptizing the people, upon whom all eyes are gazing, when a young man from a distant province, an apparent stranger there, steps forward to be baptized, and with the administrator, he walks into the stream and is buried beneath its waters. When he comes up out of the water the opening heavens reveal, in dove-like form, the Spirit of God descending upon him; and "a voice from heaven, saysaying, this is my beloved Son in whom I am well pleased." He is thus announced to be the Son of God, and sanctified, set apart to his divine ministry and mission on the earth.

And this, the same personage as in the other pictures, takes deeper hold upon the affections, and is recognized as Jesus the Christ the Son of God.

g. A crowd of friends and enemies assembled around the grave of Lazarus, presents us another striking picture, with Jesus weeping, standing before the now opened grave and calling the dead to life.

Pictures present themselves almost daily in the sayings and doings of Christ for some three years and a half, for which we have not space.

h. Scenes connected with the crucifixion will furnish material for a picture that will try the hearts. The one they have learned to love through all these pictured scenes, now nailed to the rugged cross, bleeding and dying in agony, the darkened heavens, the quaking earth, the rending rocks, with all the attendant miraculous phenomena, will make an impression upon their hearts never to be effaced.

i. Omitting many others we take the last picture, as he ascends from Mt. Olivet, and we gaze upon his ascending form till it finally vanishes out of sight, bearing with him the affections of the children that have followed him so eagerly through all these *Word Pictures.*

Final Illustration. That vine that climbed the oak, the monarch of the forest, twined its tendrils around twigs and limbs in that grand old coronal, by which it was lifted up and supported in the sunshine of heaven, has been rifted by the storm and lies prostrate upon the ground, utterly powerless to reascend, or even stand alone. How can that union and former position be restored? We will suppose that the oak, in wonderful condescension, bends down and lies by the side of the prostrate vine that had been reaching out its tendrils and taking hold on grass and weeds, and shrubs, that could not lift it up. Changing the objects of their affection, these tendrils are now transferred to the twigs and limbs, and sproutlets of the oak until the union is strong and confiding, when the oak once more assumes its erect position, in its ascent, carrying with it the confiding vine to its former position of union and companionship with the oak.

Application. Man, like that vine, had broken away from his relation and companionship with God, and lay powerless and prostrate with no human arm able to save. God in the person of his son, "God with us," in great condescension comes down, and lies even in the grave, remaining on earth long enough to gather the affections of men and unite the tendrils of human hearts to his, and returns to heaven, whither he will lift up and elevate into divine favor, all whose hearts have taken hold on him with trust sufficient to enable them to follow him.

XXXVII.
GOD'S DRAWING.

DELINEATION.

1—Power classified.	4—How drawn.
2—Adequate.	5—Faculties addressed.
3—The medium.	6—Motives presented.

SURVEY.

"No man can come to me, except the Father who hath sent me draw him." (John 6: 44.)

Looking through the hazy atmosphere of modern mystic theology, and seeing in this popular text nothing but a mysterious abstract drawing of God, by a direct impact of the Holy Spirit upon the sinner's heart, men naturally, conclude that it is useless to take any step towards coming to God, until they have felt that supernatural drawing. Under this blinding delusion, hundreds are deterred from coming to God, waiting for that mysterious something which to them, never comes, till finally they land in open infidelity, or die in despair.

It is a matter of vast importance to know how to come to God, and how men are drawn. But if the fog is so dense that we cannot read the guide boards, we may grope in uncertainty, and arrive at the wrong destination. Let us then come out of the fog, and with our common sense, learn the way in the light of God's word, with full purpose of heart to walk therein.

I. *Motive Power.* If men are drawn, or anything is moved, some power is requisite to produce that motion. Common sense says yes. And the Scriptures do not contradict the statement. Power may act upon and move *matter* or *spirit*. Material, or spiritual substances, may become the objects moved or drawn by power. When power acts upon matter, it is known as physical power. Acting upon spirit it is called spiritual power, or moral power.

II. *Power must be adequate.* To propel the locomotive and draw the heavily freighted train, the power of the steam applied must be adequate to the task of moving the pondrous load; and to propel it up a steep grade, it may become necessary to apply additional power. To lift the elevator to a higher plane, the power must be adequate. The drawing of a saw-log up an inclined plane from the river to the mill, requires the application of adequate power. So also to influence and move an intelligent spirit, the moral power must be adequate.

III. *The medium.* That which conveys the power to the object, or connects the object with the power, is called the medium. For moving matter a physical medium of communication is required. The normal medium of moral power, to move intelligent spirit is language. To move a saw-log you fasten a rope or chain to it. To move a man intelligently you speak to him.

IV. *How drawn.* As the drawing of men to lead them to God, is the drawing of intelligent beings, by the source of all intelligence, we might infer, from what is already said, that language would be the medium used. But there is so much animal nature in man, that some will shut their eyes to the light, and woo some animal impulse that is better felt than told. The mystic theories of modern theology, lead right along that befogged line.

Now brush away the fog, and use both eyes and ears, with a modicum of common sense, remanding the *uncommon sense* to the moles and bats. Do you say none can come except the Father draws them, and you are waiting for that potent drawing. Then honestly, how does God draw them? If the Savior had left us to guess how that drawing is done, there might possibly be some show of excuse for men to be waiting for God to draw them. But as the Savior told us in the next verse, how that drawing is done, I can conceive of no reasonable excuse for men stubbornly waiting, and insisting that God shall improvise some other drawing, for their special benefit than that he has offered them.

After quoting from the prophets: "And they shall be all taught of God," his clear application of it is: "Every man, therefore, that hath heard, and learned of the Father, cometh unto me." Language could not make that plainer. Those who hear and learn, come to Christ. Those who refuse to hear what "God hath spoken to us by his Son," whom God requires all to hear, of course will not learn, and therefore will not come. And yet blind mysticism tries to throw the blame on God for not drawing them.

The prophecy from which the Savior quoted, reads thus: "And it shall come to pass in the last days, that the mountain of the Lord's house shall be established in the tops of the mountains, and shall be exalted above the hills; and all nations shall flow unto it. And many people shall go and say, come ye, and let us go up to the mountain of the Lord, to the house of the God of Jacob; and he will teach us his ways, and we will walk in his paths; for out of Zion shall go forth the law, and the word of the Lord from Jerusalem." (Isa. 2: 2–3.)

The initial point of fulfillment of this prophecy was on the day of Pentecost, the natal day of the Church of Christ, when three thousand "heard and learned of the Father," and came to Christ, in accordance with the Savior's plan in our text, and the teaching of the Holy Spirit, for they heard, believed, repented, and were baptized in the name of Jesus Christ.

V. *Faculties addressed.* Should you see a stranger traveling on a road that leads to a dangerous precipice, perhaps ignorant of the danger, your method of turning him would be to convince him of the danger ahead, and point out a road that avoided the danger, and led to a delightful country.

The sinner is on the wrong road, and going further away from God. In drawing him, to induce him to turn, God speaks to him in his word addressing his *apprehensions*, his *aspirations*, and his *affections*.

His *fears* or apprehensions are aroused by convincing him that he is a sinner against God and in a dangerous road.

His *desires* or aspirations are enlisted by convincing him that there is a better way, in the opposite direction, leading away from danger and into complete happiness.

His *love* or affection is reached, as a strong motive power in turning him, by placing before him some lovely object that strongly appeals to the emotions of the heart.

VI. *Motives presented.* To each of the above faculties addressed, there is a motive presented, calculated to take hold, or reach, and move it in the right direction. These motives are respectively, *Hell, Heaven, The Cross.*

At the terminus of this broad gauge road, and down grade, on which the sinner is all thoughtlessly careering, is presented in glowing terms, the gehenna, the hell, the lake of fire, the second death, the banishment from the presence of God and from the glory of his power, into a second death from which no resurrection is intimated.

Turn around and travel in the opposite direction and at the termination of your path is heaven and all the bliss, and happiness, and glory, that cluster around that word. The glories of heaven, the society of the good and the holy of all ages, with eternal life in the presence of God, and the companionship of the Lord Jesus Christ, enter into the sublimity of the panorama of eternity, so graphically portrayed by the pen of inspiration, as revealed by the divine telescope.

Then to reach the highest and noblest, and strongest human faculty, the affection, the cross is presented with all that it implies. Love, suffering love appeals to the heart in a way that nothing else will. The story of the cross, those word pictures that trace a loving sympathizing savior from the manger to the cross, the babe of Bethlehem, the child with its parents and the magi, the journey to Egypt, the sojourn there, the return, the boy twelve years old too wise for the learned doctors, the example of obedience to parents, the young man baptized and acknowledged by his Father in heaven, the forty days' temptation, the power over diseases, the power over the winds and waves, the authority over demons, the suspension of gravitation in walking on the sea, the power over death in raising the dead, the sympathizing elements in the darkness and earthquake at the crucifixtion, the triumphant resurrection, the visible ascension, the glorification as announced on Pentecost, all emphasize the dying love of him whose benediction for his enemies was: "Father forgive them they know not what they do."

XXXVIII.
THE GREAT COMMISSION.—ANALYSIS AND SYNTHESIS.

DELINEATION.

Matthew, 28: 18–20.	Mark, 16: 15–16.
1—Authority.	1—Go.
2—Go.	2—Preach.
3—Make Dssciples.	3—Believe.
4—Baptizing.	4—Baptized.
5—Name.	5—Saved.
6—Teaching.	6—Condemned.

Luke, 24: 47:	John, 20: 21–23.
1—Repentance.	1—Sent Me.
2—Remission.	2—Send You.
3—Preached.	3—Forgiven.
4—Name.	4—Retained.

Synthesis.

1—Authority.	6—Baptize.
2—Go.	7—Name.
3—Preach.	8—Remission.
4—Believe.	9—Teaching.
5—Repent.	10—Condemnation.

SURVEY.

PENDING the forty days' interview with his apostles, before "he was taken up," Jesus gave them the Great Commission under which they were to disciple the nations and bring them into peaceful subjection to his authority. This commission is substantially recorded by Matthew, Mark, Luke, and John. (Revised version.)

Matthew.—" All authority hath been given unto me in heaven and on earth. Go ye therefore, and make disciples of all the nations, baptizing them into the name of the Father and of the Son, and of the Holy Ghost; teaching them to observe all things whatsoever I commanded you." 28: 18-20.

Mark.—"Go ye into all the world, and preach the gospel to the whole creation. He that believeth and is baptized shall be saved; but he that disbelieveth shall be condemned." 16: 15-16.

Luke.—"Thus it is written, that the Christ should suffer, and rise again from the dead the third day; and that repentance and remission of sins should be preached in His name unto all the nations, beginning from Jerusalem." 24: 46-47.

John.—"As the Father has sent me, even so send I you.........Whosoever sins ye forgive, they are forgiven unto them; whosoever sins ye retain they are retained." 20: 21-23.

I. *Analysis* gives the following elements:

Matthew.—1, Authority; 2, Go; 3, Make Disciples; 4, Baptizing; 5, Name; 6, Teaching.

Mark.—1, Go; 2, Preach; 3, Believe; 4, Baptize; 5, Saved; 6, Condemned.

Luke.—1, Repentance; 2, Remission; 3, Preached; 4, Name.

John.—1, Sent me; 2, Send you, 3, Forgive; 4, Retained.

These items are all in the commission as either expressed or implied by all the witnesses.

II. *Synthesis* gives us the following logical and Scriptural arrangement of the elements:

1. *Authority*, on which the sending is predicated, and mentioned by Mat. and John.

2. *The mission*, or *sending*, given by Matthew, Mark, and John.

3. *Preaching*: Found in the *preach*, of Mark and Luke, and the *make disciples*, of Matthew.

4. *Believe*: This is mentioned by none but Mark, yet it is regarded as essential, and implied by the others.

5. *Repentance*: None but Luke mentions this, yet nobody regards repentance as non-essential in conversion.

6. *Baptism*: This is mentioned by Matthew and Mark, and of course cannot be ignored.

7. *The Name*: Matthew and Luke both mention this; one showing that remission is in the Name; the other, that baptism brings the believer into the name.

8. *Remission*: Not mentioned by Matthew; but where John has *sins forgiven*, Luke has *remission of sins*, and Mark has *saved*, in the sense of saved from sin, that being the gospel salvation through the obedience to Christ. "For it is He that shall save His people from their sins." Mat. 1: 21. Significantly, then they must become "His people" that they may be saved from their sins.

9. *Teaching*: Found only in Matthew's record, but none the less binding. This is the teaching of Christian duty to those who have been discipled.

10. *Condemnation*: This malediction is named by Mark and John; the former against those who disbelieve the offered gospel; the other the same class, but

named as those whose sins are not forgiven through the terms announced by the apostles.

Arranged thus, we have the decalogue of the commission, as the organic law of the kingdom of Christ, under which the apostles preached remission of sins through Christ, and taught the duties and activities of citizenship, to those who were discipled.

III. *The Practice.* Analysis of the first sermon and practice under this commission, Acts 2: 14-42, shows that Peter, with the eleven, discoursed by divine inspiration, recognizing the "authority" of Christ, and his mission or "sending" of these men as his witnesses. Thus armed, he "preached" Jesus, and presented the testimony to prove that he was the Christ, and challenged them to "believe" that God had made him both Lord and Christ. Believing, and pierced to the heart, they inquire what they shall do, and the divine instruction in that inquiry meeting is, to "repent" and be "baptized" in the "name" of Jesus Christ for the "remission" of sins.

Here we have model instruction for inquiry meetings, though sadly ignored in modern times. Peter faithfully followed the commission, and they that gladly received the word were baptized, and on that natal day of Christianity three thousand rejoiced in the forgiveness of sins, and, being added, they came under the apostles' second "teaching," and "continued steadfastly in the apostles' teaching and fellowship, in the breaking of bread and the prayers."

The tenth item: "Condemnation," is not ignored by the apostles, but it is to another class of persons, recognized in 2 Thes. 1: 8, 9, as: "Them that know not God, and that obey not the gospel of our Lord Jesus Christ; who shall be punished with everlasting destruction from the presence of the Lord, and from the glory of his power."

Alterations or amendments to the organic law, "The perfect law of Liberty," are not in order, having no provisory enactment on the statute book, the word of God.—[*Published in the Pacific Church News, February 15, 1884.*

XXXIX.
THE THREE SALVATIONS. — UNIVERSAL, SPECIAL, ETERNAL.

1 Tim. 4: 10, Heb. 5: 9.

DELINEATION.

I. States or Conditions.	III. Proclamation.
a.—3 Entities.	*a.*—3 Truths.
b.—3 Kingdoms.	*b.*—3 Facts.
c.—3 Salvations.	*c.*—3 Commands.
II. Actions.	IV. Results.
a.—3 Births.	*a.*—3 Promises.
b.—3 Lives.	*b.*—3 Denunciations.
c.—3 Changes.	*c.*—3 Relations Severed.

SURVEY.

"FOR therefore we both labor and suffer reproach, because we trust in the living God, who is the Savior of all men, specially of those that believe." (1 Tim. 4: 10.)

"And being made perfect, he became the author of eternal salvation unto all them that obey him." (Heb. 5: 9.)

In this first text, God is declared to be the Savior of *all men*, and stopping at that point we might predicate *universal* salvation, by reasoning that if God is the Savior of all, then all will be saved. But quoting the remainder of the sentence, we find a *special* salvation for believers.

Then in the second text, we find an *eternal* salvation for the obedient. Here are three salvations, which, in this discourse, I purpose examining, surveying, and locating. A plot of the ground to be surveyed is given in the Delineation.

I. STATES, OR CONDITIONS.—*a*.—The *Three Entities*. Man, the subject of the three salvations, is a threefold being, combining in himself the three entities.

1. The body, a physical organism in which the spirit dwells, and constitutes him a living soul.

2. The soul, or life, the vital endowment resultant upon the union of body and spirit.

3. The spirit, the inner man, the living intelligent, thinking entity that dwells in, and guides and controls, and superintends the growth and repairs of the body.

b.—The *Three Kingdoms*. Man the three-fold being is permitted to live in three kingdoms.

1. The kingdom of nature, in which we all live and move and have our being, in common with all animated nature.

2. The kingdom of grace, or favor, the kingdom of Christ, or as Paul calls it: "The kingdom of God's dear Son." (Col. 1: 13.)

3. The kingdom of glory, the eternal kingdom, or as Peter calls it: "The everlasting kingdom of our Lord and Savior Jesus Christ." (2 Pet. 1: 11.)

c.—The *Three Salvations*. In each of the three kingdoms, there is provided a salvation peculiar to that kingdom, making three salvations, and locating them each in a different kingdom, and adapted to the three entities in man.

1. In the provision for the salvation, or preservation of the body, we find the universal salvation, or that in which God is the "Savior of all men." And this is located in the kingdom of nature, in which is the true universal salvation, as it includes "all men," and is irrespective of

moral character. God sends the rain and sunshine, upon the evil and the good, the just and the unjust; and the wicked can raise as much grain upon a given area of ground as can the righteous. If it be said that this salvation is not complete, for the bodies die; the reply is that God has provided a universal resurrection, irrespective of moral character, for: "There shall be a resurrection of the dead, both of the just and unjust." (Acts 24: 15.) "For the hour is coming, in the which all that are in the graves shall hear his voice, and shall come forth; they that have done good, unto the resurrection of life; and they that have done evil, unto the resurrection of damnation." (John 5: 28–29.) The resurrection then, is unconditional, but the life or salvation into which we are raised, is made conditional, and the terms put into our hands.

2. The special salvation, is a salvation from sin, in the remission of sins, offered to "those that believe," and is located in the kingdom of grace. "The kingdom of God's dear Son; in whom we have redemption through his blood, even the forgiveness of sins." (Col. 1: 13–14.) Clearly then, it is a great mistake to attempt to transfer universal salvation from the kingdom of nature where it belongs, into the kingdom of grace where it does not belong.

3. The eternal salvation is located in the everlasting kingdom, and is conditional, based upon obedience to Christ; for he is "the author of eternal salvation unto all them that obey him." (Heb. 5: 9.) But, "when the Lord Jesus shall be revealed from heaven with his mighty angels, in flaming fire taking vengeance on them that know not God, and that obey not the gospel of our Lord Jesus Christ; who shall be punished with everlasting destruction from the pres

ence of the Lord, and from the glory of his power." (2 Thes. 1: 7-9.) Here we have a sharply defined distinction between the eternal salvation, and everlasting destruction.

In this collocation of nine items, we have three entities, three kingdoms, and three salvations, all of which are states, or conditions, to be enjoyed.

II. ACTIONS.—*a.*—The *Three Births*. The normal method of entering each of these kingdoms, is by being born into it, making three births, or a birth for each kingdom.

1. The natural birth which introduces us into the kingdom of nature, consists of two relations, the paternal, and the maternal. The child is begotten by the father, and born of the mother, and this order is never reversed. As the natural birth is made the basis of analogy for the other two births in our lesson, we will find in them the two relations corresponding to the paternal, and maternal.

2. The new birth as it is commonly called, by which men and women are born into the kingdom of grace, conforms to the analogy, in the two relations, begotten by the Spirit, through the word of truth, or as Paul says, begotten through the gospel; (1 Cor. 4: 15) and born of water. The Savior makes these essential elements in the new birth, without which none enter. (John 3: 5.)

3. The birth from the grave through which we enter the kingdom of glory, is analogous, having the two relations, quickened by the spirit that dwelt in us, and born from the grave.

b.—The *Three Lives*. A birth into either of these kingdoms, introduces the subject to a life conformable to the laws of life and health in that kingdom.

And here again the natural is made the basis of analogy.

1. The natural life lies before the child newly born into the kingdom of nature, and the enjoyment of that life depends upon living in accordance with the laws of life and health, in the kingdom of nature.

It is one of the laws of life and health that we must eat in order to live and enjoy life. Disobedience to that law, meets with just retribution in suffering or death.

Another law of life and health, requires us to breathe the atmosphere, which is adapted to our lungs, and to which our lungs are adapted. A violation of this law is visited by swift destruction. Shut up in an air tight box, animal life, whether human or brute, pays the penalty. Let a man or child, be held under water for a time and asphyxia supervenes, followed by death if long continued, and the person suffers the penalty of violated law. Not that the water kills him, but that it excludes the air from his lungs, and the blood fails to be vitalized. The little child walking backwards and drawing its toy wagon, topples over into a tub of water and drowns. It was ignorant of the law of life it has violated, and yet it suffers the penalty.

A law of life and health bids us live in the aerial element, and forbids us to live in the fire. The violator of this law suffers the penalty. The child, innocent, and ignorant of this law of life, in attempting to reach the glowing coal on the hearth, for a plaything, falls into the fire, is badly burned, suffers, and finally dies. This child suffers the penalty of violated law, of which law it was ignorant. Does any one charge God with cruelty in punishing that innocent child for violating a law of nature? No. Intelligent men do not so construe it. God made the law with penalty annexed, and men who know the law, do not violate it. But the irresponsible infant is placed under the responsibility of friends to care for it. Then do not charge God with cruelty in ordaining and revealing laws in the kingdom of grace, with penal judgments annexed for violation.

2. The spiritual life, in accordance with the laws of life and health in the kingdom of grace, lies before those who have been born into that kingdom by the new birth. And these laws of the kingdom are found in the New Testament. Conformity to these laws of the divine life, will result in healthy spiritual growth, while their disregard will dwarf the Christian life, or tend to spiritual death.

3. The eternal life is in the everlasting kingdom, stretching away through the cycles of eternity, before those who have entered that kingdom, and will be in accordance with the laws of life and health of that kingdom, which in due time will be then and there revealed.

c.—The *Three Changes.* The transition from the kingdom of darkness, into the kingdom of grace, involves three changes in the subjects.

1. A change of heart, is the transfer of the affections from sin, and placing them on Christ as our loving Savior. This change is effected by faith in Christ, and takes hold of the *spirit* of the man, the gospel having been addressed to his understanding.

2. A change of conduct, or purpose, affecting the *soul* or life, the will determining to lead a new life, is known as repentance.

3. A change of state, or relationship, carries the person out of the state of an alien, into that of a citi-

zen of the kingdom of Christ. This last change is effected in baptism, the action of which terminates upon the *body* of this three-fold being man.

Thus the three changes, cognize the three entities in man, the spirit, the soul, the body, and bring them all into submission to Christ, and constitute what is usually known as conversion.

III. PROCLAMATION.—*a.*—The *Three Truths*. The gospel, as proclaimed by the apostles, contains three leading truths through the belief of which they were led to Christ.

1. The first truth is that Jesus is the Christ. This affirms his official character, as the anointed one, to all the offices of prophet, priest and king. When we confess him as "the Christ," we accept him as our prophet to teach us, our priest to make atonement for us, and our king to rule over us and lead us on to victory. And in so doing we virtually disclaim all authority to make laws for the kingdom of which we have acknowledged him to be the rightful sovereign.

2. The second truth is that he is the Son of the Living God. This affirms his divinity. And in confessing him we confess his divinity. Then we can trust him in everything as a divine teacher, and therefore infallible, a divine priest, and able to save, a divine king, able to lead us on to certain victory.

3. The third truth is that Jesus is Lord. At the first proclamation of the gospel of a risen Savior, Peter announced this truth for the first time on earth: "Therefore let all the house of Israel know assuredly, that God hath made that same Jesus, whom ye have crucified, both Lord and Christ." (Acts 2: 36.) This third truth affirms sovereignty. These truths believed

with the heart, were confessed with the mouth, under apostolic practice.

b.—The *Three Facts.* The leading facts of the gospel were also three, as given by Paul. (1 Cor. 15: 3-4.)

1. That Christ died for our sins. A necessity, as without the shedding of blood is no remission.

2. That he was buried.

3. That he rose again the third day.

These facts Paul calls the gospel by which these Corinthians were saved. It is a gospel of facts, as well as truths. Facts are actions, or past acts. Truths are simply things that are true. The truths believed were confessed with the mouth. The facts believed were required to be acted out, they being actions. Believing the first fact, that Christ died on account of our sins, they died to their sins. Believing that he was buried, they were buried with him in baptism. Believing that he rose, they rose from their baptismal burial. As Paul expresses it: "Buried with him in baptism, wherein also ye are risen with him." (Col. 2: 12.)

c. The *Three Commands.* Upon the presentation of the truths and facts of the gospel, with the testimony, there followed three commands.

1. Their belief was challenged. They were commanded to believe the gospel upon the testimony, if they would enjoy its benefits.

2. Having believed, they were commanded to repent, or change their will, or purpose.

3. They were next commanded to be baptized. These were instructions or directions following the proclamation of the gospel.

IV. RESULTS.—*a.*—The *Three Promises.* Upon the

obedience to the *three* commands, not to one or two of them, are the promises made.

1. The first promise upon obedience to all these commands, is remission of sins.

2. The second promise is the indwelling of the Spirit, the spirit of Christ in the heart. Peter says: "And ye shall receive the gift of the Holy Spirit." (Acts. 2: 38.) But Paul, addressing those who had "been baptized into Christ," says: "And because ye are sons, God hath sent forth the Spirit of his Son into your hearts." (Gal. 4: 6.)

3. The third promise is the adoption, the heirship, the sonship, which implies the inheritance of the eternal life at the end of the race.

None of these promises can plausibly and scripturally be claimed short of obedience to the three commands.

b. The *Three Denunciations.* The promises, and the denunciations, are to different classes; the former to those who accept, and the latter to those who reject the offered salvation through the gospel.

1. To the unbeliever is denounced, condemnation: "But he that believeth not shall be condemned." (Mk. 16: 16.)

2. To the impenitent is the assurance of judgment and wrath. Paul assures the Athenians that God: "Now commandeth all men everywhere to repent; because he has appointed a day, in the which he will judge the world." (Acts 17: 30-31.) And upon the Romans he charges: "Not knowing that the goodness of God leadeth thee to repentance? But after thy hardness and impenitent heart treasurest up unto thyself wrath against the day of wrath and revelation of the righteous judgment of God." (Rom. 2: 4-5.)

3. The disobedient are threatened with banishment: "When the Lord Jesus Christ shall be revealed from heaven with his mighty angels, in flaming fire, taking vengeance on them that know not God, and that obey not the gospel of our Lord Jesus Christ; who shall be punished with everlasting destruction from the presence of the Lord, and from the glory of his power." (2 Thes. 1: 7-9.)

c.—Relations Severed. The sinner sustains three relations to sin, each of which must be severed, in order to the enjoyment of remission of sins in the name of Jesus; and in the following order.

1. The love of sin. While the sinner loves sin he will continue to practice it. But faith in Christ separates him from the love of sin.

2. The practice of sin. When he no longer loves sin he will resolve to cease its practice and follow Christ. This is repentance.

3. The guilt or stain of past sins. This guilty stain on the character stands against him on God's book of remembrance in heaven, where also the blood of Christ is ready to cleanse the stain, when the penitent believers, in baptism, yields obedience to the commands of the gospel. Then "in the name of Jesus" he has the assurance of remission.

XL.
CHRISTIAN AND JEWISH ANTITHESES.

DELINEATION.

Packages Weighed in Contrast.

1.—The Two Messages.	4.—The Covenants and Promises.
2.—The Messenger.	
3.—The Priesthood.	5.—The Blood.
	6.—The Service.

SURVEY.

WHILE antithesis between Judaism and Christianity stands out boldly in some passages in Paul's Epistles to the Galatians and Romans, yet the Epistle to the Hebrews may, by way of eminence, be termed the Antithetical Epistle. The word antithesis is from the Greek verb *tithemi*, to place, or stand, and as a prefix, the preposition *anti*, opposite, or in front of, hence hiding, substituting, or taking the place of another.

Many of the entities and activities of Christianity are, by the apostle, in this Epistle placed in antithesis, or in front, of things in Judaism, hiding them or covering them, as type is covered by antitype. I trust it may be interesting and profitable to look at a few of these, as the apostle places them in antithetical counterpoise, and note their relative avoirdupoise, and spiritual commercial value.

God, the only self-existent and living entity, is represented as having spoken to men in the *former* message, and the *latter* message, which two messages will constitute our first antithesis. As placed upon the scales at God's mint, their relative value is registered, under the eye and sanction of that same God, "Who at sundry times, and in divers manners, spake in time past to the fathers, by the prophets." (Heb. 1: 1.)

a. This first package, and containing messages from the living God, I find labeled with antithetical insignia, as to recipients, agents, modes, frequency, and periods of time. Or, *to* whom, *by* whom, *through* whom, *how*, *often*, and *when*.

1. It was to the fathers.

2. By prophets.

3. The manner almost as various as the messengers by whom it was sent.

4. It was delivered at divers and sundry times and periods, for generations; and running down through the ages and centuries.

5. It was finished up at a period that had lapsed far into "time past," when Paul wrote this Epistle to the Hebrew Christians.

b. The second message will now be weighed in counterpoise with the first. It bears the same assurance that this same "God hath, in these last days, spoken to us by his son." (Heb. 1: 2.)

This message, either in this sentence or elsewhere, bears antithetical insignia at all the five points in the last weighed, or *former* message.

1. It is addressed to us, and is therefore *our* message.

2. It was spoken by his Son, the Lord Jesus Christ.

3. The manner is through inspired apostles, whom he had trained in person and thoroughly qualified, and to whose remembrance the Holy Spirit would bring

all things that he had taught them, when the time came for them to commence.

4. At the appointed time it was delivered "once for all."

5. It was "in these last days," and had been delivered at the time in which Paul was living.

   c. The *messenger* of the new institution appropriately comes next in order. and the eulogium pronounced upon him by the apostle, occupies the remainder of the first chapter of Hebrews. Messengers under the former dispensation there were, numerous and multifarious, but placed upon the antithetical scales of the New Covenant, they appear almost as light as the chaff that the wind drives away. Prophets and angels, and spirits, and winds, and flaming fire, as God's ministers, flit by on airy wings and scarcely leave a footprint on the balances to remove the dust, and indicate their presence and departure.

The foundation of the earth and the pillars of heaven are placed upon the scale as a very small matter, and are quickly rolled up as a garment, and laid away to change and disappear.

High above, and "so much better than the angels," sits the messenger of the New Covenant, anointed with the oil of gladness above his fellows, and radiant with the brightness of divine glory, at the right hand of the Majesty on high, wielding a sceptre of righteousness, and regnant over the angels of God.

Thus fairly is the antithesis introduced in the first chapter of an Epistle addressed to Judaizing Christians to enthuse them for the great superiority of Christianity over Judaism.

   d. The Priesthood. We. next "consider the apostle and High Priest of our profession [confession], Christ

Jesus." (Heb. 3: 1.) And considering the High Priesthood, antithetically, we find this label: "Seeing then that we have a great High Priest that is passed into the heavens, Jesus the Son of God, let us hold fast our profession." (Heb. 4: 14.) "Profession" should be rendered *confession*. Here the Judaizing Christians are encouraged to hold fast to the one they had confessed, and not to go back to Moses and the Aaronic priesthood. The antithetical points here made are: 1. Our High Priest is *great* by contrast: 2. He has passed into the *heavens*, or through the heavens, not through the veil of the tabernacle. 3. He is Jesus, Savior. 4. The Son of God, the Jewish high priests being sons of men.

Again, "And being made perfect he became the author of eternal salvation to all them that obey him." (Heb. 5: 9.) Here is antithesis in:

1. *Perfect* versus imperfect.

2. The *author* versus only instruments.

3. *Eternal* salvation versus temporal salvation from death without mercy under the law.

Again, "Whither the forerunner is for us entered, even Jesus made a high priest forever after the order of Melchisedec." (Heb. 6: 20.)

1. "Whither," within the veil as an anchor of a vessel carried inside the harbor.

2. "Forerunner," the one who has run into the harbor, carrying the anchor in advance of the vessel; and if the cable does not break we *hope* to see the vessel drawn safely in.

3. "For us," that he may bring us in after him.,

4. "Forever," in contrast with a few years service of Jewish high priests.

5. "Order of Melchisedec," in contrast with the

order of Aaron, an order of succession. Another feature in this order is, king and priest at the same time as Melchisedec was (see also Zech. 6: 13), where it is prophesied that he should " be a priest on his throne." This order is further necessitated in order to perfection. "If, therefore, perfection were by [through] the Levitical priesthood (for under it the people receive the law) what need of another." "The priesthood being changed, there is made, of necessity, a change also of the law." "But we have a *great* high priest over the house of God." (Heb. 7: 11, 12, and 10: 21.)

It is then a great favor, "grace," that Jesus is on the throne, as his presence there makes it a "throne of grace," and the apostle, after referring to the fact that our high priest had "passed into the heavens," says: "Let us therefore come boldly to the throne of grace." (Heb. 4: 16.)

He further admonishes: "Looking diligently lest any man fail of the grace of God.," or more literally "fall from the grace," thus showing that it is possible to "fall from grace." (Heb. 12: 15.) In accord with this, the same apostle says: "Whosoever of you are justified by the law, ye are fallen from grace." (Gal. 5: 4.)

There is no grace in law; the grace is through Christ, and the apostle says: "For ye are not under the law, but under grace." (Rom. 6: 14.) Then as the apostle has said, those who apostatize from Christ and go back to the law, have "fallen from grace."

e. Covenants and Promises. "But now hath he obtained a more excellent ministry, by how much also he is the mediator of a better covenant which was established upon better promises." (Heb. 8: 6.)

Here the antitheses are very clearly defined, contrasting ministry, mediator, covenants, promises. The ministry is "more excellent," being under a "better covenant," and underlying that covenant, as a basis, are the promises of God to Abraham.

God promised him a numerous progeny of fleshly descendants, and a large landed estate, extending "from the river of Egypt to the Euphrates." (See, Gen. 12: 2, 15: 18, and 17: 8.) Upon this promise was "established" the covenant from Mt. Sinai, with the fleshly descendants of Abraham, with a fleshly seal, promising temporal blessings in the land of Canaan, under a hereditary ministry, the Levites, and Moses, a mortal man, as mediator.

God made another and "better promise" to Abraham: "And in thy seed shall all the nations of the earth be blessed, because thou hast obeyed my voice." (Gen. 12: 3, and 22: 18.) Upon this "better promise" developed, was "established" this "better covenant," from Mt. Zion, Jerusalem, with the spiritual descendants of Abraham, with a spiritual seal, and promising spiritual blessings in the kingdom of Christ, under a converted and faithful ministry, and Jesus Christ, the Son of God, the divinely constituted mediator. (Heb. 12: 24.)

"And for this cause he is the mediator of the new covenant." (Heb. 9: 15.) "And to Jesus the mediator of the new covenant." (Heb. 12: 24.) "By so much was Jesus made a surety of a better covenant." (Heb. 7: 22.)

Now we will read the antithetic labeling on the two covenants themselves, in which their differentia are sharply defined. Moses gives us the covenant from Sinai or Horeb. (Dent, 5: 1-22.) He says: "The Lord our God made a covenant with us in Horeb," and then gives the text of the covenant in the language of the ten commandments, and says: "These words the Lord spake * * * and he added no more * * * and he wrote them in the two tables of stone."

As they failed to keep this covenant, the Lord promised (Jer. 31: 31,). to make a new covenant, which Paul quotes as having been made, and the one under which Christians work, and back to which he is calling these Judaizing Christians. (Heb. 8: 1-12.)

1. In the new, the laws are put in the *mind;* in the old they were on tables of stone.

2. In their *hearts:* the motives being *love* versus *authority.*

3. Those in the new covenant will not be required to teach their brethren and fellow-citizens "to know the Lord," which was required in the old.

4. The reason for the last specialty is, that *all* in the new covenant do know the Lord in order to come into covenant relation with him. There were infants born into the old covenant who could not "know the Lord," and had to be taught *to know him.*

5. *Merciful* to unrighteousness under the new. while under the old "he that despised Moses' law died without mercy."

6. Sins and iniquities rememberd no more, while under the old, there was a remembrance made of sins every year.

f. The Blood. Streams of blood flowing for ages from victims offered on Jewish altars, under the first covenant, became as dust in the balance when placed in antithetical counterpoise with "the blood of the everlasting covenant." (Heb. 13: 20.) "Wherefore Jesus also, that he might sanctify the people with his own blood, suffered without the gate." (13: 12.) "For it is not possible that the blood of bulls and of goats should take away sins." (10: 4.)

Then he who apostatized from Christ, and went back to the law, had "trodden under foot the Son of God, and counted the blood of the covenant, wherewith he was sanctified, an unholy thing." (10: 29.)

"But Christ being come, a high priest of good things to come, by a greater and more perfect tabernacle * * * Neither by the blood of goats and calves, but by his own blood, he entered in once [once for all] into the holy place, having obtained eternal redemption for us. (Heb. 9: 11–12.)

The apostolic label on the packages of *blood* now weighed, reads: "For if the blood of bulls and of goats, and the ashes of a heifer sprinkling the unclean, sanctifieth to the purifying of the flesh; how much more shall the blood of Christ, who through the eternal Spirit offered himself without spot to God, purge your conscience from dead works to serve the living God." (Heb. 9: 13–14.)

The apostle says: "We have an altar, whereof they have no right to eat who serve the tabernacle." (Heb. 13: 10.) The altar represents the *service*, which leads us next, and last, to the antithetical consideration of the service, or practice.

g. The Service. Entities and activities of typical and representative estimate, expiring by limitation, have now been placed in counterpoise with the golden coin they represented, and the Hebrew Christians are admonished to adhere to the gold coin currency of the Christian institution, in their practice, and not abandon the valuable and potent realities, for the now depreciated and valueless shadows of Jewish ritual.

"For it is impossible for those who were once enlightened, and have tasted of the heavenly gift, and were made partakers of the Holy Ghost, and have tasted the good word of God, and the powers of the world to come, [the coming age,] if they shall fall away, to renew them again unto repentance; seeing they crucify to themselves the Son of God afresh, and put him to an open shame." (Heb. 6: 4-6.)

The "powers" of sacrifices and Jewish ritual, as a foundation of "repentance from dead works," has vanished with the covenant under which they existed, and "the powers of the coming age," that have come in their place, are the gospel powers, in "the good word of God," through "the blood of the everlasting covenant," to "purge the conscience from dead works to serve the living God."

Hence, it is impossible to renew the once enlightened ones, who have fallen away to Judaism, because they have abandoned the only living power, and resorted to the extinct forms of an abrogated law, like seeking for fire amongst the ashes, and debris of an extinct volcano.

Fearfully have antithetical *consequences* culminated in this terribly suggestive admonition, which the apostle introduced by this precautionary advice: "Therefore, leaving the principles of the doctrine of Christ, let us go on to perfection; not laying again the foundation of repentance from dead works, and of faith toward God, of the doctrine of baptisms, and of laying on of hands, and of resurrection of the dead, and of eternal judgment." (Heb. 6: 1-2.)

Here the *service*, or practice, is thrown upon the antithetical scales and weighed out for practical use. The meaning and purpose of this wonderfully antithetical Epistle, to some extent, centers in the sentence above quoted, making it a sort of key to the mysteries of the apostolic panorama. Apply the key wrong side up and turn it the wrong way, and a clashing of inconsistencies will follow the error.

If any have used the key the wrong way, take the apostle's advice and turn it right. The popular error at this point is, that some have supposed these six principles to be gospel principles, and having placed the key wrong side up, persist in using it that way, and twist and turn, in irreconcilable confusion.

I have seen preachers *try* to fit these six principles into Christianity; but I never yet saw one make them fit. There will be collision and friction somewhere, in every such attempt.

The time has come when Bible students ought to abandon the fantastic architectural feat, of attempting to poise the beautiful gospel structure, on six rusty foundation pillars exhumed from the debris of a defunct system of typical ritualistic service.

Regard this sentence as *antithetic*, and it accords with the whole antithetical structure of the Epistle.

a. The apostle says: "Therefore leaving the principles." The revised version says: "Cease to speak of the first principles." Now whatever these principles are, the apostle says leave them, or cease to speak of them. But some modern preachers will not leave them, or cease to speak of them.

b. The apostle had prepared these brethren for this lesson (5: 12,) by reminding them that they had overlooked the *antitheses*, and needed to be taught which were the *first* or typical lessons, "The first principles of the oracles of God." (5: 12.) What are these? [*ta stoicheia tees archees ton logion tou theou.*] Translate these by phrases and we have: *ta stoicheia*, the rudiments; *tees archees*, of the beginning; *ton logion*, of the oracles; *tou theou*, of the God. Put these together and read: "The rudiments of the beginning of the oracles of God." These are clearly not gospel principles, but those first and typical teachings concerning a coming Christ, and lamb of God.

c. The world, *stoicheia*, translated principles, in the 12th verse, is used seven times in the Greek New Testament, and translated elements, and rudiments, but never used to represent gospel principles. The passages are: (Gal. 4: 3, 9; Col. 2: 8, 20; 2 Pet. 3: 10, 12; Heb. 5: 12.)

d. "*Therefore*," based upon the above corrections, they should leave the typical.

e. "Principles of the doctrine of Christ." The word for "principles," is not in this verse. It is *ton tees archees tou Christou logon*. The phrases translated read: *ton logon*, the teaching; *tees archees*, of the first; *tou Christou*, of the Christ. Put together they read: The teaching of the first of the Christ. Or, the first teaching concerning the Christ, which were the typical teachings.

f. These things laid aside, our work now is on something else, and we should, literally, "proceed upon the maturity." [*epi teen teleioteeta.*] The gospel is "the maturity," or majority, of which these first rudiments were the minority. In other words, we should leave the boyhood and proceed with the manhood.

g. "Not laying again the foundation." Here is a foundation of six pillars, *not to be laid again;* a sufficient evidence that it is not the gospel foundation, which must be laid, or presented, again and again, wherever the gospel is preached.

The gospel foundation is *Jesus the Christ*. And the

same apostle says: "Other foundation can no man lay than that is laid, which is Jesus Christ." (1 Cor. 3: 11.) Then why persist in trying to lay that "other foundation," which "no man can lay?" Better stand by the one foundation of unity, a firm foundation.

The "six principles," here weighed and found wanting, antiquated, layed aside, and not to be laid again, are:

1. "Repentance from dead works." That foundation was laid in the types when repentance, and the offering of a lamb, averted the death penalty for a sin of ignorance.

2. "Faith toward God." Gospel faith is faith toward Jesus Christ.

3. "Doctrine of baptisms." These baptisms were very numerous in the typical ritual, but there is but one baptism required in Christianity, and no man who regards these as gospel principles, ever has, or ever can, reconcile Paul with himself on the plural "baptisms." It will stand: (Eph. 4: 5, *versus* Heb 6: 2,) or, Paul *versus* Paul.

4. "Laying on of hands." This foundation was laid in numerous instances in typical service by laying hands on the heads of animals offered for sins, of individuals, officers, priests, rulers, the congregation; also the laying hands on the scapegoat.

5. "Resurrection of the dead." This foundation was laid, in the living scapegoat that succeeded the dead one, and the living bird flying away with the blood of the dead bird upon its body.

6. "Eternal judgment." The judgment for sins, was pronounced by the priests. In case of sins of ignorance, a foundation is laid for "repentance from dead works," and the terms being complied with, the

judgment is rendered: "and it shall be forgiven him." This was typical of the "eternal judgment" rendered by Christ "once for all." He, "having obtained eternal redemption for us."

In all these antitheses, the antecedent entities have yielded, and given place to the "perfection."—*Published in Pacific Church News, Aug. 15, Sep. 1, and Oct. 1, 1884.*]

ERRATA.

Page 16, bottom line, for "story," read stony.

Page 129, 9th line, after "around," insert "him."

Page 157, bottom line, for "hydrogen," read nitrogen.

Page 308, lines 20 and 21, for "whosoever," read whose soever.

Page 326, 7th line, for "receive," read received.

Page 332, 7th line, for "world," read word.

691

Deacidified using the Bookkeeper process.
Neutralizing agent: Magnesium Oxide
Treatment Date: April 2005

PreservationTechnologies
A WORLD LEADER IN PAPER PRESERVATION
111 Thomson Park Drive
Cranberry Township, PA 16066
(724) 779-2111

LIBRARY OF CONGRESS

0 014 087 833 9

www.ingramcontent.com/pod-product-compliance
Lightning Source LLC
Chambersburg PA
CBHW030320240426
43673CB00040B/1231